Sarah I
VEGET

Over a hund
food — espec … Britain's most famous
vegetarian cook.

Sarah Brown's
VEGETARIAN LONDON

A Thorsons Guide

THORSONS PUBLISHING GROUP

First published 1986 by Sky Books
This fully revised and reset edition first published 1988

British Library Cataloguing in Publication Data

Brown, Sarah
Sarah Brown's vegetarian London.
Fully rev. and reset ed.
1. London. Vegetarian restaurants.
Directories
I. Title
647'.96421

ISBN 0-7225-1652-5

Published by Thorsons Publishers Limited,
Wellingborough, Northamptonshire NN8 2RQ,
England

Printed in Great Britain by
Richard Clay Limited, Bungay, Suffolk

10 9 8 7 6 5 4 3 2 1

Contents

Acknowledgements

All this eating out has been tremendous fun, and has only been possible with the help of a terrific team.

I'd like to thank Paul Street particularly, who has often asked 'what are we doing this evening?' and continued smiling when the reply comes – 'something beginning with R'. Fortunately he's a bottomless pit as far as food is concerned, which is a good qualification for an eating companion!

Thanks also go to Jo Wright, William Sewell, Valerie Greenberg, Frances and Peter Miller and Pauline Robertshaw who have all trekked to and checked up on a number of places. Others involved include Tom Ferguson, David Sulkin, Beverly Muir, Ged Young and the many people who wrote to me since the last edition with most helpful comments.

I am indebted to Vegetarian Edinburgh for the initial inspiration.

Introduction

The food scene in the Capital has changed tremendously in the two years since the publication of the first guide to Vegetarian London. You'll find many new places reviewed, and it's been a challenge searching them all out to see if London is still one of the best places to sample vegetarian food. I've also had good fun revisiting favourite haunts, noting the improvements made. So you'll find that nearly every entry has something new to say.

Of the places that have sprung up, several are completely vegetarian but have none of the worthiness associated with that word. They are smart, sophisticated and, above all, have developed menus that would win over the most hard-hearted carnivore. Many are run on a very professional basis and this means you can eat out safely in some style.

I've felt there has been more willingness to cater for vegetarians, almost as a matter of course. Vegetarian food is appealing to more and more people on either an occasional or a regular basis. Plenty of restaurants now have at least one option, many places asterisk food that is suitable and understand the requirements of a strict veggie, — not eating any product of slaughter. It is a pity there is a growing confusion about whether or not we eat fish.

Apart from the widening choice and availability of vegetarian food, there have been some other notable changes. More restaurants now have no-smoking areas and, on the alcohol front, several places now offer a selection of interesting organic wines and beers. You'll see from the geographical index that the West End and North of London still have the widest selection of restaurants, but I hope the few brave souls trying to make a go of things south of the river have some success.

Sadly, a few of my favourite eating places from the previous guide have disappeared. Some of these were small restaurants, lovingly run by individuals who may have found for one reason or another they were unable to continue. In vegetarian catering, it still seems as though devoted amateurs play a very important part in the development of new ventures, but they face fierce competition and need something quite special to succeed. The ethnic vegetarian restaurants appear to survive better on the whole.

With my team of helpers, we've visited a variety of venues from the chic and expensive to the cheap and cheerful, and a wide range of cuisines that manage well without meat. Do remember that places will change in all sorts of ways, opening times and menus particularly, so please do check by ringing up before venturing miles off the beaten track.

This guide is not only for vegetarians and vegans but for the many people who want to eat good food that is both delicious and healthy. Bon appetit!

SARAH BROWN

How to use the guide

Finding your way about

There are three main sections to the guide:

1. Restaurants
2. Theatres and galleries that serve meals
3. Wine bars

In each section the reviews are listed alphabetically. At the back of the book there are two indexes: one by postal district and one by type of cuisine or style of restaurant. Also, there's some information on major restaurant chains and where to eat outside London. There is a tube map on the last page.

The symbols

The star ratings are my opinion of the restaurants. Use them as a quick guide if you haven't time to read the whole review.

★★★★ EXCELLENT

Go a long way to visit these places at least once. The stars are not an indication of prices but rather that the restaurant achieves really well what it sets out to do. Only awarded to completely vegetarian restaurants.

★★★ HIGHLY RECOMMENDED

Good food and something special in terms of menu, decor, style or price that make these above average.

★★ GOOD

Worth making an effort but not a long detour.

You should get decent food and some, but probably not all, of a good choice, efficient service, atmosphere and value for money.

★ USEFUL

You may not get much choice but you needn't enter with trepidation.

Completely vegetarian restaurant — in most cases cheese, if used, is vegetarian, and eggs free-range.

£ The average price of a three-course meal if it is table service, and of a two-course meal otherwise — prices do not include alcohol.

This symbol indicates those places where wheelchair access is possible, although you may find that there is a small step or perhaps not all that much space between tables in the smaller places.

American Express

Access

Diners Club

Visa

A note on the reviews

We have visited every restaurant at least once. For a restaurant to be included in this guide, it must either claim to be completely vegetarian or, without making such a claim, offer a choice of vegetarian dishes. This may be two or more main courses, or a selection of starters or side dishes that add up to a good meal. We looked primarily for good, tasty food, imaginative and well-cooked meals and use of wholefoods, organic produce, including wine, and whether there was any sugar-free cooking. We've described any dishes that were especially good, to give you some idea of the menu.

We've tried to convey the style of each place — whether it's the atmosphere you should go for, the friendly service or the spotless loos. We've indicated places that are great for a special night out and those more suitable for a casual meal or snack.

We've only included restaurants of a certain

standard. Some places, vegetarian or otherwise, where the food was either unreliable or the general atmosphere and service dreadful, have been left out as I think a bad review is a waste of space.

Your comments

I hope you have the same enjoyable experiences we've had. I would be delighted to hear your comments about places reviewed and recommendations for places you think should be included in subsequent editions.

Please use the form at the back of the book. With your help this guide will keep Vegetarian London on its toes.

RESTAURANTS

Ajimura Japanese Restaurant

★★

51–53 Shelton Street, WC2
☎ 240 0178
£12

A mainly meaty traditional Japanese restaurant that does a variety of special vegetarian meals. There is the vegetable tempura for around £10 that features classic dishes in the Japanese cuisine. The Vegetarian Dinner in a Box is a selection of vegetables cooked according to the Zen temple traditions, with rice and soy soup and fresh fruit to follow. There are also vegetarian hors d'oeuvres, including plenty of interesting combinations of seaweed, plus a vegetable sukiyaki that you cook yourself at the table! A busy, pleasant atmosphere, quite up-market with a fair smattering of media people.

Open: 12–3, 6–11 (closed Saturday lunch, all day Sunday)

Covent Garden tube 50 seats

Al Basha

★★★

222 Kensington High Street, W8
☎ 938 1794/5/6
£12

This is an opulent Lebanese restaurant where great care and attention has been paid to the decor. This care extends to the service, which is extremely efficient to the point of cleaning your table with a miniature hoover between courses. The main vegetarian dishes are the many hors d'oeuvres which can be ordered in profusion – falafel, tabblouleh, baba ghannough, for instance – with muhallabieh (milk pudding) or very sweet pastries afterwards. The best bet is to go for the vegetarian mezze where you get something of everything. It is beautifully presented and extremely filling, especially as it all tastes so good that it's hard not to carry on eating until all the plates are clean. Either go feeling hungry or armed with a doggy bag!

Open: 12–12 daily
High Street Kensington tube,
then a walk or bus 9, 27, 28, 33

65 seats

The Angel Gate

★★

51 Queen Caroline Street, W6
☎ 748 8388
£5

The new chef/manager here has shown what can be done within a very simple formula. There is a choice of two hot main dishes, a soup of the day, a few salads and two puddings.

On the day we went, there was a spicy Moroccan casserole with succulent potato salad and, for pudding, a plain cobbler that had a light, fragrant sponge. The freshly pressed orange and carrot juice is excellent.

There is plenty of space in this bright, airy, upstairs café. It is attached to a church and both are run by the Steiner movement, but no propaganda intrudes on the lunchtime atmosphere so, if you have an excuse to be in Hammersmith, do try it. Evening opening times vary so phone beforehand.

Open: 12–3, 5–8.30 Monday-Friday
Credit cards: none
Hammersmith Broadway tube 35 seats

Baalbeck

★★

18 Hogarth Place, SW5
☎ 373 7199
£8.50

A quiet retreat with a decor designed to soothe fragile nerves. This Lebanese restaurant has a separate vegetarian menu which isn't displayed outside – so don't be dismayed if at first there seems little on offer. The starters are varied enough for you to make a complete meal without having a main course and, on the whole, they are much better than the main dishes, which seem to consist of four rather disappointing stews. The felafel is nutty and crisp, fatoush is a special salad, quite strong on the garlic, and there are also fried aubergines in yoghurt and brown beans in a Lebanese dressing. The service and the stirring Turkish coffee were excellent.

Open: 12–11 Monday-Saturday
Credit cards: none
Earl's Court tube — 24 seats
♿

Baba Bhelpoori

29-31 Porchester Road, W2

221 7502
£7

One of the original London bhelpoori houses which has recently moved around the corner and now has smart decor with bright paint and red tables and chairs. This restaurant serves the usual cuisine of South India – samosas, dosas, thali, dahl vada and lassi. The food is good, though I feel that the Drummond Street restaurant is better. The service is extremely friendly and attentive and the 'Baba' of the name is a guru of the Indian family that owns and runs the place.

Note: This restaurant is now licensed.

Open: 12–3, 6–11 Tuesday-Saturday
7, 15, 27 bus to Westbourne Grove 40 seats

Bambaya

★★★

1 Park Road, Crouch End, N8
☎ 348 5609
£9

A warm and welcoming restaurant with a spacious feeling and lots of interesting pictures, plenty of plants and one wall still decorated with beautiful old tiles with fruit motifs which are echoed on the menu.

This is a fish and vegetarian restaurant, Caribbean in style, and there was a wide range of interesting dishes for vegetarians: such as Hoppin' John, a colourful mixture with ackee (a most unusual, custard-like vegetable) served with rice and beans; or Vegetable Rundown, which was a mixture of carrots and courgettes cooked in coconut milk. There was also a bulgar pilaff and a more standard curry. For starters you could have a spicy green pea fritter, but check on the stock used if you go for the soup. Many of the typical Caribbean vegetables can be had as side dishes, such as plantain, yams or green bananas, and there is also cornbread and a terrific arame coleslaw. For pudding there are delicious heavy cakes and pumpkin pie.

I thought the food was very tasty. Perhaps, for anyone new to the cuisine, the menu could give a little more guidance on what goes best together. It might encourage a more adventurous choice.

Bambaya is busy and friendly, and is an excellent place for an evening out. They don't use cheese.

Open: 12–2.30, 6.30–11 (Sunday 10.30, closed Sunday lunch and all day Monday)

14, 4, W7 bus to Crouch End Clock Tower 46 seats

The Beehive

11a Beehive Place, off Brixton Road SW2
☎ 274 1690
£4.50 (day) £11 (evenings)

Now open in the evenings, this is a pretty cool restaurant in a pretty cool part of town. It is set on the first floor and has a spacious feeling, relaxed atmosphere and friendly staff.

At lunchtime there is a choice of full meals or snacks such as pizza, falafel or rice balls. It is all good quality stuff and they do use organic ingredients whenever possible. The menu changes daily. Having said that, the food is rather ordinary during the day. Salads are poor and the choice is limited. Don't go for a very late lunch as the food tends to run out around 3 o'clock.

In the evenings there is table service, groovy music and a different, more exotic menu. Service is enthusiastic but a little slow. The artichokes in orange and white wine sauce were good, the tofu 'treasure boxes' filled with stir-fry vegetables and a sweet and sour sauce were delicious, as were the irresistable banana and walnut crêpes. There was unlimited coffee and an extensive organic wine list. Every few months you can have a lot of fun at the Italian Opera evenings. Do book as these are popular events.

Open: 11–4, 7–10 (10–5 Saturday, 7–10.30 Friday and Saturday, closed Sunday)
Credit cards: none
Brixton tube 50 seats

The Blue Gardenia

★★★

136 Barking Road, East Ham E6
☎ 471 6685
£7

Since opening, this Caribbean and vegetarian restaurant has expanded its kitchen and added real plants and tablecloths to make the place more comfortable. The menu has also changed, and they are offering a choice of four main courses; stuffed cabbage Trelawn with mushrooms, carrots and courgettes; mixed nut roast; vegetable curry; and soya bean balls. In addition, there are all the usual Caribbean special vegetables – yam, plantain and sweet potato. There are puddings made with these as well, including an interesting banana and sweet potato pudding and a carrot cake. At the weekends there is sometimes a singer and the restaurant may stay open until much later. It's a place that feeds you well, relaxes you and makes you feel well looked after. It can be found on the second bit of the Barking road, which starts at the Green Street junction – the numbering is rather confusing. The main courses tend to be vegan. Cheese, where used, is not vegetarian.

Open: 6.30–10.30 (12.00 Friday and Saturday)

Upton Park tube 50 seats

Bombay Bhelpoori House

★★★

194 Stoke Newington High Street, N16
☎ 923 1425
£7

Newly opened in 1988, the Bombay Bhelpoori House looks set to occupy a leading place in the myriad of Indian Vegetarian restaurants in North London. The decor is completely modern whilst retaining a traditional flavour with 'Raj' fans, cane furniture and Indian music. There is a spacious waiting area and extra touches, such as a free Indian aperitif and hot towels, are offered.

The poori and other starters are light and served with delicately spiced sauces. Of the main courses, the Uthappam Mixed Lentil (pizza with peppers and coconut) and Idli Sambhar (steamed sponge rice cakes) are well worth trying, and there are the usual dosas. There are a dozen side dishes and a good choice of puddings. The sophisticated surroundings, attentive and efficient service plus super food make this place excellent for a night out.

Open: 12–11.30 daily
73 bus to Stoke Newington

50 seats

The Bombay Mix

★★★

7–9 Woolwich New Road, SE18
☎ 854 0035
£6.50

This spacious, modern, well-decorated restaurant opens its arms to vegetarians and vegans. The owner, Mr Karia, prides himself on product knowledge and the ability to cope with people with allergies and other special needs. 'People only have to ask,' he says. There are different utensils and separate storage for all the vegetarian food.

The cuisine is Madras – deliciously fragrant and spicy – and starters such as the bhelpoori are recommended. The matir panir is very satisfying, and the kulfi ice-cream delicious. Check on the ingredients in the English ice-cream.

Once a month there is a gourmet evening, exploring the cuisine of different parts of India. It is best to book, as these are very popular, and also to let them know you are vegetarian.

Open: 10–10 (11.30 Friday and Saturday, closed Tuesday pm)

Woolwich Arsenal B.R. 60 seats

Bunjie's Coffee House

27 Litchfield Street, WC2
☎ 240 1796
£4

Right in the heart of London is this monument to that daring institution of the fifties – the coffee bar. It is down in the basement and suitably dark and dingy, with posters advertising the excellent flamenco and folk music played here in the evenings. Along with the authentic frothy coffee or Barleycup (in authentic Pyrex cups) you can have a good pizza, curry, and now fresh pasta at a very reasonable price. Not everything is made on the premises so, although the food is advertised as being all-vegetarian, it's best to check on ingredients, especially with pastry and cakes.

Open: 12–11 (5–11 Sunday)
Credit cards: none
Leicester Square tube 45 seats

Café Flo

★★

205 Haverstock Hill, NW3
☎ 435 6744
£10

Up-market, fairly expensive French-style restaurant. Smart and efficient service, with good French bread brought to the table. The choice for vegetarians isn't huge but what there is is beautifully presented and tasty, particularly the warm lentil salad. It comes served in a large white bowl and virtually makes a meal on its own. The fresh pasta dish was excellent, while the risotto was rich and creamy but rather bland. For pudding, there was an extremely delicious chocolate mousse (containing no gelatine), sorbets or poached fruit.

Café Flo is a good place for a smart business lunch or leisurely evening meal. The same group owns Le Bistroquet on Camden High Street.

Open: 12–3 Monday-Friday, 12–3.30, 6.30–11.30 Saturday, 12–3.45, 6.45–11 Sunday

Belsize Park tube — 40 seats

Café Pacifico

★★

5 Langley Street, WC2
☎ 379 7728
£8

This is where streetwise latent Mexican bandits hang out when shopping in Covent Garden. You can act out one of those John Huston movies here, what with the ceiling fans, fading yellow walls and long bar. The service is positively American in its friendliness – it is owned by a consortium of Californians – and the food is a good example of its kind. Some of it is even wholefood, using brown flour and so forth. The guacamole, nachos, enchiladas and beans are great, but be warned, you can come away feeling rather bloated with all those beans. Above all, this place is fun and very different.

Open: 11.30–11.45 (12–10.45 Sunday)

Covent Garden tube | 125 seats

Café Pelican

★★★

45 St. Martin's Lane, WC1
☎ 379 0309
£12

This very French café is open for *le petit dejeuner* until the small hours and, apart from the typical croissants, good coffee and excellent salads, there is a complete vegetarian menu available. It offers such delights as Crème Antillaise, which is a spinach and coconut cream soup, or Gâteau de Ratatouille as starters, with main courses of Apple and Blue Cheese in Filo Pastry, Tarte à l'Oignon, tagliatelle and the inevitable omelette. It's not cheap with main courses starting at £4 and plenty of trimmings to make the bill add up, but I feel it's worth it for the special atmosphere. The front part of the café is set out like a traditional French bar and the spacious, more formal, restaurant is at the back. It's a good place to go for pre-theatre meals but, as the service can be a little erratic, give yourself plenty of time so as not to miss curtain up. Checking on some of the more hazardous ingredients (fats, etc.) can be tricky as they don't seem (or want) to understand why it's important for a non-meat-eater to know.

Open: 11–1 am daily
Leicester Square tube 250 seats

The Cherry Orchard

241 Globe Road, E2
☎ 980 6678
£4

This is still one of the cheapest vegetarian restaurants in London, and seems to go from strength to strength with an expanded and more imaginative menu. The atmosphere is light, relaxed and warm. In the summer you can eat outside in their little garden.

The food is simple, reliable and very tasty: good salads, nut roasts, pizzas and an excellent range of herb teas and fruit juices. The range of vegan food is good. The cheese is vegetarian and the eggs free-range.

At lunchtime it is self-service, during the afternoon only cakes and drinks are available. In the evening it changes to table service, and this certainly creates a more stylish atmosphere. The staff are very attentive. This restaurant, owned and run by a Bhuddist community, is well worth a visit.

Open: 12–11.30 Tuesday-Saturday
Credit cards: none
Bethnal Green tube — 55 seats
♿

Chiang Mai

★★

48 Frith Street, Soho, W1
☎ 437 7444
£12

Delightful Thai food served by delightful Thai people in clean, friendly surroundings. The low wooden ceiling, covered with hanging plants, adds greatly to the atmosphere.

There is a generous number of choices for vegetarians, but the main problem is making it absolutely clear exactly what 'no animal products' means, as there is a language difficulty. One of our starters tasted vaguely of fish, although we were assured that the frying of non-meat foods was separate. Som Tam is a delicious papaya salad, very hot due to mega-quantities of fresh chilli. The Thai vegetable curry was full of exotic ingredients with a fragrant sauce. Rice is white. Puddings are a little bit disappointing as there is not much more than fresh fruit and ice-cream. Good place to go if you are just on the brink of vegetarianism and so wouldn't spend the meal wondering about the nature of all the ingredients.

Open: 12–3, 6–11.30 (6–10.30 Sunday)

Leicester Square tube — 40 seats

Christy's Healthline

122–126 Wardour Street, Soho, W1
☎ 434 4468
£11

This is a smartly-decorated restaurant, done out in a black and white theme with marble tables, with every intention of attracting the typical Soho-ite. Upstairs is the main restaurant and downstairs the wine bar. Definitely a place to be seen, whether you are staff or customer.

The salad bar has been good on every occasion I've visited, with a wide choice of ingredients used and a selection of dressings. You can help yourself to as much as you can pile on the plate so it's good value. Main courses tend not to be so reliable in standard. On offer is some ordinary fare such as pancakes, stir-fry and lasagne. Some other imaginative-sounding items have also been on the menu but have generally been 'off' by the time my order has reached the kitchen. I'd recommend you to go for the special of the day or eat what's on show to avoid disappointment.

I feel the food and service at Christy's don't live up to the surroundings but, at the time of writing, they are making substantial changes to the menu.

Open: 8–11.30 Monday-Friday, 10–11.30 Saturday

Leicester Square tube 150 seats

Chutney's

124 Drummond Street, NW1
☎ 388 0604
£7

Relatively new Indian vegetarian restaurant opening in competition to Ravi Shankar and Diwanas. The surroundings are more stylish, with a black and white theme. Service was attentive and friendly, the prices are extremely reasonable and, above all, the food is good. I had a main course of lentil uppertham (described in a rather off-putting fashion as a lentil pizza). It is delicious, lightly spiced with a coconut flavour. The vegetable curry was good and the side dish of okra excellent. The special thali is tremendous, both for its variety and value. To follow there are the classic puddings of shrikand and kulfi. I think it's certainly worth going to Chutney's with a good appetite so that you can manage a main course and some side dishes, as they are generally splendid and well cooked. At lunchtime there is a help yourself buffet for a set price of £3.75. Again, excellent value.

Open: 12–2.45, 6–11.30 daily

Euston/Euston Square tube — 75 seats

Compton Green

14 Old Compton Street, W1
☎ 434 3544
£8

Relatively new completely vegetarian restaurant and one that certainly tries to be stylish, which is definitely to be encouraged: streamlined modern decor, long wine list and an excellent choice of fun-sounding non-alcoholic cocktails. Its table service, and the staff are mostly friendly and helpful.

The dishes come from all sorts of cuisines – Indian, Mexican, Middle-Eastern and so on – so most of the classic meals are featured. There's a good choice of starters and side dishes, such as baked potato with filling for 85p. I've had some splendid meals here, but also some rather disappointing experiences when the food did not live up to its description. On one occasion the only pudding available was fruit salad, the excuse being that the kitchen staff were very rushed after an exceptionally busy night.

Invariably restaurants do suffer teething troubles when they are trying to establish themselves, one day very busy and no customers the next. I do hope Compton Green can keep its standards high and consistent, as competition in the West End is fierce. It's a good place to go for a smart lunch or an evening out.

Open: 11.30–11 Monday-Saturday

Leicester Square tube 80 seats

Cordon Vert

136 Merton Road, SW19
☎ 543 9174
£7

Plain café-style place with simple stripped pine decor and a completely vegetarian, but rather ordinary, menu. They usually have a choice of 5-6 starters. I had a very tasty nut and brandy pâté. There are several main courses with all the standard ideas such as nut roast, curries, casseroles and salads. Often, the flavouring used for stocks is Marmite, and I found it rather overpowered the dish I had. The cakes are good and simple, made with wholemeal flour. The desserts always include a fruit salad and usually a crumble. They have vegetarian Cheddar but other cheeses are not vegetarian. It is not licensed but you can bring your own and pay a 90p corkage charge.

A trip to the loo involves a journey outside and a visit to their pantry to wash your hands. However, it was all very clean.

Open: 11.30–10 Tuesday-Thursday, 11.40– Friday and Saturday, 12–3 Sunday
Credit cards: none
South Wimbledon tube — 40 seats

Country Life

1 Heddon Street, W1
☎ 434 2922
£3.80

A haven for vegan and vegetarian gluttons and surely what must be the best value for money in London. All you can eat for £3.80, and all the food is wholesome, tasty and dairy-free though you wouldn't notice.

It is a help-yourself buffet system, priced according to what you eat. Stick with soup, salads, bread and spreads and that will cost you £2.95, add a hot special and it's £3.30, or go for the lot at £3.80. You get a small tray and appropriate plates then work your way round. I had a delicious Russian potato soup with rye bread and sunflower spread, followed by a heaped plate of different raw vegetables and some tofu and cashew nut dressings. Three hot specials were available including a spinach quiche and chick pea stew. For pudding, there are separately-priced cakes, or a fruit salad in the all-in-one price that can be enhanced with different toppings such as granola, dried fruits, nuts and seeds. As you stagger off with your loaded tray, the person handing you your bill (which you pay on the way out) kindly explains that you can come back to the table for as much as you want again, all you do is show the ticket! Drinks are priced separately.

The atmosphere is quite relaxed considering what a busy place it is. You'll almost certainly have to share a table. I'm sorry that the decor isn't better, and I hate eating off the polystyrene plates they provide, and even more eating with plastic cutlery. However, as someone pointed out to me, you could easily take your own! And really I feel nit-picky making any criticisms, in view of the fact that such excellent food is offered in a genuinely generous and warm-hearted way.

Open: 11.30–2.30 Monday-Thursday, 11.30–2 Friday
Credit cards: none
Piccadilly Circus tube — 80 seats

The Covent Garden Pasta Bar

★★

30 Henrietta Street, WC2
☎ 836 8396
£8

If you are the type of person to allow yourself non-veggie cheese when up against it with a healthy appetite, zoom off to the Covent Garden Pasta Bar, or its other branch at St Martin's Lane – the Pizza and Pasta Bar.

In the Covent Garden branch, there is excellent pasta, yummy sauces, professional service and a good atmosphere. In the St Martin's Lane branch they make huge, tasty pizzas and you are served very quickly. My only grumble is that there isn't a non-smoking section and it can spoil your enjoyment if the people on nearby tables light up. These places are good for pre-theatre suppers or business lunch dates as long as you are not discussing anything too confidential – they are quite noisy.

This group also has branches at Chelsea, Kensington and Kingston Riverside. These branches close at midnight.

Open: 12–11.30 daily
Covent Garden tube — 74 seats

Cranks

(Addresses and details listed over the page.)

Cranks has, for the last twenty years, been one of the mainstays of vegetarian eating in London. Whilst the flagship still remains Marshall Street, a number of other branches have opened in the last couple of years. Plans are underway to centralize the cooking and baking in one unit that will supply all the branches, thus maintaining even standards but hopefully not formularizing the food so it loses its character.

Food at Cranks has never been cheap, but they don't cut corners in terms of the quality of ingredients they use, nor do they run out of stuff. The queues are usually long but it is worth waiting to sample the wonderful savouries, salads, puddings and cakes.

The decor is simple, often with bench seating. At both the Tottenham Road and Adelaide Street branches, good use is made of plain wood and lighting which is very pleasing. There's a feeling that no expense is spared in the design, down to eating off beautiful craft pottery that inevitably increases the prices.

The wine and dine is at Marshall Street. Started some years ago in a small area, it has now expanded and become more sophisticated with candles on the tables and other trimmings, so it is an excellent place for a special night out.

There are innovations at the new branch at Adelaide Street, with a downstairs eat-as-much-as-you-like buffet for £5.50, and table service upstairs. It was good to be welcomed in and shown to a table and then served in a friendly manner. Generally, though, I have found the service at the self-service counters to be offhand and abrupt.

Cranks is professionally organized. It comes in for a fair share of knocks because it is well-established and expectations are higher. Although the food remains the same, it is always well-presented and wholesome. My favourite branches are Marshall Street and Adelaide Street as they are spacious, whereas some of the new places are rather pokey, especially Covent Garden.

8–10 Adelaide Street, WC1 ★★★★
☎ 379 5919
£5.50 buffet

Open: 8–7 (10–6 Saturday, closed Sunday)
Credit cards: none
Charing Cross tube 60 seats

23 Barrett Street, W1 ★★★
☎ 495 1340
£5

Open: 8–8 (closed Sunday)
Credit cards: none
Bond Street tube 35 seats

11 The Market, Covent Garden, WC2  ★★
☎ 379 6508
£5

Open: 10–8 (10–5 Saturday and Sunday)
Credit cards: none
Covent Garden tube 30 seats

17–18 Great Newport Street, W1  ★★★
☎ 836 5226
£5

Open: 8–8.30 (10–8.30 Saturday, closed Sunday)
Credit cards: none
Leicester Square tube 40 seats

8 Marshall Street, W1 V buffet ★★★
☎ 437 9431 V wine and dine ★★★★
£5 buffet, £11 wine and dine

Open: buffet: 8–7 Monday-Friday (9–7 Saturday)
wine and dine: 6.30–11 Monday-Saturday

Oxford Circus tube 170 seats

9–11 Tottenham Street, W1 V ★★★
☎ 631 3912
£5

Open: 8am–9pm (Saturday 9–9, closed Sunday)
Credit cards: none
Goodge Street tube 60 seats

Di's Larder

62 Lavender Hill, SW11
☎ 223 4618
£4

A shop and tiny café combined, with stripped pine and stripey tablecloths and magazines to read while you eat.

The staff here are extremely friendly and very helpful. They make their own bread, which was terrific, and a thick, creamy yoghurt which comes in liberal helpings on the puddings. There is only a small menu with soup, a couple of hot main courses, which change daily, quiche, hummus and two or three salads. Some of the cheese is vegetarian and the eggs are always free-range. The shop, which is open standard hours is well stocked with basics as well as some more unusual items (I bought a delicious organic marmalade). Di's Larder is a small cosy place, deservedly popular. There are plans at the moment for it to change hands, so the future is uncertain.

Open: 12–3 daily
Credit cards: none
45, 156 or 77 bus — 20 seats

The Dining Room

Winchester Walk, SE1
☎ 407 0337
£10

This restaurant is unusually situated among warehouses near London Bridge station. It has little residential trade which is why it is closed at the weekend and on Mondays.

The menu changes weekly and usually includes a vegan option. They try out many imaginative combinations of food – some work well, others don't. For confirmed wholefooders the food can be exciting but some newcomers have found it difficult to swallow. An overall comment is that the dishes tend to be heavy, so they could perhaps do more on the salad side. The plus points are that they use 80 per cent organic vegetables, organic wine, live Greek yoghurt, and the bread, pastry and mayonnaise are home-made.

It is a good place for a casual meal; the service is sometimes abrupt, and you may have to share a table in the evenings.

Open: 12–3, 7–10 Tuesday-Friday
Credit cards: none
London Bridge tube 30 seats

Diwana Bhelpoori House

121 Drummond Street, NW1
☎ 387 5556
£5

Probably the original bhelpoori restaurant in London, from which the bhelpoori industry sprang. It is now showing its age and the service seems to suffer from terminal boredom amongst the waiters. It is usually full and has a loyal following of regulars. There's no doubt that the food is good, especially the lacy dosa, and the prices are still remarkably cheap. Each of the Drummond Street Indian restaurants has something slightly different to offer and it's a good idea to try them all.

Open: 12–12 daily
Euston tube

40 seats

Diwana Bhelpoori House

50 Westbourne Grove, W2
☎ 221 0721
£5

The same ownership as the restaurant of the same name in Euston (and Paris!) but somehow better food and atmosphere – the latter because you are not squashed onto hard pine benches. Instead, there are comfortable chairs plus friendly staff to serve you and explain the menu. The matar panir (peas and cottage cheese) is quite the best and the mango sorbet knows no equal. The aloo papri chat is superb as is the salty lassi, which is well seasoned.

Open: 12–2.45, 6–10.45 (Saturday and Sunday 12–10.45)

Bayswater tube 70 seats

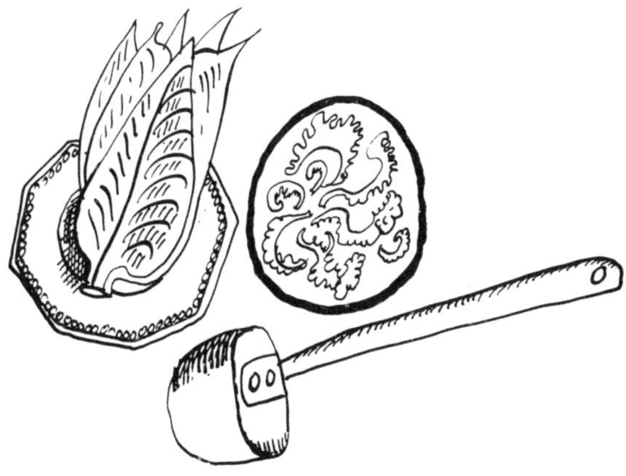

The East West Centre Restaurant

★★

188 Old Street, EC1
☎ 251 4076
£5

The one and only macrobiotic restaurant in Britain. The East West Centre has a peaceful and relaxing atmosphere which makes this a good place to eat and escape the frenetic world of the City just down the street. The staff are friendly and certainly healthy looking. The food, however, takes some getting used to.

Macrobiotically-balanced meals provide unusual tastes and textures, the dishes are often salt-, sugar- and dairy-free. However, the set meal (£3.25 for a small portion) of brown rice, pressed radish with nori, millet and tempeh bake with mushroom sauce, steamed kale, green beans, daikon and carrots looked and tasted good. The sugarless pear trifle was sweet and delicious. The dandelion mousse had a weird flavour that seemed to improve the more you ate. That rather sums up the place — go with an open mind and be prepared to experiment, as it's no good trying to compare macrobiotic cooking to any classic wholefood cuisine. The restaurant is certainly always crowded at lunchtimes and evenings, which is evidence of the great demand for this balanced approach to eating.

There is a wide range of organic beers and wines, including an organic Beaujolais Nouveau!

Open: 11–9.30 daily (lunchtime only on Sunday)
Credit cards: none
Old Street tube 57 seats

The English Garden

★★

10 Lincoln Street, SW3
☎ 584 7272
£22

I've included this charming restaurant, which serves variations on traditional English dishes, as it is useful to know about places to go for special occasions even if the choice for a vegetarian is not extensive. The elegant decor includes a light, airy conservatory which is delightful in summer. The staff are always courteous and attentive.

Starters include chilled melon soup or a similarly creative fruit and vegetable soup, a cheese pudding and a 'red' salad of leaves, fruit and cheese. There is usually only one possible vegetarian main course – a light pastry pie filled with seasonal vegetables – but I've found that you can always ring beforehand and ask for an alternative. Do save room for the desserts, which are divine concoctions of spun sugar, nursery puddings and fruit tarts or syllabub. Coffee comes with excellent home-made petit fours.

The sister restaurant, The Lindsay House, 21 Romilly Street, W1, is a more opulently-decorated version with a different menu based on the same themes.

Open: 12.30–2.30, 7.30–11.30 daily

Sloane Square tube — 50 seats

The Equatorial

★★

37 Old Compton Street, W1
☎ 437 6093
£10

This seems to be the main Singaporean restaurant in London. It is busy, cosmopolitan, and friendly; the service is quick and the delightful staff will explain the menu in their broken English. There are 60 seats on three floors. The menu has no vegetarian starters but 6 or 7 main dishes and 3 or 4 puddings. These include meehon with rice vermicelli, gado gado (salad with hot peanut sauce) and the excellent tauhu goreng which is a bean sprout and vegetable stir-fry with deep-fried tofu. Try crunchy banana fritters to follow. A good place for an exotic but not too slap-up meal before the cinema in the West End.

Open: 12–11.30 daily
Leicester Square tube — 60 seats

Falafel House

★★

95 Haverstock Hill, NW3
☎ 722 6187
£7

The surroundings are simple and the atmosphere casual at this popular little restaurant. The friendly staff are prepared to find out exactly what is vegetarian on the menu, which turns out to be an excellent choice of side dishes that easily make up a substantial meal. All the classic Middle-eastern offerings are available, such as falafel, hummus, aubergine dip and pitta. There are also some main-course specials such as guvetch (a ratatouille type of stew) or savoury rice and beans. It's quite cheap and a good place to go with a party. They also do take-aways.

Open: 6–midnight Monday-Saturday
Barclaycard / Visa
Chalk Farm tube — 40 seats
♿

Fatso's Pasta Joint

★★★

13 Old Compton Street, W1
☎ 437 1503
£4

This restaurant was one of the first to offer the tempting 'eat as much as you can' style pasta meal, and at an extremely tempting price of £2.80 which, at the time of writing, has only increased slightly in the last 2 years. It's a popular place, needless to say, and though you may have to queue for a while, once you're at your table they don't rush you. The service is crisp and efficient. There are quite a few choices in the vegetarian line now, all helpfully marked with an asterisk. The mushroom and garlic, and the cheese and spinach sauces were great, making the one described as vegetarian seem dull by comparison. The cheese and ice-cream (other than sorbets) are not vegetarian.

Open: 12–11.30 (midnight Friday and Saturday, 10.30 Sunday)
Credit cards: none
Leicester Square tube — 109 seats

Food For Thought

31 Neal Street, WC2
☎ 836 0239
£4

Always busy at feeding times, when you will certainly have to queue down the stairs. The wait can be at least 10 minutes but it is thought worthwhile, mainly because the food is very reasonably priced. Main courses are around £1.50 and a mega-salad is £2.20. The menu changes frequently and it is all wholesome fare, tasty savouries and luscious cakes and puddings, and some choice for vegans. Now real addicts can buy the cookbook featuring the restaurant's recipes. (*The Food for Thought Cookbook* by Guy Garrett and Kit Norman, Thorsons Publishing Group, 1987).

The main drawback at Food for Thought is the lack of space. There are only 35 seats which are extremely crammed together, and this tends to make you feel rushed and hassled – rather like eating on the 5.45 to Surbiton, albeit a rather trendy Surbiton.

The cheese used is not vegetarian, which is a pity.

Open: 12–8 Monday-Friday
Credit cards: none
Covent Garden tube — 35 seats

Fountain Restaurant

★★

181 Piccadilly, W1
☎ 734 8040
£5

This is the restaurant linked to the Fortnam & Mason store. It has the sophisticated, calm atmosphere you would expect, and very attentive service. There isn't a large selection here for vegetarians but the management are certainly willing to oblige.

I would recommend this place as an ideal stop off when shopping for a light snack, or afternoon tea, or for a light supper before or after the theatre. There is a good choice of sandwiches, elegantly served, and two interesting salads: Fruit and Cheese Quartet, which consists of a salad base with cottage cheese, peaches, chopped walnuts, tomato wedges and prunes; and Blue Cheese Salad, which consists of half a pear stuffed with blue cheese on a salad base. Both of these dishes cost £4.25. To follow, there is a huge selection of gateaux, cakes and pastries all baked in Fortnam's own kitchen, so it is easy to check what is suitable. Prices for these range from 95p to £1.35.

Note that after 5.30 p.m. the entrance to the restaurant is off Jermyn Street.

Open: 9.30–11.30 Monday-Saturday
AMERICAN EXPRESS · ACCESS · DINERS CLUB · BARCLAYCARD VISA
Piccadilly or Green Park tube 150 seats

Gaby's Continental Bar

★★

30 Charing Cross Road, WC1
☎ 836 4233
£4

A useful place for quick lunches, snacks and take-aways. This is a Middle-eastern café that looks all the world like a greasy spoon but is actually something better. Sometimes the service is solicitous and friendly and sometimes not so warm, likewise the quality of the food. The choice for vegetarians includes many Middle-eastern specialities such as falafel, hummus and spinach rolls. For under £3 you can have a special platter that gives you a taste of everything. The stock and cooking fat are vegetarian. Gaby's also do most of their food to take-away.

Open: 9–midnight Monday-Thursday, 9am–3am Friday, Saturday, noon–10pm Sunday
Credit cards: none
Leicester Square tube — 45 seats

Gaylord

★★★

79 Mortimer Street, W1
☎ 580 3615
£15

The very tasteful decor, seating and crockery are all top quality – this is Indian food for the Nouveau Raj – as is the excellent service. The menu has a good selection for vegetarians and there are some main dishes for vegans. Unusual foods such as lotus root curry gives this place a feeling of ultimate opulence, as does the cost. All the food is freshly prepared – the pakora and samosas were heavenly and you get free coffee refills. As it is the little things that add up you may be best going for the Thali at £7.50

Open: 12–3, 6–11.30 daily (6–11 Sunday)
Oxford Circus tube 96 seats

The Golden Duck

★★

6 Hollywood Road, SW10
☎ 352 3500
£15

The vegetarian menu at this popular restaurant comprises mainly of a seven-course vegetarian feast. For this you get tasty spring rolls on pickled cabbage, sweetcorn soup with peas, and little dumplings with a spinach filling, which are rather bland. The main courses include a very good tofu and beansprout filling for pancakes, plus a savoury mixture of Chinese vegetables, served most attractively. Tinned lychees made a rather uninspiring pudding. The service here was efficient and friendly, but so it should be as you end up paying a cover charge of 75p per person plus 12½ per cent service. Be warned, it can make the bill add up to more than you expect.

The stock, fat and gelatine situation is OK for vegetarians.

Open: 7–11.30 Monday-Saturday

14 bus from South Kensington — 80 seats

Le Gourmet

★★★

312 King's Road, SW3
☎ 352 4483
£12

I thought we had arrived in the middle of a party — but no, this is the regular atmosphere at Le Gourmet, and it's great either to observe or be part of. As soon as you open the door, Gus hails you from the other side of the restaurant and fits you in somewhere. An extraordinary banter is kept up about the food, the customers and Joan Collins is kept up for the rest of the meal. There are 3 or 4 choices for vegetarians, and the main courses were tasty and the salad excellent. Eating here is good fun and could be part of a special night out (do book), or go for a lazy Sunday lunch and take the papers. The cheese is non-vegetarian.

Open: 6.30–11.30 Monday-Saturday (12.30–3, 6.30–11 Sunday)

Sloane Square tube — 62 seats

Govinda's

 ★★

9 Soho Street, W1
☎ 437 3662
£5

Just off the eastern end of Oxford Street, Govinda's is in a very convenient location. It is a clean, functional place with tray and counter service. The staff are always unruffled and friendly – some of them dressed in the robes of the Hare Krishna movement which owns the restaurant. There are posters and leaflets available but you are not pushed to read them or hassled in any way.

Usually there is a good range of hot savouries such as pizza, ratatouille, and vegeburgers, which come in good portions at a reasonable price. There are also fresh salads, and a variety of cakes and puddings many of which are sugar-free. However, the choice can depend on the time you go. Recently I've hit times when the selection has been rather limited – once, surprisingly, at around 6pm.

They use vegetarian cheese and no eggs at all in the cooking.

Open: 12–8 Monday-Saturday
Credit cards: none
Tottenham Court Road tube — 60 seats

The Greenhouse

16 Chenies Street, WC1
☎ 637 8038
£4.50

This is a busy basement restaurant that is pleasantly unpretentious with simple decor, attractive pictures and plants, whitewashed walls, and a certain cosy, welcoming quality. I do like this restaurant as the food looks and tastes good, the portions are generous and the prices very reasonable. There is a varying menu of wholesome savouries, pizza, quiche, vegetable bakes and so on, as well as some tempting cakes and puddings. At times it can become extremely crowded and a little oppressive – you may have to share a table and clear your own space, and there could perhaps be a little more light by which to see what you are eating. The eggs are free range but, sadly, the cheese is non-vegetarian. Note that Monday evening from 6.30-9 is for women only.

Open: 10–10 Monday-Friday (1–10 Saturday)
Credit cards: none
Goodge Street tube 50 seats

Grunts

★★

12 Maiden Lane, WC2
☎ 379 7722
£6

There isn't exactly a choice; what you get is a basic deep pan, doughy pizza for which a choice of toppings come extra. The menu contains some of the worst puns and innuendos ('son of Grunts' small pizza) but the unadulterated salad (from an old bath hence the 'shower' of salad) including whole tomatoes, chunks of lettuce, cucumber, sweetcorn, beetroot, shredded cabbage and grated carrot – to which you help yourself – is excellent and, at £3.25 for a main course plateful (£1.95 for a side dish), excellent value. The pizzas are cooked to order so you have to wait 25 minutes, but that's good time for your starter or a lovely non-alcoholic cocktail. Coffee is served in beakers afterwards. This place is best for a fun meal while marauding around Covent Garden or on your way to the flics. Be warned, however, that you may have to queue some time before getting the chance to order. The cheese is non-vegetarian.

Open: 12–11.30 Monday-Saturday (12–10 Sunday)

Covent Garden tube 120 seats

The Hat Shop

★★

11 Goldhawk Road, W12
☎ 740 6437
£5.50

The rather austere display of hats outside this restaurant give little away about the atmosphere inside. There is an intimate, downtown American feeling to the place and the service is fast, friendly and efficient.

Since the last edition, they have expanded their range of vegetarian dishes. The starters now include chilli beans, tortillas and choice of dips, garlic bread and stuffed mushrooms. Soup is usually made with chicken stock. There is a variety of deep pan pizzas on offer, starting with the very basic at £4.30 to serve two people, which is good value. The salad was crisp and fresh, and can be part of a main course. For pudding there is American ice-cream which is just made with cream, but the special pudding of the day is often bought in so you'll have to check on the ingredients.

I found the staff most helpful concerning vegetarian requirements. Also, the menu has little V signs on it for, as it says, 'our non meat eating friends'.

The restaurant section is on the ground floor, there's a wine bar in the basement which does different food at lunchtime, and a room upstairs can be booked for parties, which I'm sure would be good fun.

Open: 12–11 daily
Access, Barclaycard Visa
Goldhawk Road tube — 130 seats
♿

Herbs and Spices

★★

26 Greek Street, W1
☎ 439 0648
£8

Fairly run-of-the-mill Indian restaurant, with a good selection of small vegetable dishes that can be put together to make quite a feast. You have to wait some while for your order and get the feeling that it is specially prepared. The food is well-flavoured with subtle spicing. The special nan e moglai bread stuffed with almonds and sultanas was delicious and virtually a meal in itself. A nice touch is that they sell a range of Indian spice mixtures – useful if you feel inspired after the meal to go home and try something yourself. One feature that could be improved is the music. We sat through two renderings of famous film soundtracks whilst lingering over lunch.

Open: 12–12 daily

Leicester Square tube

36 seats

Hockney's

98 High Street, Croydon
☎ 688 8624
£8

'The food works on the principle that you don't have to suffer when eating vegetarian', says the publicity blurb in the hand-out describing the Arts Centre which houses Hockney's restaurant, and it's certainly true. It's a most pleasant place with an excellent and imaginative menu. The restaurant is upstairs and consists of a large, open room, brightly decorated. There's a spacious, airy feeling with plenty of room between the tables and good lighting. The menu includes ideas from different cuisines such as Mexican, Greek and Malaysian. They make some very imaginative meals too. I had the 'Peacock Pie' which consisted of a layer of onion, black eye beans, cashews and creamed coconut, covered with a topping of puréed cauliflower, tomato and cheese. Delicious! The puddings consist of home-made ice-cream, parfaits and concoctions made with fruit salad, as well as a choice of cakes.

Although it may be a bit of a treck to Croydon, a visit to Hockney's is worth it, and why not combine your meal with one of the events organized at the Arts Centre to make a memorable evening.

Open: 12–10.30 Tuesday-Saturday
B.R. to Croydon

80 seats

Huffs

★★

Chelsea Farmers Market, 250 Kings Road, SW3
☎ 352 5600
£5

Even on a cold, damp, autumnal day, which is when I visited, this is a pleasant, light place to have lunch or tea. The restaurant is very simple, with mainly wooden fittings, self-service style, and you have the impression of sitting in a rather large greenhouse or garden shed! Service is quick and friendly but the menu is set out on a blackboard rather confusingly, so I wasn't entirely sure what choices there were or how the total bill was arrived at. The hot dish is good value whilst the salads are expensive. Puddings were substantial helpings of crumble or delicious-looking cakes. As some of these are not made on the premises you are advised to make sure of ingredients. One plea – why do they have to use ghastly plastic teapots?! The cheese is non-vegetarian.

Open: 10–5 daily
Credit cards: none
Sloane Square tube, then 19, 22, 11 bus
down King's Road — 65 seats
♿

India Club

★★

143 Strand, WC2
☎ 836 0650
£6

A rather old-fashioned Indian restaurant, up two flights of stairs, which is amazingly cheap for the centre of London – all the main courses are around £2. You can get chilli bhajis (extremely hot, but you are warned), sambar, and a good masala dosa. They also do an excellent lassi. The chapatis and puris were a little greasy and the vegetable curry was disappointing. The decor is to be ignored rather than enjoyed. However, it's more than made up for by the charming service, which is unflustered even when busy, and the friendly, casual atmosphere. They quite clearly have a good following amongst local office workers – not surprising as the food is excellent value, and you should add this restaurant to any list of cheap lunchtime places.

Open: 12–2.30, 6–10 (12–2.30, 6–8 Sunday)
Credit cards: none
Charing Cross tube — 50 seats

Inigo Jones

★★★

14 Garrick Street, WC2
☎ 836 6456
£29.50

You certainly get vegetarian food with all the trimmings at Inigo Jones, and service that is wonderfully attentive. The sommelier wanders around with the traditional silver cup round his neck, but you wouldn't expect anything less in a restaurant that has so much style. The set vegetarian meal costs £29.50 but it is six courses so, although not cheap, it does seem good value for a really special night out. The menu does change. At the moment there is a pear and watercress starter, followed by consommé with barley, a wild mushroom tartlet, sorbet to clear the palate, then on again with fresh herb ravioli, cheese selection and filled choux pastry swans. If you didn't like the sound of any of the courses, I'm sure they would be only too willing to make changes. The food is not wholefood, nor is the cheese vegetarian.

Open: 12.30–2.30, 5.30–11.30 (closed Saturday lunch and all day Sunday)

Covent Garden tube 70 seats

Jai Krishna

161 Stroud Green Road, N4
☎ 272 1680
£3.50

This cheerful red and white modern-styled Indian restaurant offers a good selection of dishes. You order food at the counter and there is also a take-out service.

The food is interesting – light kachouris flavoured with fennel seeds, dudi dal (lentils with squash) and the creamy dahi vardi with subtle guvar were especially memorable. A thali at £3.50 is a way for newcomers to try a variety. The desserts include a deliciously rich shrikand made with yoghurt.

Fresh exotic juices are served, together with lassi and other non-alcoholic drinks. A small charge is made for corkage if you bring your own wine or beer, and there's a handy off-licence opposite.

The only complaints are a rather heavy masala dosa, indifferent coffee and a cold trip to the outside loo! However, Jai Krishna remains a useful place for a cheap, well-spiced and filling meal.

Open: 12–2, 5.30–10.30 Monday-Friday (11–11 Saturday, closed Sunday)
Credit cards: none
Finsbury Park tube then W7 bus 42 seats

Jazz Café

56 Newington Green, N16
☎ 359 4936
£7

Opened in 1987, described as a café, wine bar, vegetarian restaurant and jazz venue, this place is the find of the year! The decor is smart but simple, with black tables and mesh chairs, terrific lighting and the walls hung with an exhibition of prints or paintings. The menu is displayed behind the bar; it is all-vegetarian and consists of fairly standard ideas such as lasagne, moussaka or cheesy vegetable bake, but they are very tasty and well-presented, with a very fresh salad garnish. I had a subtle bean and olive pâte for starters and couldn't resist a huge portion of almond cake which was very light and fragrant with lemon. The prices are reasonable, not just for the food but the wines too. We had an organic Muscadet which was crisp and dry.

Unless you go early, it is advisable to book, as space is limited. There are different musicians each night and a programme is available. Ask for a front table if you are particularly interested in the music, otherwise sit in the back section where you can still hear but needn't feel overwhelmed.

My only worry for this place is that, because it is so small, it will always be overcrowded. The ordering system at the bar is a little annoying as you have to spend time queuing in the middle of your meal if you decide to have a pudding. However, there are obviously imaginative minds behind the venture and teething troubles will be sorted out.

Open: 12–3, 6–12 (7–12 Sunday)
Credit cards: none
73 or 30 bus

65 seats

Karna Phuli

★★★

42 Stoke Newington Church Street, N16
☎ 254 0301
£6

Established in 1970, the Karna Phuli continues its high-quality cooking and service. The menu is mixed, but they understand how important it is for vegetarian food to be kept separated. They offer vegetarians plenty of choice with 16 starters and numerous main courses and thali. The paneer dishes using home-made cheese are particularly good, the three potato dishes are well spiced and there's a particularly delicious peshwari nan stuffed with almonds. The portions are generous and the quality consistent.

The Karna Phuli solves the problem of going for a meal with non-vegetarians and, in an area well served with suitable restaurants, it stands head and shoulders above the rest.

Open: 12–3, 6–12 Monday-Thursday (12–3, 6–1 Friday, Saturday and Sunday)

73 bus to Stoke Newington 50 seats

Kettner's

★★

29 Romilly Street, W1
☎ 437 7437
£7

Fast food in a slow food setting. Kettner's is a long-established restaurant taken over by Pizza Express, but the decor is not spoilt in any way. The atmosphere is very pleasant and intimate – the style is 1940s, smart and comfortable. There is a choice of 5 vegetarian pizzas all marked with the Vegetarian society Ⓥ symbol, and several salads that make good main courses. They use free-range eggs but the cheese is not vegetarian. There's live music at lunchtime and after 8pm.

Open: 12–12 daily
Leicester Square tube

200 seats

Knoodles

★★★

30 Connaught Street, W2
☎ 262 9623
£10

This was one of the early restaurants to specialize mainly in fresh pasta. Sauces are all home-made and there are some interesting ones for vegetarians, such as the cultivated or wild mushroom sauce and stir-fry vegetables with Oriental sauce. To go with the sauces, there are 5 types of noodles to try – white, wholemeal, spinach, orange and tomato. There is also the house speciality called Knoodle Roll which is a sheet of pasta stuffed with spinach and cheese, rolled up and served with rich tomato sauce. There are non-pasta choices, too: home-made soup (sometimes made with vegetable stock), Mozzarella cheese with fresh basil or baked garlic mushrooms. I feel that the food here has a much more personal quality than most of the pasta chains and, as the non-vegetarian food is also interesting, it's a useful place to take mixed parties.

Open: 12–3, 6.30–10.45 for last orders
Monday-Saturday

Marble Arch tube, then 15 bus — 46 seats

La Reash Cous Cous House

★★

23–24 Greek Street, Soho, W1
☎ 439 1063
£10

Family-owned restaurant specializing in Moroccan and Algerian cuisine. It's a pleasant place and, although essentially a meat-based menu, the owners are very aware of vegetarian needs and happy to answer all the familiar questions about animal fats, etc. The vegetarian mezze for under £7 was extremely filling with 8 dishes including an Arabic moussaka. There is a 50p cover charge, but for that you get bread, olives and pickled turnips which are terrific. If you don't drink alcohol the choice is rather limited and the mineral water expensive. Overall, an enjoyable place for a casual meal out.

Open: 12-12 daily

Leicester Square tube — 80 seats

The London Ecology Centre

V★★★

45 Shelton Street, WC2
☎ 379 4324
£3

Millwards, who run the restaurant in Stoke Newington, took over the café at the Ecology Centre in mid 1987. They offer a range of basic savouries such as pizza, quiche, veggie bangers and burgers at very reasonable prices. There is a choice of about six fresh-looking salads, again all fairly basic. There is also a daily special for around £2. For afters there are some hefty wholefood cakes, and I had a delicious cheese scone which they were thoughtful enough to suggest warming up. The coffee was excellent, and there are also plenty of herbal teas.

The café is actually in the heart of the Centre so there is plenty to look at, and there's a gift shop in the back if you are tempted. I particularly like the fact that it is non-smoking. Although a little off the beaten track I do hope it gets known as it may ease the burden on the other overcrowded places around Covent Garden.

Open: 10.30–5 approx. Monday-Saturday
Credit cards: none
Covent Garden tube 26 seats

Mandeer

21 Hanway Place, W1
☎ 323 0660
£5 day, £12 evening

Situated in a labyrinthine basement in a rather seedy back street behind Tottenham Court Road, Mandeer is a surprise. One of the first completely vegetarian Indian restaurants in England, the decor is darkly oriental with great brass lamps. There are two sections, a self-service canteen, which serves a variety of snacks and simple main courses at wonderfully cheap prices, and a regular, more formal restaurant with a full menu and waiter service. This is a good place for a pre-theatre meal or a night out. There's a very good choice with some adventurous items such as puffed lotus savoury, and tofu dishes. The portions are quite small for the price and the thali is probably a better bet for economy's sake. The wholemeal Indian breads are excellent. The puris arrive at the table puffed up and tasty. Most of the sweets are milk-based, flavoured with sweet spices, brown sugar, saffron and nuts, but there are Himalayan apricots and fresh fruit for vegans. The staff are very helpful with decisions when you are faced with a dauntingly large menu and, as you're given plenty of time, you can eat at leisure.

Open: 12–3, 5.45–10.30 Monday-Saturday

Tottenham Court Road tube 100 seats

Manna

4 Erskine Road, NW3
☎ 722 8028
£8

Manna is well established and, though it changed hands at the beginning of 1987, it still remains a warm and welcoming place to go for an evening meal. It is a very casual place – you have to fend for youself looking for a seat and attracting the staff's attention. As it's often busy you may have to share a table but, as everyone gives the impression they are enjoying their meal, there is an overall atmosphere that makes you want to go back.

The standard of the food does tend to be a little inconsistent. I had an excellent salad starter of arame (not to everyone's taste, I know) and followed it with a delicious vegetable stew. The puddings had sold out, unfortunately, and although the waiter was very enthusiastic about the banana brulée, it was no more than banana shrouded in cream, and rather dull.

Manna is good for a reasonably-priced, casual night out.

Open: 6.30–11.30 daily
Credit cards: none
Chalk Farm tube
45 seats

Maxim Chinese Restaurant

★

153–5 Northfield Avenue, W13
☎ 567 1719
£15

A very large, moderately plush, above average Chinese restaurant. The decor and lighting are simple but effective. There are not many more vegetarian dishes on the menu than in most Chinese restaurants but they have been cleverly bunched together under the heading 'Vegetarian Menu'. The most interesting moments are the vegetarian hors d'oeuvres (delicately prepared raw vegetables topped with pickled cabbage), crispy seaweed topped with sweetened grated nuts, red fried tofu, and toffee apples with sesame seeds. They do a set vegetarian menu at £9.50 which does miss out some of the more interesting dishes, but has main courses such as savoury noodles, sweet creamed cabbage and bamboo shoots. Fats used are vegetarian, but the soup stock is liable to be chicken.

Open: 12–2.30, 6.30–midnight (12.30am Friday and Saturday, closed Sunday lunch)

Northfields tube 120 seats

Melate

★★

31 Peter Street, W1
☎ 437 2011
£5

This is an Indonesian restaurant in the heart of strip-joint country. The waiters are friendly and wish you '*selamet makau*' (good eating) as you embark on your Far-eastern culinary journey.

The decor is straightforward and no-nonsense, the clientele at lunchtime largely Soho media people. The vegetarian dishes on the menu are all asterisked, including the one that says grilled vegetarian! The gado gado (peanut sauce stir-fry with salad) and ketoprak (nutty beansprout and tofu dish) are particularly good. But do ask for advice if you are not familiar with the cuisine as you may end up eating dishes that are rather similar. Some of the savouries tend to be sweetened with a lot of coconut and can be overwhelming. The puddings sound spectacular but are not always available. Check about the gelatine content and whether the ice-cream is vegetarian.

Open: 12–3, 6–12 Monday-Saturday
Leicester Square tube — 30 seats

Millward's

97 Stoke Newington Church Street, N16
☎ 254 1025
£8

Millward's, which was quite new in the last edition, has now established itself as a good and most popular place to eat. Booking is certainly advisable – the night I was there no fewer than 10 people were turned away.

The food is imaginative and well presented. The starters are displayed on the central bar, and every dish is served with a little garnish. The main course comes on a large plate with your choice of side salad or selection of vegetables coming in a separate dish. We had a hefty nut and parsnip roast served with apple sauce, and a very good ravioli. There were several appetizing puddings, and I couldn't resist a fresh fruit cheesecake which was exceptionally light.

You can still try the 'tasty maisy' – a little bit of everything on the menu – which is a good idea for the sceptical diner or the fascinated quasi-vegetarian.

The restaurant is full of charming touches, like the well-cared for plants, interesting music and olives to nibble while you wait for your meal. As they are open twelve hours a day, you can go there for afternoon tea after a brisk walk round Clissold Park, which is just down the road, as well as for lunch or dinner.

Open: 12–12 daily
Credit cards: none
73 bus from Tottenham Court Road, 76 from city
42 seats

Myra's

★★

240 Upper Richmond Road, SW15
☎ 788 9450
£6

Myra's is a small, motherly place dominated by the large and motherly Myra. She has now created a special menu for vegetarians with a choice of 4 dishes: risotto, crêpes, croquettes and lasagne. Myra is willing to make a real effort for anybody and, as there was no lasagne left the night we went, she hastily dived into the kitchen to make one specially. Although it wasn't up to her usual standard, I'm sure, I thought it was terrific that she was prepared to try and give us what we wanted. The food is certainly not wholefood; the sauce I had with the broccoli pancakes was white as snow, rich and creamy. She obviously has a strong local following, many of whom were eating on their own, who know they will be warmly looked after. That's very much the style of the place – not necessarily the choice for a special night out, but somewhere cosy for the sort of meal you might have at home but without the bother of preparing or washing up!

Open: 12–2.30, 6.30–11 Monday-Saturday (closed Sunday pm)

East Putney tube — 25 seats

Narmada Indian Vegetarian Restaurant

V ★★

152 Haverstock Hill, NW3
☎ 722 5047
£10

This is a small restaurant set in a converted room of a terraced house. It offers Gujarati cuisine including a very good mini thali as well as a main course thali, both of which come on the traditional large circular tray. There are all the usual starters such as samosas and puris, as well as mohgo fries, a delicious snack of slices of cassava served in a tangy sauce. there are various dosas, the classic rice pancake, and a choice of eleven vegetable dishes. The ringda auro (roasted pulped aubergines) was particularly good.

I didn't find the decor very inspiring or comfortable, but that was more than made up for by the helpful service and good choice of food. As usual with this style of restaurant you get an interesting meal for a reasonable price.

Open: 6–11.30 Tuesday-Sunday (plus 12.30–2.30 Saturday)

Belsize Park tube 40 seats

Neal's Yard Bakery and Tea Room

6 Neal's Yard, WC2
☎ 836 5199
£4

Neal's Yard doesn't seem to change at all as the years go by! You are still likely to get a seat under which the next week's supply of fruit juice is stacked, and they can certainly do nothing about the lack of space. However, what does not change either is the quality of the food. It is good and wholesome – nice, chewy pizzas, tasty scones and well-made salads. They have a range of excellent cakes, some vegan and others sugar-free.

Neal's Yard really works best as a take-away, as it is extremely crowded at meal times. If you do manage to penetrate the upstairs tea room then the choice of herb teas is excellent and all are served in comfy brown tea pots. Lunch starts at noon and, on the evenings when they are open late, there is a separate menu from 5.30. The prices are very reasonable for such good-quality food.

The eggs used are free-range but the cheese isn't necessarily vegetarian. There is also a small vegetarian take-away food bar on the opposite side of the Yard.

Open: 10.30–7.30 Monday-Saturday (closes Wednesday, 4.30 Saturday)
Credit cards: none
Covent Garden tube 20 seats

Nouveau Quiche

★★★

301 New Cross Road, SE14
☎ 691 3686
£11

This is worth a trip to Dartford, even in the thick snow and cold of a winter's night. The Art Deco style is bold and imaginative. The service is friendly and the food good. There is a lot of information on the menu to explain exactly what is suitable for vegetarians and vegans, so it is one of the few mixed meat and veggie places that I feel completely comfortable eating in.

The menu changes occasionally. We had an excellent smoked tofu dish as a main course, and very good, large portions of salad. The gnocchi weren't quite as good. To follow, there was a terrific blackcurrant syllabub. The eggs are free-range but the cheese, unless specified, is not vegetarian.

They do have an endless stream of traffic hurtling by which, sadly, drowns the beautiful music.

Open: 12–3.30, 5.30–10.30 Tuesday-Saturday (12–3, 7–10.30 Sunday)

New Cross B.R. 45 seats

The Nuthouse

26 Kingly Street, W1
☎ 437 9471
£3.50

The Nuthouse, conveniently situated just behind Liberty's, is a pure vegetarian restaurant in the heart of the West End and therefore spot-on for shopping trips. It is somehow a rather dingy place. There are a wide variety of savouries on show, mostly of different combinations of vegetables and a choice of basic salads. Unfortunately the food on display tends to look a little tired, so it's best to go for items such as burgers that stand up to more hanging around. There are also various cakes and puddings but, again, watch out for freshness. It's a shame with such a good site that the Nuthouse isn't better. The eggs are free-range and some of the cheese is vegetarian.

Open: 10.30–7 (10.30–5 Saturday)
Credit cards: none
Oxford Circus tube — 90 seats

The Olive Tree

★

11 Wardour Street, W1
☎ 734 0808
£4

The Olive Tree is a well-established Middle-eastern restaurant in the heart of the West End. You pass a large display of savouries as you go through to the tables behind. The food served is very cheap and most of the classic Middle-eastern vegetarian dishes are available. The portions are generous, but not much time is given over to presentation. It's definitely best to go to the Olive Tree for a snack-style meal, which may end up being quite substantial, rather than a special night out. Hummus, pitta and a mixed salad will only set you back £2 or so.

I've sometimes found the service very sloppy, or else abrupt, which is a shame. You may be ignored as you enter and no indication is given as to whether there is a table free. You can sometimes wait rather a long time to order. However, as it's such good value for a tasty snack before an evening out, do your best to ignore it.

Open: 12–12 daily
Picadilly Circus tube 40 seats

Oodles

★

42 New Oxford Street, WC1
☎ 580 9521
£5.50

This small chain of healthy fast-food restaurants has closed two of its branches leaving only the flagship in New Oxford Street and the one in High Holborn. Part of the problem I'm sure must be the competition from the fresh pasta places and the new, more up to date fast-food bars such as Piazza. There's no doubt that Oodles does seem dated, especially with spring orchard look of blossoming trees made of plastic blooms.

However, the food is quite acceptable and there is a reasonable choice for vegetarians: ratatouille, vegetable curry, broccoli gratin, all of which is microwaved individually. There is also a good range of fresh salads. The pastry is made with unspecified margarine, not necessarily vegetarian, and that may also be the case with many of the cakes and puddings. However, the fresh fruit salad and compôte looked delicious.

Oodles makes a good place for a fairly wholesome lunch whilst out sightseeing or shopping. The High Holborn branch is closed on Sundays.

Open: 11–9 Monday-Saturday (12–7 Sunday)

Tottenham Court Road tube 72 seats

Phoenicia

★★

11–13 Abingdon Road, W8
☎ 937 0120
£15

A Lebanese restaurant that does two excellent and very filling set meals for vegetarians. The salad comes in chunks: whole beef tomatoes, baby cucumbers and half lettuces, but watch out for the greenfly! The usual Middle-eastern menu follows with felafel, tabbouleh, hummus, pitta bread, moutabel (aubergine in a delicious sauce) and moujadarah (rice and lentil salad). The pastries cannot be vouchsafed, though usually filo pastry is vegetarian. As the mezze is substantial you may be better picking individual dishes from the menu. This place is expensive, but you pay for the spacious surroundings and attentive service which may, at times, be a little overwhelming. The cheese is not vegetarian.

Open: 12–12 daily
High Street Kensington

90 seats

Piazza

★★

92 St Martin's Lane, WC2
☎ 379 5278
£3

Is this the shape of things to come? A fast-food, health food snack bar and take-away. They serve a range of fillings in either granary bread or wholemeal French bread. I paid £1.05 but thought the portion and salad garnish were very generous. The hot savouries on offer are standard wholesome fare: bulgar wheat pilaf, lasagne, risotto and curry, heated for you in the microwave. The portions are small, made more obvious by the irritatingly small plate. However, it's only £1.50 and, for the centre of London, that seems good value. There's a wide choice of salads that are vegetarian, and some non-wholefood-looking cakes and pastries. Fresh orange juice is available as well as a selection of coffees and herbal teas. They had only been open a month when I went and were certainly keen. There's limited seating, but it's adequate enough for the time it takes to snack (there are plans to have a restaurant downstairs).

Open: 8.30–9 Monday-Friday, 11–7 Saturday
Credit cards: none
Leicester Square tube 25 seats

Pizzeria Castellos

★★

20 Walworth Road, SE1
☎ 703 2556
£8

A non-vegetarian restaurant that is in this guide principally because of its location and terrific lively atmosphere. It does also have a good selection of vegetarian and vegan pizzas and pastas. It has authentic Italian murals and tiled floor, checked table cloths and waiters shouting at each other in Italian.

You can choose any combination of toppings on your pizza, which is especially useful for vegans. There is also a vegetarian pasta dish. The waiter will grind fresh black pepper on your food as requested. The ice-cream, trifle, and profiteroles are excellent, though you should check what fats are used.

Apart from being good fun in the evening, it's also fine for a business lunch in the Elephant and Castle area.

Cheese is non-vegetarian.

Open: 12–11 Monday-Friday (5–11 Saturday)

Elephant and Castle tube 100 seats

Plummers

★★★

33 King Street, WC2
☎ 240 2534
£12

Martin Plummer, the owner, makes sure there is always a choice of three main courses for vegetarians that are guaranteed not to contain animal fats or meat products, and this policy has now been extended to include some vegetarian soups and vegetarian choices on the weekly special menu - 2 courses for £7.95. The standard main courses are a pie with a good chunky filling, a casserole and a cream cheese and spinach crumble. The portions are quite small and may seem expensive, so the special menu could be better value. Some of the dishes on offer on that menu are a chilli casserole or a spinach and peanut pancake.

The atmosphere is pleasant: Laura Ashley and muted Victorian decor with efficient and attentive service (12½ per cent). A good place for a business lunch, a night out, or a meal before the theatre or cinema.

The ice-cream is Loseley and therefore safe, but the cheese is non-vegetarian.

Open: 12.20–2.30, 6–11.30 Monday to Saturday (closed Saturday lunch)

Covent Garden tube 80 seats

Pollyanna's Bistro

★★

2 Battersea Rise, SW11
☎ 228 0316
£12

Pollyanna's is a very pretty place where a dinner is a really pampered night out, and you do have to be prepared to take your time as the service is not quick. The chef is a great enthusiast and goes to great lengths to create authentic French cuisine. There are always three vegetarian main course dishes on the menu. However, as with many meat restaurants that serve vegetarian food (whilst that is to be encouraged), some of the vegetarian-sounding meals are not so. The night we went the vegetable mousse was made with gelatine. So do check carefully on the ingredients with the waiter. The cheese is not vegetarian.

Open: 7–12 daily (plus 1–3 Sunday)
Clapham Junction B.R. 80 seats

Rainbow

153 Clapham High Street, SW4
☎ 622 1230
£3

Rainbow is fine if you want something cheap and filling at lunchtime. The café, which is at the back of a small wholefood shop, seems to open when the food is ready, though, luckily, this does coincide with lunchtime, and shuts when the food runs out, any time between 2 and 4 o'clock. The soup and dish of the day change daily, and cheeseburgers, soysage and pizza are standard. There is a choice of about 4 salads and several cakes and puddings. Cheese is vegetarian and eggs, not widely used, are free-range.

Try not to be put off by the surroundings, which are a little messy, and the service, which is abrupt almost to the point of being begrudging. I had a generous portion of pizza slice which was very tasty. It is whisked away and heated in a microwave and they shout at you as soon as it is ready. I also tackled the salad, a large helping served in the smallest bowl – inevitably half of it went on the table but no one seemed to care much. It is a pity because, whilst the food is good, a little effort could make the place a pleasure to eat in.

Open: 12–3 or 4 Monday-Saturday
Credit cards: none
Clapham Common tube 36 seats

The Raj Bhelpoori House

V ★★★

19 Camden High Street, NW1
☎ 388 6663
£5

One of the newer bhelpoori houses that has now become well-established. It serves good-quality pure vegetarian Bombay cuisine at reasonable prices. It is a pity they haven't done anything more interesting with the decor.

The menu offers all of the standard Bombay dishes, and a thali for under £4. This restaurant is not licensed but you are welcome to bring your own wine.

Open: 12–11.30 daily

Mornington Crescent tube — 46 seats

Rani

3–5 Long Lane, N3
☎ 349 4386
£7

Rani is a small place, decorated in a cheerful modern style, serving excellent Bombay-style food. The cooking, by the women of the Brahmin family who own the restaurant, is delicate and subtly spiced. The poppadoms – plain or fiery – come folded; the dal cakes with a wonderful coconut chutney; paper thin dosas with a tasty sauce; and the most delicious savoury rice. There are also some most imaginative dishes on the menu. I tried the odd-sounding banana methi, a combination of spinach and banana with fenugreek leaves which was simply terrific. Apart from the choices on the menu there are different daily specials such as stuffed aubergines and potato curry on Wednesday with Al Tiki with tamarind and yoghurt sauce as a starter, and stuffed green chilli bhajia on Saturdays. The service is discreet and friendly and the whole evening out doesn't cost an arm and a leg. Rani sets out to give you delicious food in unpretentious style and it certainly achieves this. Highly recommended.

Open: 12–3, 6–12 daily (closed Monday and Tuesday lunch)

Finchley Central tube | 20 seats

♿

Ravi Shankar

133 Drummond Street, NW1
☎ 388 6458
£5

Now established three years, Ravi Shankar is still one of the best bhelpoori houses in London. It's always crowded at peak times and you may have to wait a few minutes or be prepared to share tables.

The food is well spiced, authentic and downright delicious – especially the matar panir (pressed cottage cheese and peas) and the paper masala dosa (a great cone of crisp rice flour pancake with various fillings.) The service is fast and mostly friendly. The kitchen is fully visible behind the counter where they make the bhelpoori – it's good to know they have nothing to hide. It is a pity though that they couldn't have been braver in terms of design and broken away from the ubiquitous stripped pine furniture, which is hardly comfortable.

Open: 12–11 daily

Euston tube — 75 seats

Raw Deal

65 Paddington Street, W1
☎ 262 4841
£4 (minimum charge £1.75 between 12 and 3 and from 6)

Raw Deal has been in business for at least 20 years, and deservedly so. It is a small restaurant with counter service that is quick and friendly. The decor is simple, with dark polished wooden tables. The salads are fresh and imaginative, but don't be deceived by the name of the place, it's not just raw food on the menu. There's a small selection of other dishes including soup and a hot daily special. It can get crowded but you don't have to wait long for a table. The cheese is vegetarian and the eggs free-range. It is not licensed but you can bring your own wine.

Open: 10–10 Monday-Friday (10–11 Saturday)
Credit cards: none
Baker Street tube 40 seats

Sabras

263 High Road Willesden, NW10
☎ 459 0340
£9

'London's most authentic Indian vegetarian restaurant' is the claim made on the front of the menu, which is extremely extensive, listing dishes by the part of India from which they come. After a Monty Pythonesque dialogue with the waiter, it became clear that the only way to discover what was actually on the menu was to name each item and be told yes or no – he was simply not able to give us a list of what was on the cooker that night.

The food we did get was absolutely delicious in its delicacy and subtlety. Beautiful potato cakes with tamarind and yoghurt, or whole aubergines in a very subtle sauce. If you are adventurous and love Gujarati food, do go to Sabras, but don't expect much of the surroundings.

The gypsy caravan decor, with the enormous TV dominating the back wall, is either charmingly authentic or tacky – depending on your taste – and continues when you go to the loo where you are greeted by a sign telling you 'pull cable very slowly to flush'. But, for vegetarian gourmets, it is easy not to be bothered by such things in the light of the excellent food.

Open: 12.30–3, 6–9.30 Tuesday-Friday (1–9.30 Saturday and Sunday)

Dollis Hill tube | 24 seats

Seasons

4 Chatterton Road, N4
☎ 359 0341
£7 (minimum charge £6)

This individual little restaurant just off the Blackstock Road reflects the owner's personality in its informal bistro style, with chalked-up menu and seasonally-based dishes (hence the name?) pretty china and well-chosen wine list. This usually includes good value North African labels. Music is jazz or classical but never intrusive. All without a hint of pretentiousness.

There is generally a choice of three substantial main courses surrounded by an imaginative list of starters, including aubergines and Roquefort, or spinach and avocado soup, and desserts such as mousses and creamy cakes (but nothing is *too* sweet). Coffee made to order is excellent.

Smoking can be intrusive in such a small place and the loos are rather basic. However these niggles are outweighed by the excellent cooking, service and atmosphere which are highly recommended and will more than satisfy vegetarians and non-vegetarians alike.

Open: 7.15–11, closed Monday
Credit cards: none
Arsenal tube 30 seats

Shahanshah

60 North Road, Southall
☎ 574 1493
£4

A pure Indian vegetarian restaurant in the heart of Southall that mainly caters for take-aways – but has 20 seats and counter service. The food here is authentic and absolutely delicious and still incredibly cheap. The samosas, a speciality of the place, are huge, crisp, spicy and only cost 25p including the mint sauce. The bhaluka (fluffy, puffy, spiced bread with a crisp outside) are amazing. The range of sweets is enormous and the carrot halva is light, moist, scented and sweet. You can gorge yourself well and truly for under £4. It certainly deserves 4 stars for the truly excellent food and value. Their other branch is at 17 South Road, Southall and it is closed on Wednesdays. The closing days at both places have changed since the last edition. If you are making a special trip, try to check. They also cater for weddings and tea parties.

Open: 10–8 daily (closed Tuesday)
Credit cards: none
Southall B.R. 20 seats

Slenders

41 Cathedral Place, EC4
☎ 236 5974
£5 (minimum between 12–2: £2)

A self-service restaurant that caters for the daily crowds that work in and around the City/St Paul's area. They serve good, wholesome, basic fare in the now time-honoured vegetarian tradition. Generally there are a couple of hot savouries for around £3, plus a standard cashew nut burger with sauce. A large bowl of mixed salad can be had with portions of cheese, cottage cheese or hummus. There are some splendid cakes and home-made breads and puddings such as blackberry crumble with cream. The specials are listed at the back but some of the smaller dishes are not, so it can be a little confusing if it's your first visit. But at least the prices are very reasonable.

For people who have to spend a great part of their lives in the stressful sardine-like city environment, such food served by friendly people is essential to maintain health and morale. It's good that there is a no-smoking area. For those occasions when the restaurant gets very crowded, there's a take-away bar and some pleasant seating areas on the terraces nearby.

Some of the cheese is not vegetarian.

Open: 7.30–6.15 Monday-Friday
Credit cards: none
Saint Paul's tube 100 seats

Smollensky's Balloon

★★

1 Dover Street, W1
☎ 491 1199
£10

It is quite possible to forget the hustle and hassle of London's Piccadilly as soon as you enter Smollensky's Balloon. There's a New York atmosphere, smart yet relaxed, with live piano music of the 'thirties and 'forties played on muted keys. Set on two floors, you can sit in the open and attractive area downstairs, choose an intimate alcove table in the upper part, or sit around the balcony and look down on the diners and pianist below. There appear, at first glance, to be 5 vegetarian main courses but, irritatingly, two of these contain fish. The true choices are a vegetable curry with raita, hot harvest pie and a delicious pasta filled with Ricotta and spinach and served with a good mixed green salad. The portion is very generous. For starters the soup, when vegetable, is made with safe stock, otherwise try the crudités. The rich chocolate mousse to follow, if you have space, is made with egg yolks.

Come here for a leisurely lunch or somewhere special for pre- or post-theatre trips. Do leave yourself enough time as it is not fast food. Sensitive vegetarians may like to know that the carnivores choice is mainly steak, served on large wooden platters.

Open: 12–11.45 Monday-Saturday, 12–10.30 Sunday

Green Park/Piccadilly tube 210 seats

Something Else

49 Cross Street, N1
☎ 226 6579
£8

Homely style vegetarian restaurant serving good food but nothing particularly memorable. The menu is chalked up on a blackboard and there's a choice of soup, pâté with toast, dips and crudités. The service was quick – almost too quick as the pâté arrived well before the soups so we sat watching the toast go cold. There is a choice of main courses which come with rice or salad. The portions are reasonable but rather swamped by the salads which are all heaped on the same plate. Puddings offered were cake or cheesecake, and crumble, which was delicious except I was horrified to be offered yoghurt containing gelatine! It was brought in the pot, as they had run out of jugs, so I happened to read the label.

I enjoyed the meal at Something Else; the place has a lot of potential but could do with losing the amateur elements that prevent it from being more memorable. Good, though, for a casual meal out.

Open: 12–3 Monday-Saturday, 6.30–11 Monday-Thursday, 6.30–12 Saturday, 7–10.30 Sunday
Credit cards: none
Angel Islington tube — 47 seats

Spices

30 Stoke Newington Church Street, N16
☎ 254 0528
£9

Reopened in 1988 and tripled in size, Spices has undergone transformation. Decor and logos reflect muted spice colours and textures but strictly 'eighties in concept with bright spotlights and uninterrupted street views. The prices have increased too. There was a reasonable choice of eight starters and six main dishes, plus a set meal, various side dishes and desserts. The wines are from Corney and Barrow with one Indian white, and they vary from £5.50-£11.

When reviewed, Spices had only been open a few weeks in its new format and so they probably have a little sorting out to do. However, the service is very unhurried. The food could do with improvement as the cashew pakoras and vegetable cutlets were dry, whereas the 'award-winning' sweetcorn korma was very liquid. The panir was tasty and the fruit shrikand delicious. In an area well-provided with good vegetarian restaurants, they will have to work hard for a share of the trade, and will need to offer more in comparison to the cheaper, more traditional places. There are plenty of choices for vegans, and from spring 1988, a free crêche will be available Sunday lunchtimes. Do they know what they are letting themselves in for?

Open: 12.30–11.45

73 bus to Stoke Newington High Street 100 seats

Sree Krishna

★★

192–194 Tooting High Street, SW17
☎ 672 4250
£8

This is a mixed meat and vegetarian restaurant specializing in Indian cuisine so there is the usual choice of samosas, dosas, thali etc. It is fairly cheap and has minimal decor but they do offer a take-away service if you wish to go and eat in more comfort.

Open: 6–11 Monday-Thursday & Sunday;
6–12 Friday & Saturday

Tooting Broadway tube 130 seats

Twenty, Trinity Gardens

★★

20 Trinity Gardens, SW9
☎ 733-8838
£10

Twenty, Trinity Gardens is a pretty restaurant in a pretty street just south of Brixton tube. It gives veggies a chance to sample 'Modern English Cooking', though in fact the dishes we tried were neither modern nor English! There are two set menus which change frequently and each contains at least one vegetarian starter and main course, sometimes more. Often vegans are well catered for, though it's best to check. The food is generally good and imaginative, with such starters as vegetable terrine with coriander sauce and goat's cheese salad, but you may have the odd disappointment. Certainly the vegetarian dishes at this restaurant stand on their own merits and are probably tried and enjoyed by meat eaters as well. The only niggle was the sticky PVC tablecloths. Do check for animal-free stocks and gelatine in mousses. Cheese is non-vegetarian.

Open: 12.30–2.30, 7–10.30 (closed Saturday lunch, all day Sunday)

Brixton tube 45 seats

Veeraswamy's

★★★

99–101 Regent Street, W1
☎ 734 1401
£15

Veeraswamy's was opened in 1922, so it has claim to being the oldest Indian restaurant in London. The setting is very sumptuous, luxurious and very, very Indian. The whole experience begins when you meet the costumed lift attendant who ushers you upstairs. The staff are very friendly and attentive and only too willing to explain about the food. There is a good choice for vegetarians. The mint paratha was unusual, the panir makhri had a delicious fragrant sauce. Vegetable kofta are light dumpling-like balls of fried vegetables with a hot spicy sauce. Everything was well presented. To follow, one of the more unusual desserts on offer was a tamarind sorbet with a distinct sweet and sour taste. The more classic Indian puddings are also available.

Veeraswamy's is certainly the place to go for a stylish night out, especially for parties with mixed eating habits. Most of the vegetarian dishes are cheaper.

Open: 11.30–3, 6.30–midnight daily
Piccadilly Circus tube — 80 seats

The Viceroy of India

3–5 Glentworth Street, NW1
☎ 486 3401
£9

As the name would imply, the Viceroy is rather grand with comfortable and spacious surroundings. It has a plush, calm atmosphere. At lunchtime it is fairly quiet and the service is extra attentive. In the evenings it is busier, making it good for a smart night out. The food is tasty and well-presented. This restaurant is certainly not run of the mill, but the menu has no hidden delights either. Probably a good place to take a mixed party.

Open: 12–3, 6–11.30 daily (6–11 Sunday)

Baker Street tube 100 seats

The Wholemeal Café

1 Shrubbery Road, Streatham, SW16
☎ 769 2423
£5 daytime

This place is clean and pleasant, with pine tables and chairs, and lots of plants. You order at the counter and the food is then brought over to your table. The selection is good and I had a particularly tasty mixed salad – a huge bowlful for £1.20. The savouries are kept warm on a hotplate at the back. The selection changes daily. Their breads, cakes and puddings are delicious. Large, slightly marmaladey tasting muffins alone are worth the journey to St. Reatham!

On Friday and Saturday evenings there are special three course meals and I imagine the staff do everything they can to create a cosy atmosphere. The Wholemeal Café is licensed, and non-smoking, and remember it is open on a Sunday.

Open: 12–10 daily (closed 6–7 on Friday, Saturday, Sunday)
Credit cards: none
159, 3, 133, 109 buses — 40 seats
♿

Wilkins Natural Foods

61 Marsham Street, SW1
☎ 222 4038
£3.50

Definitely a place for Westminster workers. Between midday and 2pm there is a permanent queue. A lot of people resort to getting take-aways to save time. The staff serving at the counter are rather laid back so it all takes rather longer than necessary.

The food, though the menu is ordinary, is well cooked and tasty. There is always a soup, two main courses and a salad bowl. They bake their own bread, which is excellent, and the puddings consist of sticky flapjacks and the like, fruit salad and yoghurt.

In the summer there is a little space outside and, of course, plenty of lovely places to sit quite close by.

Open: 8–5.30 Monday-Friday
Credit cards: none
Westminster tube or 3, 159, 88 buses 28 seats

The Windmill

486 Fulham Road, SW6
☎ 385 1570
£6

The Windmill is a cheerful and very informal restaurant. The food is always imaginatively prepared, tastefully presented and delicious. There is a frequently changing choice, all fully described so you can tell exactly what is vegan or what has been organically grown. There's also a wonderful range of fresh-looking salads and tempting puddings. I couldn't resist a rich carob and butterscotch flan. The portions are good and the meals here are excellent value. Being so small, The Windmill soon gets full and has little space for queuing, but it is worth the hassle. The surroundings are not especially comfortable — PVC tablecloths and hard chairs — but they do put candles on the tables in the evenings to create an atmosphere. Good place for a casual night out, and somewhere you could feel happy eating on your own. The eggs are free-range and the cheese vegetarian. They sell organic wine.

Open: 12–11 (7–11 Sunday)
Credit cards: none
Fulham Broadway tube 28 seats

Woodlands

77 Marylebone High Street, W1
☎ 485 3862
£10

This excellent chain of restaurants reaches from Delhi through London to New York, serving the now familiar Bombay cuisine. The dishes taste individually spiced and are prepared by expert chefs from India. There's a very wide choice of pancakes, dosas and different rice dishes. The Royal Thali is a sumptuous feast with delicate samosas, the lassi with saffron and almond is luscious. But it is pricey compared with other bhelpoori houses, justified perhaps by the impeccable service and luxurious surroundings. All three restaurants are highly recommended, as is the food which is consistently excellent.

OTHER BRANCHES AT:
37 Panton Street, W1
Tel 839 7258

402 High Road, Wembley, Middlesex
Tel 902 9869

Open: 12–3, 6–11 daily

Bond Street tube 120 seats

The Wren At Saint James

★

235 Jermyn Street, SW1
☎ 437 9419
£4

Attached to the New Age church, you can reach The Wren through the church from Piccadilly or from Jermyn Street. It is bright, modern and extremely busy, particularly at lunchtime and the early afternoon. You take your tray to tables on the ground floor or a cleverly-designed upper gallery or, in the warmer weather, outside. Quite frankly, the vegetarian food is not as good as it was, which is a shame as it is such a useful location. There are veggie pasties and a standard Harvest Pie served with a reasonable salad. The soup, made on the premises, is not usually safe. When I visited, the main course, which changes daily, was hot pot that consisted of little more than stewed chickpeas. The flapjack and apple crumble were great, whilst the apple streudel was stale.

I've decided to include The Wren even though the standard of food has gone down, as they do a good range of herbal teas, use some wholefoods, and it is all non-smoking.

Open: 10.30–6 daily (but tends to vary)
Credit cards: none
Piccadilly Circus tube 60 seats
♿

Zen

★★★

Chelsea Cloisters, SW3
☎ 589 1781
£15

It's nice to eat good vegetarian food in plush, spacious and comfortable surroundings. There is a page on the menu for vegetarian dishes, which confusingly includes a fish dish. However, there was certainly no muddle about the food we ordered. It was all beautifully presented in delicate portions leaving you room to get through a lot of different dishes. There were tiny spring rolls with chilli sauce, crisply-fried sweet and sour seaweed, and minute parcels of tofu stuffed with fragrantly spiced vegetables. When you are feeling adventurous, try some of the more unusual puddings such as the sago and melon dessert. To my surprise it was delicious, light and refreshing.

The same management own I Ching, which also offers a range of vegetarian dishes.

Open: 12–3, 6–11 (12–11.30 Saturday)

South Kensington tube — 150 seats

Zona Rosa

★★★

3 Long Acre, WC2
☎ 836 5255
£10

This is the London branch of a successful New York restaurant and it's a treat for vegetarians, with an excellent choice of 3 main courses. All sounded so appetizing that I found it extremely hard to choose. Hongos Guisados con Chilli is a succulent mixture of dried mushrooms in a sauce which was quite delicious, and Zapellitos Relleno is stuffed courgettes. All the food is very well presented and well flavoured. There are also light bites if you are not so hungry, with a choice of dips and tortillas, and 15 frozen Margarita cocktails to make your evening go with a swing. The staff are very friendly (and so they should be with service at 15 per cent!) and the whole place has a lively atmosphere added to by the live music played late at night. Highly recommended.

Open: noon–3am Monday-Saturday (noon-midnight Sunday)

Covent Garden, Leicester Square tube 55 seats

Zzzzz's

238 Gray's Inn Road, WC1
☎ 833 4466
£3

Tucked away behind a pine bed shop, this deservedly popular vegetarian take-away is a good place for tasty filling lunches. You can choose from freshly-filled baps, and an interesting selection of 8 or more salads including imaginative combinations such as wheatberry or broccoli and seaweed. There are jacket potatoes, soup, and tremendous wholemeal quiches packed with different vegetables, nuts, seeds and sometimes chewy cheese topping. The cakes and puddings are also a great temptation and their crumble is excellent. There is limited seating – well, room to perch on high stools, anyway, but I think it's better to take the food away and enjoy it in more comfort. There are plans, however, to expand the seating area. There is a minimum charge of £1.75 from 12-2.

Open: 8.30–3.30 Monday-Saturday
Credit cards: none
King's Cross, Chancery Lane — 10 seats

THEATRES AND GALLERIES

Galleries seem to be leading the way when it comes to an improvement in food for vegetarians. I was most impressed by the major ones such as the National Gallery and the Tate, as well as some of the smaller places like the ICA and the art gallery at Whitechapel. The theatre museum in Covent Garden is also excellent. The Arts Centre in Croydon is terrific. (Hockney's, the restaurant there, is reviewed in the Restaurants section.)

Sadly, the theatres don't seem to be nearly so imaginative and it's often best to eat at a nearby restaurant. Smaller theatre venues like the Almeida and the Unicorn have developed excellent ranges of food. What is on offer at the National Theatre is uninspired, and the Barbican reminds me of eating in an airport canteen. Having said that, they both have a vegetarian option at their smarter restaurants but it is often limited to one dish and is the same for lunch and dinner.

Some cinemas have a small selection of wholefood savouries and snacks. The Screen on the Green (Islington) and The Screen on the Hill (Belsize Park) are particularly worth a mention, and the NFT is reviewed.

Institute of Contemporary Arts

★★★

The Mall, SW1
☎ 930 3647
£4

It's well worth the 60p daily membership fee to eat at the ICA. The restaurant itself is most attractive with pastel blue-green walls and black seating. There's always a hot vegetarian dish which could range from lentil and nut roast to cauliflower potato pie or spinach and feta in filo pastry. All very reasonably priced at around £2. The salads look absolutely terrific, and you can have a large plateful for £1.95. Normally the soup is vegetarian, though on the occasion I went it wasn't so do always check. If you are still hungry there is a good range of breads – sometimes a 'secret recipe' chilli bread as well as scones, cakes and puddings. Live music may well be going on in the nearby bar, and there are exhibitions to see, plus a bookshop and lots of unusual postcards to buy. Always a plus point to eating in a gallery.

Open: 12–9 daily
Credit cards: none
Charing Cross or Piccadilly Circus — 50 seats

National Film Theatre

★★

South Bank, Waterloo, SE1
☎ 928 5362
£6

The NFT houses the Riverside Restaurant and coffee bar. I used to feel it was forward-thinking in its catering for vegetarians but some of the other theatres and galleries have overtaken it somewhat. Having said that, there is a very good choice of fresh salads — 13 in all when I last went. The ingredients all looked crisp and some of the combinations were quite imaginative, with sultana and courgette side by side with carrot and yellow pepper. The rest of the vegetarian menu is sadly restricted to a quiche. Occasionally there is a hot savoury such as lasagne and sometimes the soup is safe. I said I wondered what was in the trifle and the reply came — 'so do I!' In the coffee bar there are tasty vegetarian pasties which are quite cheap, and some wholesome flapjacks. Being near the bar it tends to get a little smoky, but in the summer you can eat outside.

Open: 12–2.30, 5.30–9 daily (coffee bar 12.30–3 Monday-Saturday, 12–10 Sunday)
Credit cards: none
Waterloo tube 90 seats

National Gallery

★★

Trafalgar Square, WC2
☎ 839 3321
£4

The restaurant at the National Gallery is in the depths of the building, but it is surprisingly light and airy with high ceilings and long windows. There is plenty of space as the seating area spreads into several rooms. There is a quick service bar for snacks, mostly of the sugary, refined type and a second bar for more substantial meals. The choice for vegetarians is good and imaginative. Possible cold dishes include vegetable mille feuilles, spinach roulade or mushrooms à la grecque, and the hot savoury was lasagne. There were four salads to choose from, all were colourful and included a good mix of ingredients. There was decent bread. It's certainly a useful place to escape the hubbub of Trafalgar Square.

Open: 10–5 daily (2–5 Sunday)
Credit cards: none
Charing Cross tube — 130 seats

The October Gallery Restaurant

★★

24 Old Gloucester Street, WC1
☎ 242 7367
£3

The restaurant is at the far end of the gallery (dedicated to Third World artists) and is cheap and good. All the cooking is done by Suzanne and so it's a relatively simple menu: lack of choice is made up for by the fact that everything on offer looks appealing and is very tasty. Soup with bread and butter is £1.50, main courses change daily and they are usually suitable for vegans. They cost around £2.20. There's normally one choice of mixed green salad with a well-flavoured dressing. You help yourself to fruit juices and coffee. There is a relaxed, friendly atmosphere. The tables are generally shared by several people but are large enough for you to hold your own conversation.

Open: 12.30–2.30 Tuesday-Saturday
Credit cards: none
Holborn tube 40 seats
♿

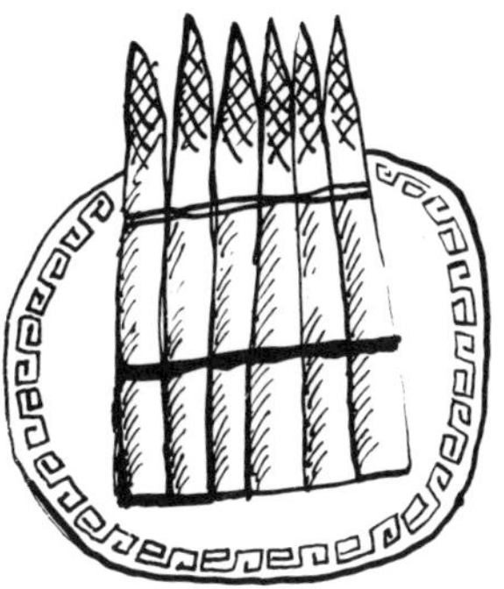

Royal Festival Hall

★★

Belvedere Road, SE1
☎ 921 0800
£5

The eating spaces at the Festival Hall are beautifully airy and spacious, and in the pasta and salad bar there is a large no-smoking area. The choice for vegetarians isn't huge, but what there is is well done. At the salad bar there is hummus and good bread; you can then help yourself to a wide range of interesting mixed salads – coleslaw, rice, Italian, green, etc. At the adjacent pasta bar there is, so far, only one choice but it was very tasty. Puddings and cakes mostly look bought in so do check on ingredients.

When eating at the Festival Hall, you get the benefit of a pleasant environment and foyer music from 12.30–2, and 5.30–7.

Open: 12–2.30, 5.30–10.30 daily (pasta bar closes 10pm)

Waterloo tube 300 seats

Saint George's Theatre Café ★

Tufnell Park Road, N19
☎ 607 7978
£4

The range of food available at this café has unfortunately diminished drastically during the last eighteen months, as have the hours of serving food. It is now really a lunchtime place and only coffee and cakes are available before the performances. For lunch, there was quiche, being kept warm on a hotplate, and a choice of two salads, including white rice, and jacket potato. Pudding consisted of cakes, not wholefood. It is still a useful place to know if you are local or work in the area but certainly not worth a special trip. Maybe they will reconsider the provision of food in the evenings.

Open: 12–2.30 Monday-Saturday
Credit cards: none
Tufnell Park tube 100 seats

The Tate Gallery

★★

Millbank, SW1
☎ 834 6754
£10 restaurant; £3 coffee shop

A beautifully-designed restaurant and coffee shop are both to be found in the bowels of the Tate. The restaurant is very stylish and it is essential to book. They are very friendly and go to great lengths to help vegetarians. There are two starters, both of which can be made into main courses. Most tables are for non-smokers.

The coffee shop is also beautiful to behold. One welcome change since the last edition is the development of a large no-smoking area, leaving just the small room for smokers. They do a wide choice of salads, layered vegetable pie and pasties which were both made with vegetarian pastry. Apparently the demand for these items has increased tremendously and the management show great concern to introduce more wholefoods. Cheese used is not vegetarian.

Open: restaurant: 12–3 Monday-Saturday;
coffee shop: 10.30–5.30 (2–5.15 Sunday)
Credit cards: none
Pimlico tube or 77 bus — 110 seats in each part

The Unicorn Café Bar

6 Great Newport Street, WC2
☎ 240 3787
£6

Since the last edition this café has changed hands, but it is operating on the same principles though a few more of the snack-type savouries, such as samosas and burgers, and cakes are now bought in. The full menu is served from midday. There is still a good choice of hot daily specials such as chilli bean casserole, mushroom stroganoff and Indonesian curry. You can also have filled jacket potatoes, hummus, soups and bread. Salads are fairly basic, simple mixed greenery and grated carrot, etc. However, it all looks fresh and everything is very reasonably priced. The staff serving at the counter are very friendly and the atmosphere in this crowded basement is welcoming. My only regret is that the delicious carrot cake has vanished from the menu.

This is a fun daytime place and is fine in the evenings, too, if you remember that a sudden deluge appears from the theatre in the intervals.

Open: 10–11 Monday-Saturday
Credit cards: none
Leicester Square tube — 40 seats

Victoria and Albert Museum

★★

Cromwell Road, South Kensington, SW7
☎ 581 2159
£5

Run by Milburns (who also run the restaurant at the Museum of London as well as unlikely places such as Durham Cathedral), this restaurant has the most lovely spacious feeling cleverly created with use of unpainted brickwork, arches, and long windows. The choice of food for vegetarians is not extensive but what there is is good and, as they don't have a deep freeze on the premises, things are certainly made freshly. Of the two daily hot dishes one will be vegetarian – pasta and vegetarian mornay, for example – and there is a choice of several cold main courses as well as a help-yourself salad table with at least 8 salads. There is usually a vegetable-based soup, but it's advisable to check on the stock. There was a good selection of wholefood cakes amongst the refined varieties. Certainly everything was tempting and had a nice home-made look. The wine bar section is open 12-2.15, and there are no-smoking areas too. It was heartening to be told by the manager that, apart from the increasing demand for vegetarian and wholefood, about half his staff were now vegetarian.

Open: 10–5 Monday-Saturday (2.30–5.30 Sunday)
Credit cards: none
South Kensington tube 250 seats

The Whitechapel Art Gallery Café

★★★

Whitechapel Road, E1
☎ 377 6182
£5

This is an innovative 'people's' gallery where you can see the work of modern artists and sculptors. There is now an entry fee of £2.50 but, if you explain that you are just there to eat, you may be allowed through -- the exhibitions, though, are very interesting.

The café is smart and clean with a varied range of dishes suitable for vegetarians. There's a hot savoury, baked potatoes with a range of fillings and plenty of salads. The cakes are good, but check on the ingredients. Soups and pastries are usually OK. The gallery is always very busy on a Sunday.

Open: 11–6.30 Tuesday-Sunday
Credit cards: none
Aldgate East tube — 64 seats
♿

Wine Bars

The five places reviewed in this section are more than just wine bars as they offer a comprehensive selection of vegetarian food. They make good venues for more casual evenings out as you can have snacks or a full meal.

Around the capital, there are quite a few others that offer some limited vegetarian dishes. I particularly like Rebato's (169 South Lambeth Road, SW8), a wine and tapas bar, which has a wonderful atmosphere and good Spanish omelette. In Clapham is Ormes (67 Abbeville Road, SW4) which is a wine bar and restaurant. They offer several vegetarian starters, such as garlic mushrooms or deep fried cammembert, and usually one main course. Opposite the Young Vic is a small Spanish-style bar with a good choice of cold hors-d'oeuvres.

Almeida Theatre Wine Bar

★★

Almeida Street, Islington, N1
☎ 226 7432
£6

This popular wine bar next to the Almeida Theatre always has about half of its menu suitable for vegetarians. All of the food is cooked on the premises so it's easy to ask about soup stock and type of fat used. Generally, there is a hot savoury and a choice of a couple of different quiches. For lighter meals, there is hummus, cheese (non-vegetarian) and choice of several excellent salads. The puddings are tempting chunky cakes and crisp apple tart.

Food is not served in the evenings until six o'clock, nor after ten. They also stop serving food 30 minutes before curtain up.

Open: 11–3.30, 5.30–11 (closed Sunday unless there's a special event)
Credit cards: none
Angel tube 40 seats

The Archduke

★★

Concert Hall Approach, South Bank, SE1
☎ 928 9370
£5

A spacious, friendly wine bar built under the railway arches next to the South Bank, it has plenty of windows, split levels and plants to add atmosphere. Queuing at the bar is a grisly experience even for the hardened vegetarian, as you are confronted with a choice of cold meats! But don't despair, as behind lurks a good selection of salads, and there's often hummus, vegetarian pâté or a hearty ploughman's lunch, all served with good chunks of granary bread. It is a popular place so sometimes the vegetarian options run out. It would be lovely if they could develop a non-smoking section. The cheese is not vegetarian.

If you want something more than a hefty snack, there is a smart table-service restaurant on the upper floor which has vegetarian choice. The menu changes every month. It could be spinach pancakes with sherry sauce, ratatouille or onion tart and they cost from £4. Usually about half the starters are suitable and there are some safe puddings.

Open: 11–3, 5.30–11 (closed Saturday lunch and all day Sunday)

Waterloo tube 160 seats

The Fallen Angel

65 Graham Street, N1
☎ 253 3996
£5

The Fallen Angel is a refreshing, bright, café-bar which, as a free house, has an excellent selection of real ales. The decor is adventurous: spacious and airy rather like a French café. Whilst I still think the Fallen Angel has a wonderful friendly atmosphere, they do seem to have had problems during the last year on the food side. If it's there, then what is served is good and tasty but the choice is often very limited. The salad section has diminished and sometimes consists only of mixed greenery and rice. Usually there are two cakes or puddings on offer.

Open: 11.30–12 daily
Credit cards: none
Angel Islington tube — 70 seats

Quaffers

★★★

8 Norfolk Place, London, W2
☎ 724 6046
£12

Quaffers is the kind of wine bar everyone would like to have close by. Pleasant decor, warm welcome, helpful staff, and a good choice of well-prepared vegetarian dishes at a very affordable price. The menu changes daily, but a permanent fixture by popular demand is the deep-fried potato skins, which are terrific. Other starters include soups made with vegetable stocks, crudités and mushroom stuffed with cream cheese. Regular main courses include pancakes, mushroom stroganov or an exotic fruit, nut and cottage cheese salad. There are always a few daily specials and hot dishes are served with at least four vegetables. The desserts are imaginative, too, with home-made cheesecakes, apple and sultana crumble or hot brandy bananas.

Open: 12–2.30, 5.30–11.30 (closed Saturday lunch and all day Sunday)

Paddington tube 45 seats

Tea Rooms Des Artistes

★★

697 Wandsworth Road, Clapham, SW8
☎ 720 4028
£5

You name it and you'll probably find it at this lively casual wine bar south of the river where you can enjoy a spontaneous evening and don't have to be in a crowd to savour the party atmosphere. Allcomers are welcomed by the exceptionally friendly — if a little whimsical — staff behind the bar. Those serving the food have less time for the banter as they are busy turning out a whole range of meals from a tiny kitchen hardly ergonomic in design and with a selection of catering equipment that the V & A might like to get its hands on!

Not all the fare is vegetarian, but the emphasis is that way. There's a standard menu which includes vegetarian terrine, baguette fromage (non-veggie cheese), scrambled egg, help-yourself salads, and country pie. Hot main dishes vary daily. I had a delicious ratatouille with a light topping liberally sprinkled with pine kernels and a piping hot pasta and vegetable layer was just being brought out of the oven. These were served with side vegetables, described as honey-roasted but I think my portion must have missed out! To follow there were cakes and various non-wholefood puddings. You'd need to check what was suitable on the day.

There's a good selection of wines, beers, soft drinks and tea, coffee or hot chocolate.

On the first Sunday of the month, they have a breakfast club, with entertainments, food, drink and newspapers starting at the civilized time of 11.30.

Open: 11–11 Monday-Saturday (11–10.30 Sunday)
BARCLAYCARD VISA (for over £10, if possible)
Clapham Common tube — 120 seats

FURTHER OPTIONS

Apart from all the individual places reviewed in the book, there are an increasing number of chains, particularly the pasta and pizza types as well as leading hotel groups, that do make a commendable effort to cater for vegetarians. Look out for pancake places, too, which often have some imaginative fillings that are safe for vegetarians.

Pasta Mania

Bright, modern pasta places offering a variety of different sauces and different types of pasta. There's also an eat-as-much-as-you-like deal which is good when you are hungry.

Pizza Express

All vegetarian dishes are marked with a Vegetarian Society ♈ sign on the menu. The service is fast and friendly, the decor Italian and the food good.

Pizza Hut

More American in its approach, with plush upholstered seating, self-service salads and a wide range of vegetarian food.

Spud-U-Like and Wendy

Take-away and eat-in baked potatoes with a wide variety of fillings, quite a few of which are vegetarian.

Stations

Waterloo wins hands down as far as I'm concerned. There is a great variety of fast food places with quite good pizzas, some so-called healthy nibbles such as nuts, raisins and dried fruit (standard fare for the travelling vegetarian!) and, best of all, really good coffee from the Costa Coffee Boutique. There's also a range of snacks at Victoria station and a Costa Coffee Boutique just outside on the Vauxhall Bridge Road. If you are stuck at either King's Cross or Euston, you are best advised to walk along to Drummond Street.

Brick Lane

If you find yourself in Petticoat Lane or the Columbia Road Flower Market on a Sunday morning, it's also worth walking down to Brick Lane or the Commercial Road for lunch. There are a great many Indian and Pakistani restaurants offering a wide variety of authentic vegetarian food. They all offer good value and are too numerous to list.

Camden Lock

Plenty of places here that serve take-away savouries and the excellent cakes made by Rose and Antoine. It is extremely busy, especially on a Sunday. Further down the road by Camden tube is Inverness Street which has a little, but very good, vegetarian take-away in the wholefood shop Buzz. Pity about the tuna sandwiches.

Some vegetarian places within easy reach of London

There isn't the space in this book to review all of these though I've managed to visit most during the last few months and had some very pleasant meals. Especially recommended are Barts, Stones and Huckleberries.

Ashtead (Surrey)	Barts, 34 The Street ☎ 03722 75491
Avebury (Wilts)	Stones, High Street ☎ 067 23 514 (seasonal opening)
Bath	Huckleberries, 34 Broad Street ☎ 0225 64876
Berkhamstead (Herts)	Cook's Delight, 360 High Street ☎ 04427 25003
Brighton	Food For Friends, 18 Prince Albert Street ☎ 0273 25003
Cambridge	Nettles, 6 St Edward's Passage ☎ 0223 59302
Croydon	Munbhave, 305 London Road ☎ 01 689 6331
Tunbridge Wells	The Pilgrims, 37 Mount Ephraim ☎ 0892 20341

Geographical Index

Cuisine Index

Type	Name	Page
	Pollyanna's Bistro	87
Indian	Baba Bhelpoori	19
	Bombay Bhelpoori House	23
	The Bombay Mix	24
	Chutney's	32
	Diwana Bhelpoori House	42
	Gaylord	52
	Herbs and Spices	59
	India Club	62
	Jai Krishna	64
	Karna Phuli	66
	Mandeer	71
	Narmada Indian Vegetarian Restaurant	77
	The Raj Bhelpoori House	89
	Rani	90
	Ravi Shankar	91
	Sabras	93
	Shahanshah	95
	Spices	99
	Sree Krishna	100
	Veeraswamy's	102
	The Viceroy of India	103
	Woodlands	107
Indonesian	Melate	74
Italian	The Covent Garden Pasta Bar	36
	Fatso's Pasta Joint	48
	Knoodles	68
	Pizzeria Castellos	85
Japanese	Ajimura Japanese Restaurant	15
Macrobiotic	The East West Centre Restaurant	44
Mexican	Café Pacifico	27
	Zona Rosa	110
Middle-eastern	Al Basha	16
	Baalbeck	18
	The Falafel House	47
	Gaby's Continental Bar	51
	La Reash Cous Cous House	69

Type	Name	Page
	The Olive Tree	81
	Phoenicia	83
Singaporean	The Equatorial	46
Thai	Chiang Mai	30
Theatres/galleries	Almeida Theatre Wine Bar	126
	Institute of Contemporary Arts	114
	National Film Theatre	115
	National Gallery	116
	The October Gallery Restaurant	117
	Royal Festival Hall	118
	Saint George's Theatre Café	119
	The Tate Gallery	120
	The Unicorn Café Bar	121
	Victoria and Albert Museum	122
	The Whitechapel Art Gallery	123
Vegan	Country Life	35
Wholefood	The Angel Gate	17
	The Beehive	21
	The Cherry Orchard	29
	Christy's Healthline	31
	Compton Green	33
	Cordon Vert	34
	Cranks	37
	Di's Larder	40
	The Dining Room	41
	Food For Thought	49
	Govindas	55
	The Greenhouse	56
	Hockney's	60
	Huffs	61
	Jazz Café	65
	The London Ecology Centre	70
	Manna	72
	Millwards	75
	Neal's Yard Bakery and Tea Room	78
	Nouveau Quiche	79
	The Nuthouse	80

Type	Name	Page
	Rainbow	88
	Raw Deal	92
	Seasons	94
	Slenders	96
	Something Else	98
	Tea Rooms des Artistes	130
	The Wholemeal Café	104
	Wilkins Natural Foods	105
	The Windmill	106
Wine bars	Almeida Theatre Wine Bar	126
	The Archduke	127
	The Fallen Angel	128
	Quaffers	129

Your comments

Please send this page, or a photocopy, (you don't need stamps) to:

Sarah Brown's Vegetarian London,
Thorsons Publishers Limited,
FREEPOST,
Wellingborough
Northamptonshire NN8 2BR

Name of restaurant: ....

Address: ....

....

....

Phone no.: ....

Date of last visit: ....

Completely vegetarian, or do they serve meat as well?

....

What was the atmosphere like? ....

....

....

....

Were the staff friendly and helpful? ....

....

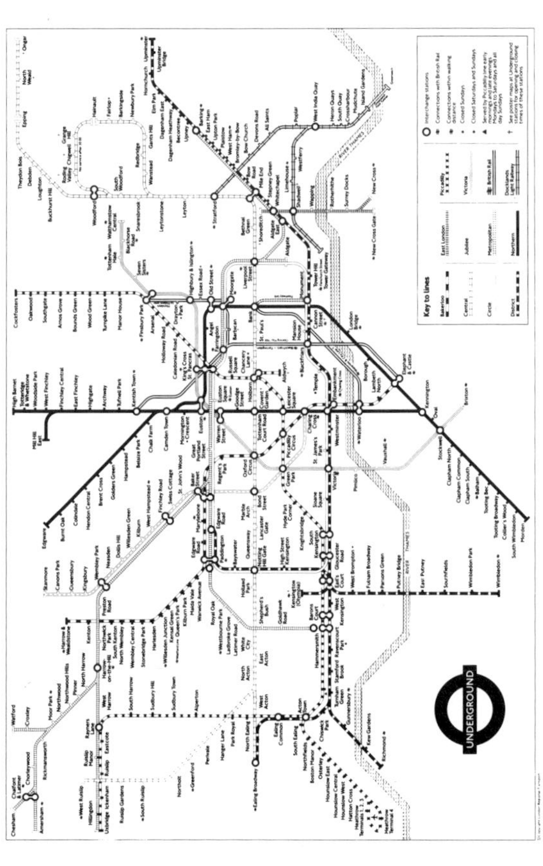

London Regional Transport Underground Map
Registered User Number 88/834

What dishes are especially worth mentioning? ....

....

....

....

What did your meal cost? ....

Any other comments?..

....

....

....

Your name and address:.......................................

....

....

....

A LIFE ON THE WILD SIDE

BY

COLIN WILLOCK

The adventures and misadventures of a wildlife film-maker

®

Other Publications

Come Fishing with Me
Come Fly Fishing with Me
In Praise of Fishing
Coarse Fishing
Death at Flight
Death at the Strike
The Gun Punt Adventure
Red, Pole or Perch
The Angler's Encyclopaedia
The Man's Book
The Farmer's Book of Field Sports
Death in Covert
Kenzie, The Wild Goose Man
Duck Shooting
Look at African Animals
The ABC of Fishing
The Survival Series of Books
The Enormous Zoo
The Animal Catchers
The Bedside Wildfowler
The Penguin Guide to Fishing
Landscape with Solitary Figure
Hazanda
The Coast of Loneliness
The Fighters
Town Gun
The ABC of Shooting
The Great Rift Valley
Gorilla; Dudley, The Worse Dog in the World
The World of Survival
Town Gun 2
In the Rut
The Complete Dudley
Kingdom of the Deep
Kingdoms of the East
Wildfight
The New ABC of Fishing
The New ABC of Shooting
The Book of Wood Pigeon

This book is for the family and
especially our grandchildren in
the hope that they will have as much
fun out of life as we have had!

Published in the United Kingdom by the

WORLD PHEASANT ASSOCIATION

PO Box 5, Lower Basildon, Reading, Berkshire RG8 9PF

ISBN 0 906864 65 8

Cover photograph: Charging elephant by Lee Lyon
Printed in Great Britain by Trio Graphics Ltd., Gloucester

CONTENTS

Acknowledgements

My thanks must go first and foremost to Keith Howman, President of the World Pheasant Association, whose enthusiasm made the publication of this book not only possible but a positive pleasure.

Second to Alaric Jackson, my young computer Guru, without whose help in the early days of owning a new Samsung word processor, I doubt whether I would have got a single line on paper. And my undying thanks to Jane Clacey whose computer magic turned my shambling efforts into a faultless manuscript. She also did the lay-out.

As to illustrations, I am deeply indebted to Alison Aitken of Survival and Tom Walshe of Anglia Television who trawled through the depths of musty filing cabinets to find a number of pictures that illustrate this book. And, of course, to the wildlife and Anglia Television photographers who took those pictures, particularly Alan and Joan Root, Des and Jen Bartlett, Dieter and Mary Plage, Lee Lyon, Mike Price, Cindy Buxton and Annie Price and Allan Cash, who though not a member of Survival, took some of the rhino-catching pictures. My thanks, too, to the Daily Mirror for the picture of the Queen at a Survival gala premier and to Mrs Bob Ashby who lent me her late husband's picture of Kenzie Thorpe. The splendid front cover picture of the charging elephant is by Lee Lyon.

Lastly, I owe an immeasurable debt to Aubrey Buxton who created the Survival unit and thus made these adventures possible.

A tribute to the wonderful world of pheasants

This book is not about filming pheasants, a fact which makes me all the more surprised, honoured and delighted to have the WPA as my publisher. However, in nearly thirty years of wildlife film-making for the long running ITV wildlife series 'Survival', we were never far away from the galliformes and frequently right among them. In many 'Survival' films, galliformes played a walk-on and, not infrequently, a starring part. And when they did, I knew where to turn for advice and invariably did so, usually to Keith Howman and always to the WPA. In fact we did quite a lot of captive filming of rare species at Keith and Jean Howman's home at Ashmere, Middlesex.

In the field we were often close to some of the more exciting members of the WPA's avian members—even the megapodes. In Australia, Des Bartlett, the daddy of all wildlife cameramen, who features prominently in this book, shot a remarkable film about the malleefowl, the clever bird that buries its egg in compost heaps and returns daily to test the temperature of the heap for incubation purposes. In Sulawesi, 'Survival's' cameras covered the even smarter megapode that has discovered that hot volcanic ash or sand can do the job equally well for it.

In Sumatra, while filming orang-utans, I saw the display mound of the biggest pheasant of them all, the Argus, though sadly not the bird itself. And in Sri Lanka while making a leopard film with Dieter Plage—another star of this book—I recall the frustrations of trying to persuade red junglefowl to pose in the open sunlight of a jungle glade. They always seemed to prefer to lurk in the shadows. Peafowl, on the other hand, were generally willing to show off their finery for the cameras in full display. But then they are not known as vain birds for nothing.

I never, alas, saw a Congo peafowl though in Africa our cameras were never far away from pheasant relatives, the helmeted guineafowl that haunt the waterholes of Namibia and the Vulturine guineafowl of northern Kenya with their bare predatory beaks and faces and striped blue, black and white breast feathers that excite the acquisitive instincts of fly-tyers! I am not sure if the diminutive button quail qualifies for inclusion. For some reason , this tiny game bird lacks the rear toe of true quails but I've no doubt they can still find shelter under the WPA's worldwide umbrella.

And talking of quail, in Arizona while filming the inhabitants of the giant saguaro cacti in the Sonoran Desert, I became totally enslaved by the diminutive Gambel's quail with their seductive gait and nodding top-knots.

When making wildlife films the first rule should be never to succumb to anthropomorphism, that cardinal sin which persuades you, however briefly, to imbue animals with human feelings and qualities. With Gambel's quail I confess that I went over the top. In the ruins of Tombstone we made a western in which Gambel's were presented as saloon girls and rattlers as quick-draw gun-fighters. When I add that Rolf Harris wrote the songs and spoke the commentary, I believe you will get the picture. I can see no harm in just occasionally having some fun with wildlife film-making, provided you don't go too far. Maybe with the Gambel's dancing girls we went OTT, or over the top as they say in show business. I can't say that I ever regretted this one lapse from the straight and narrow.

And, of course, there were the truly straight wildlife films in which galliformes played the leading roles. At 13,000 feet in the Himalayas of Nepal, Ashish Chandola made a brilliant study of the national bird of that country, the Monal, Impeyan or, as it sometimes known, and the film was called, 'The Bird of Nine Colours'. I recall. too, that blood pheasants and kalij pheasants also played prominent parts in Ashish's film.

Toby Bromley, a talented amateur film-maker with real professional ability, shot a brilliant half hour about red grouse and peregrines in which it was conclusively proved that the grouse could outfly the falcon in level flight and even knew how to evade capture by flying between the strands of a barbed wire fence.

Blackcock on a lek, yes, and 'The Old Man of the Woods' featuring a bird in the wild forests of Tayside that stars frequently at WPA Game Fair displays, the largest grouse of all, the Capercaillie.

I'm sure I have left some galliforme wildlife film performers out . They seem to crop up almost everywhere. I will conclude with a film made with the help of no less an eminence than the Director General of the Game Conservancy himself, Dick Potts. At the time, Dick was doing field work on grey partridges and generously gave time and advice to our wildlife cameramen.

Oh, yes, I nearly forgot to mention Merriam's wild turkey, Attwater's prairie chicken and the sage grouse of North America, all of which were captured by Des Bartlett's camera. As I said, this book is mainly about the adventures and misadventures of wildlife film-making with the larger members of the animal kingdom. But I hope I have said enough to reassure my readers that the galliformes were usually in the supporting cast and not infrequently in leading roles.

Colin Willock
Walton-on-Thames
2001

A Gentle Beginning

If there is a turning point in everyone's life then maggots, or gentles as they are sometimes more politely known, were mine. Maggots may not be to everyone's taste. As a life-long angler I have always had a soft spot for them, even though I know that, left to their own devices, they will turn into exceptionally nasty blue- or maybe green-bottles. My wife, who features a good deal in this narrative, is not fond of them. Maybe this is because in the first years of our marriage I kept them in the fridge. Occasionally, I made the breathing holes in the tin a half millimetre too large. This is all the encouragement an enterprising maggot needs to escape. I recall one horrific dinner party at which the guests found unexpected living additions to the salad. But let that pass. I will return to the dramatic turn maggots gave to my life.

In the nineteen fifties I had left Fleet Street, along with other magazine editors and journalists, and landed rather to my surprise in television. By a process too complicated to go into here, I found myself deputy editor of the current affairs programme *This Week*. It was the flagship political programme of the long defunct London TV company Associated Rediffusion. It was a role for which, apart from my journalistic qualifications (editor of *Lilliput* and assistant editor of *Picture Post*) I was totally unsuited or anyway wrongly oriented. The trouble was that my interests were with the birds and bees, with fish, flora, fauna and fowl. I cannot explain this. I am the only member of my family thus obsessed. As far as *This Week* was concerned I was far too often pointing in the wrong direction. There cannot have been a more urban company that Rediffusion. I doubt whether most of their programme bosses had ever set foot in a cowpat. So whenever possible, as a change from interviewing George Brown (when sober) and Randolph Churchill (usually when not), I dragged *This Week's* camera crews to country fairs, point-to-points, terrier races, river banks and hunter trials. On the whole, this was tolerated as lightweight counterpoint to the major political items of the day which in my view got far too much air-time. I can now see that my item on Frank Murgett's maggotorium was judged by the upper echelons of Rediffusion, and in particular, by Captain Brownrigg, who ran the TV company as though it was a naval dockyard, as crossing several bridges too far.

The way it happened was this. David Kentish, who was editor-in-chief of the programme, wanted a light item for the show going out on June 16. David was the one person who sometimes lent a sympathetic ear to my loonier suggestions. "David," I said, expecting the answer "no," "June 16 is the opening of the coarse fishing season. There are possibly one hundred thousand coarse fishermen in Greater London. Most of them go fishing with maggots for bait. I happen to have a friend called Frank Murgett who runs a maggot factory."

Unexpectedly, he took the bait. "Where?"

"Not far from Heathrow. Near Yiewsley in fact."

"Okay," he said, "I'll give it three minutes maximum and it had better be good. How will this man Murgett come across?"

"Enormously." An easy boast to justify. Everything about Frank Murgett was enormous.

So, on a sweltering June day, I lead a film crew into the wasteland that lies between Heathrow and Yiewsley, a wilderness of stubby grass, overgrown ditches, collapsed barbed wired fences, dog turds, abandoned and usually wheeless cars and a group of Nissen huts that constituted Murgett's maggotorium.. There could be little doubt that this was an ideal site for such an enterprise.

In those days, to capture the most fleeting image on film along with the appropriate dialogue and sound effects required a crew of between twelve and fifteen people,most of whom were called upon to do nothing but be there. The film unions were in complete control of a labour situation which managements were helpless to alter. Thus we had gaffers and grips and best boys (whatever they were), lighting men and sound men, a cameraman and assistant cameraman, a director, and naturally his personal assistant. This was before we even got down to such essential personnel as the driver and the chap who was actually going to do the interviewing. The latter was often backed up by a writer and researcher who told him what questions to ask, both parts, in this case, played by me.

The lot that dismounted at Murgett's maggotorium was at full battalion strength. Most film crews with whom I worked in those days struck me as being of a delicate disposition. I am not talking, mind you, about the battle-scarred news gatherers who appear to relish being dropped by parachute into the middle of a civil war. Those heroes could probably have faced the maggotorium without flinching. But not our boys.

We had an admirably tough little director called Sheila Greig. Because of the position and the suitably unphotogenic nature of the rear of the factory, Sheila correctly decided that the only possible set-up for the camera was downwind of the maggotorium.

As you undoubtedly know, the most noticeable bi-product of the manufacture of maggots on a large scale is a blinding, choking cloud of ammonia. This, combined with the odour of rotting meat on which the maggots feed, has been known to fell a strong man at fifty paces. This assault on the olfactory senses was something which Murgett described with some pride as 'the pong'. The pong had made itself felt as far as the borough of Yiewsley, some mile and a half downwind. So much so in fact that the municipal authorities had several times threatened legal action. Murgett's reply had been to install large fans which distributed, not entirely to Yiewsley's satisfaction, a 'deponging agent'.

It was unfortunate for the more sensitive members of the film crew that they had to wait downwind for half an hour while Murgett unloaded a fresh, if that is the word, consignment of condemned meat from Smithfield Market.

"This stuff won't keep, you realise," he told Sheila.

"Won't be a mo."

By the time Murgett was ready, the interviewer,Michael Nelson,. who couldn't work unless he had a hang-over, had turned a light shade of jade. The 'grips' had thrown up in the bushes. Meantime, Sheila had requested that Murgett make his entrance through the double corrugated iron doors at the rear of the main breeding chamber.

The moment, when it came, was a show-stopper. The doors rattled open. This huge, red-faced man appeared as if wafted on a visible cloud of pong. In each hand he held up an Aylesbury duck in such an advanced stage of decomposition that its flesh glowed putrescently green through its feathers. Looking benignly round the shuddering film crew, Murgett spoke his opening lines. "I am going," he said, "to see that each one of you has a duck like this to take home."

I cannot remember now whether the item ever made the programme. On the whole, I think not. Up on the bridge at Rediffusion, Captain Brownrigg probably decided that maggots, let alone Murgett, wouldn't mix too well with the breakfast food commercials. I am not suggesting for a moment that someone said the hard word: "Willock must go." But I am fairly sure that it was felt by the management that a more suitable outlet for my talents must be found. One turned up almost immediately. *This Week* found that it could honourably dispense with my services. I was about to start a life on the wild side.

Shortly after the maggot episode, I was transferred on loan to the newly formed Anglia Television. Anglia had thoughts about starting a natural history programme. I was working at home on a prototype for this project when the phone rang and a rather plummy voice asked: "Could you go to Uganda next Thursday and help catch some white rhinos?" "Why, yes," I said. "That sounds interesting."

Interesting! At that precise moment in 1961, I didn't know a white rhino from a black one. I just had this nasty feeling that both species had a long sharp horn at the front end which they quite often stuck into people who interfered with their preferred way of life. The voice at the other end seemed to be suggesting that this was more or less what we were proposing to do—for their own good, of course. But would they know that? I wondered about this but didn't like to ask. The voice explained that I wasn't expected to catch them myself but to bring back a film about their capture and translocation to a place of safety.

My vagueness about the colouring of rhinos extended, I discovered, to the exact location of Uganda. A glance at the world atlas quickly cleared that up. It was more or less where I had expected it to be, somewhere between the Sudan in the north, Kenya (which the ignorant pronounced: some people still do— K*ee*nya), the Congo to the west and Ruanda-Burundi to the south. Altogether a pretty exciting location and just the sort of place you might expect to encounter rhinos, either black or white. This was turning point number two. You can possibly loosen the hold which maggots have on the imagination but not rhinos, no definitely not rhinos.

There is, of course, the boring bit about how I obtained my transfer from maggots to rhinos so I will get it over as quickly as possible. About the time the political pundits of Rediffusion had decided that I was unsuited for heavy work in the political arena, Anglia Television started transmitting from Norwich. Anglia's song was the fluting trill of the skylark and the call of the wild goose. Rediffusion's, if it had a song at all, was the rumble of the Underground and the hoot of the London taxi. Most of Anglia's directors were farmers. Had not the ancestor of their Chairman, Lord Townshend, invented the agricultural revolution or at least the rotation of crops? This is not to say that Anglia's directors were not shrewd businessmen. You have to be if you're going to get top price for your sugar beet. But they also knew about the birds and bees. Most were pretty handy with a shotgun. To be a proper kind of shooting man is not so far from being a proper kind of naturalist as some townsmen might think. And so we come to that plummy voice requesting that I go to Uganda. The voice belonged to Aubrey, later Lord Buxton, Managing Director of Anglia. Aubrey summed up all the qualities and skills, inherited or learned, required of a director of Anglia Television, sometimes referred to as the Sugar Beet Network and once memorably described by David Niven as Nineteenth Century Fox. Aubrey farmed. He had been a successful industrialist. He had spent a good deal of his youth along the north Norfolk coast among the longshoremen, fishermen and wildfowlers who are about as close to nature as it is possible to be without having been born in a seabird's nest. He could probably have found a place in a team of the best eleven game shots in Britain. He was enormously knowledgeable about birds and was what is often pompously referred to as 'a distinguished ornithologist'. He was also an accomplished water colour artist. More important, he knew as friends a lot of the right people in the wildlife game, including Peter Scott, Prince Philip and Sir Solly Zuckerman, scientific advisor to the government. In short, he packed a lot of the essential clout necessary to start anything in the then uncharted world of commercial television. It all started in a very mild way.

Aubrey had invented a nice little show called *Countryman*. It was like the BBC's *Look* with Aubrey playing the Peter Scott part and local naturalist cameramen, amateur for the most part, showing their bits of film about red squirrels or badgers, and very nice, too. It went down extremely well in good old birdy East Anglia. Encouraged by this reception, Aubrey took a tape of his modest programme to the big city and showed it to John MacMillan, Controller of Programmes at Rediffusion. MacMillan was smart as an Indian tracker at finding his way through the jungles of commercial TV but was likely to faint if exposed to genuine fresh air. MacMillan took a look at *Countryman* and, true to his remit, said: "make me a programme about wildlife in London and I might be willing to listen."

Lesser men would have blanched, but not Aubrey. "Easy." he said, and then looked round for someone to do it. *This Week* had been hoping for an opportunity to unload the maggot man without actually firing him. "Take Willock," they said. And that was how I got the job.

No one asked for my scientific qualifications which was just as well as I didn't have any. But then television has never rated academic training too highly. What I did have was the undying curiosity and desire to find out that distinguishes the journalist from normal people. And, having found out, I have an equally strong, if not stronger, desire to tell the rest of the world what I have discovered. It's sometimes called a compulsion to communicate. And if the subject turns out to be the natural world and what we are doing to it, what more could any communicator with the world's most powerful means of communication at his disposal ask?

Amateur naturalist? Yes, since schooldays. My consuming interest in what was then called natural history was sparked at the age of ten by a set of fifty Player's cigarette cards wonderfully depicting British butterflies. If such beauty, diversity and adaptation could exist in the British countryside,what might the wider world have to offer? It would be a long time before I had the chance to find out. I had, however, discovered one very important fact. And, if that was the sum total of education I received from two expensive schools, then my parents' money hadn't been entirely wasted. I got this knowledge, not from the class-room or playing field, God forbid, but from a few inspired masters and the natural history societies they sponsored and encouraged. There was, naturally, a price to be paid. Members of such societies were considered by their fellow scholars to be weedy or wet and taunted accordingly. It was well worth this minor ridicule. The all-important truth you began to realise was that once you have learned what makes badgers, butterflies or tawny owls tick, it isn't too difficult to apply the same principles to rhinos or fish eagles. Nowadays, it's called ecology. To find out about it, all you have to do is to ask the right people the right questions and study the right scientific papers and books. And the right people are the second thing this book is all about.

So we made John MacMillan's programme about wildlife in London. Rediffusion lent me to Anglia to do it. My recollection is that it was brash and pretty dire, but it also broke new ground. We took a fox in a laundry basket to Hampstead Heath in order to film a genuine London fox. It obviously knew its way round. It escaped before we could film it and disappeared in the direction of 'The Spaniards' pub. Aubrey did the links and introduction, filmed in St James' Park and other well-known London wildlife locations. Most of the wildlife footage was bought in from other sources. My researches had discovered that a puffin had once made a forced landing in Hyde Park. The puffin that appeared in our programme, however, had been filmed on the cliffs of Pembrokeshire. No one seemed to notice, certainly not the then unsophisticated viewers. It would be different now! The brightest thing was the introduction by our director, Bill Morton, of a little-known jazz musician, John Dankworth, to write the score. Dankworth caused a lot of fluttering in naturalist dovecotes. "Disgusting," said the natural sound purists. It was some years before dear old Auntie BBC hitched up her skirts and danced a jig to her own wildlife programmes.

Brash or not, we had started something. Rediffusion was already muttering about an occasional series. A series had to have a title. *Survival* seemed a good one. Aubrey claims that he thought of it. So, as a matter of fact, do I. It really doesn't matter. What does matter is that forty years later, *Survival* was still surviving.

So we made a second one about the return of a wading bird, the avocet, to nest in England. That, too, consisted of other people's footage stuck together with filmed links. It couldn't go on like that. We had somehow to originate our own wildlife material. As I said, I was at home working on a new script exploring this idea when the phone range and Aubrey Buxton said: " can you go to Uganda next Thursday to help catch some white rhinos?"

My life on the wild side had really begun.

The author in the Falklands. Just after this picture was taken, a large bird of prey, a caracara, seized his binoculars and flew off with them.

Aubrey Buxton, founder of *Survival* on seldom visited Central Island in lake Rudolf. The sign must be one of the loneliest jokes in the world.

Peter Scott, scientific advisor to *Survival* outside the East Lighthouse, Sutton Bridge, Lincolnshire, where he started his first collection of wildfowl.

A gala premiere for *Survival.* The Queen talks to the wildlife camera team, Alan and Joan Root. Film director Stanley Joseph, centre. Author waits his turn, left.

To Catch a Rhino

My wife came to see us off at Gatwick. Though her lip trembled a bit she put a pretty brave face around it. After all, no one in our family had ever been rhino-catching before. I say 'us' because I now had a partner and a very intrepid one at that.

I honestly don't believe that until quite late in the day it had occurred to any of us that to make a film about rhino-catching we would need a special kind of cameraman. Not the ten men, two girls and a boy that the film unions demanded for immortalising maggot factories, but one, or possibly two, commando type cinematographers who knew one end of a rhino from the other. What we needed, in fact, was what later came to be known as a wildlife cameraman. In those days, there weren't many around unless you count Hans and Lotte Hass, dear mermaid-like Lotte with her hair streaming amongst the coral reefs like golden seaweed; or, for that matter, Armand and Michaela Dennis who didn't shoot a foot of the film used in their *On Safari* series. It was all filmed by the Australian Des Bartlett of whom much more later. So we turned to Aubrey's cousin John Buxton who lived at Horsey Hall in Norfolk and specialised in capturing black and white images of bearded tits and marsh harriers.

In fact, John's father, Anthony Buxton, himself a distinguished naturalist, had bought Horsey Hall just because marsh harriers nested in the reed beds there.

What John lacked in advanced camera technique he more than made up for in true grit. I always had the feeling that this charming, brave and modest man had been born out of his century. He should perhaps have commanded a British square when charged by the Mad Mahdi's dervishes at Omdurman. That might have given both the fuzzies and Rudyard Kipling something to think about. Only when we arrived in Africa did I discover that John had packed his dinner jacket to go rhino-catching—an obvious first for the *Guinness Book of Records*. As he explained: "you never know who you may meet. There are Buxtons all over the world." He was quite right. There is one behind practically every tree.

Our wives saw us aboard the Viscount late one spring evening. Travelling by Viscount en route to Entebbe was a bit like taking the stage-coach to Dodge City. It stopped everywhere. I have always felt sad that I never experienced the years of stately air travel in the mid-and late thirties aboard those huge Imperial Airways monsters with biplane wings somehow bolted on top of their boat-like fuselages. They had names like Hercules, Heracles, Hannibal and Argosy and descended like gracious dragon-flies at Croydon Airport. Even nobler were the Empire flying-boats—later the wartime Sunderlands—that carried you to East Africa alighting for overnight stops and gin-slings along the Nile and southward towards the wondrous chain of Rift Valley lakes. Those must have been the days with the first-class passengers reclining in wicker chairs while uniformed butlers served the drinks—or so I like to imagine. Utter bliss! The good old Viscount never quite lived up to those standards but it did stop everywhere, Rome and Khartoum and best of all, Benina, formerly Bizerta. We refuelled there in the middle of a velvet night. The ground staff reminded one of conflicts past since they wore the discarded greatcoats of British, German and Italian armies to guard them against the desert chill.

As we flew southwards, I stared out of the Viscount's windows, trying to identify lakes and savannas that I would come to know well at ground level during the next thirty years. Was that Lake Rudolf and were those volcanoes at its southern end with the black lava streams pouring over the crater lips still active? We landed at last at Entebbe where years later the Israeli commandos liberated Idi Amin's hostages. The hot herby scent of Africa made one's head swim, a form of delightful intoxication from which mine was never to recover. A signpost pointed back the way we had come. It said six thousand and something miles to London. But it felt much further than that.

John Blower met us off the plane. John had been head of the Uganda Game Department. He was now the game boss of the Uganda Development Corporation, a concern created for and geared up to sell this game-rich country to an expected and hoped-for invasion of European and American hunters, photographers and wildlife viewers.

Blower fits my theory that big countries produce big characters. Glorious eccentrics need room in which to expand and bloom. Africa, and especially East Africa, provides, or, anyway, provided, ideal space and the perfect environment for both expansion and blooming. With silk scarf threaded through a leather ring just below the Adam's apple, immaculately clad in well-ironed bush jacket and kahki shorts, Blower was so laid back that he was almost horizontal. A tall, lean man,

Blower possessed that deceptive form of languid horizontality that one associates with the Long Range Desert Group of World War Two or the Bengal Lancers of an earlier age.

As we roared out of the airport in his battered yellow Land Rover, Blower waved his hand in the direction of a neighbouring swamp and drawled: "would you believe there are sitatunga in there?"

At that moment I would have believed anything, even if I had known what sitatunga were. Maybe they were a swamp tribe like the Seminole Indians of old Florida. Not so. Sitatunga were marsh antelope, Blower explained, their elongated hooves evolved and adapted to cope with their watery environment and the reeds among which they waded. Had we, in Blower's eyes, failed the first test by ignorance of the habits of marsh antelope? I began to wish that Player's Cigarettes had followed up fifty cards on British butterflies with a similar series on African antelope. But apparently we had not fallen at the first hurdle. We had scored at least six out of ten, four for genuine interest and an obvious desire to learn and two for humility in the face of total ignorance. There were other tests to come.

The next test was ordeal by Trimmer. Bombo Trimmer was that night giving a small party in his house in Kampala to welcome the greenhorns from the old country. Bombo, a former Colonel in the King's African Rifles, was named after the garrison town in which the 3/4th battalion of the KAR was based. What he had done to earn the accolade of the township's name I never discovered, and, even when I knew him well, didn't like to ask. The nickname suited this small, cherubic, humourous and immensely out-going man down to the soles of his desert boots. Bombo sounded as though he might be one of the small volcanoes in which East Africa abounds. He certainly always looked as if he was about to explode, if only from blood pressure. In fact, he was not at all the ex-Army chuffer-duffer Colonel he sometimes appeared to be. Bombo, I soon learned, was an excellent Director of the newly created Uganda National Parks who understood, amongst other things, the need to introduce the best scientists into the parks to unravel their ecological mysteries. A most unusual man in many respects. I discovered from his wife, Kay, that he would sometimes sit up far into the night writing a one-act play about some burning issue of the day. This was then invariably locked away in his desk drawer never to be seen, let alone performed, by anyone else.

Bombo's alcoholic regime was fierce though strictly regimented. Come six p. m., the gin would be broken out. It would then be punished severely until nine p. m. when total abstinence took over. A lot of gin can, however, be consumed in that time and usually was. The routine both recognised the need for alcoholic support in tropical climes as well as the dangers of over-indulgence. In Bombo's case, and that of his splendid wife, Kay, the system appeared to work excellently. On party nights, such as the one given to welcome John Buxton and myself, the rules were, however, somewhat relaxed. The most vivid impressions I have of that evening was of the long slim form of John Blower sliding elegantly down the side of a Volkswagen Beetle and disappearing downhill into a rose-bed. As far as I can recall, no one commented on this phenomenon or tried to salvage him.

Apparently, we passed this test also. In a few days, Bombo told us, we were to be posted for a brief course of indoctrination to Murchison Falls National Park. The rhino-catchers, it seemed, weren't quite ready to receive us yet. Some crisis involving vehicles and hippos. In the meantime there was the urgent need to find not only some transport, but, if it were at all possible, a second cameraman.

The Land Rover we hired had lived a hard life. It was a Series One model, the type that was fitted with two spring clips to hold its bonnet closed. I have a feeling that the clips were holding the whole ancient vehicle together. The man who hired it to us admitted that the clutch sometimes slipped. This, he said, was easily and instantly remedied by pouring a bottle of Fanta Orange into the clutch housing. Apparently this sticky citrus drink renewed the grip that the clutch plates had lost in years of what he described as bundu-bashing, East African for cross-country work in unfriendly terrain.

The road north to Murchison had a uniquely unfriendly surface. The ruts were corrugated at one yard intervals so that each revolution of the wheels hurtled the vehicle from the pit of one corrugation to the crest of the next. It seemed that every vehicle that passed, our own included, aggravated this situation by digging deeper pits in exactly the same place as its predecessor. The soil excavated from the pit served to increase the height of the next crest. The only cure for this was to regrade the entire road surface by scraping it more or less flat again.. This happened about once a year. It seemed that we were caught more or less in an inter-grading period. The grader wasn't due to tackle this 150 mile stretch between Kampala and our immediate destination, a small town called Masindi, for another six months.

Masindi is notable for two things. It was the scene of a great battle in 1872 at which Sir Samuel Baker, discoverer of Lake Albert, defeated the overwhelming forces of the local Bunyoro King, Kabarega, who, not unnaturally, objected to Sir Samuel attempting to set up an independent province, to be called Ismalia, on his home patch. Masindi was also the home of Uganda's only British settler, Chiels Margach. Bombo and Blower had recommended that we contact the owner of this African-sounding name as he was not only a Trustee of the Uganda National Parks but also a keen naturalist and owner of a 16mm Bolex cine camera.

The owner of Kinyala Plantation turned out to be a small, soft-spoken Scot. As to the name... Margach was pronounced Margo and Chiels was a Scottish diminutive for child The only child-like thing about this kindly and welcoming man was his complete resignation to, and apparently happy acceptance of, what Africa and Africans could do to one's way of life and way of making a living.

Chiels' father had decided to settle at Masindi in the 1920's. Whereas most Brits, including the wild and womanising Happy Valley lot, had romped off to grow coffee or raise cattle in Kenya, Margach senior had for some reason been one of the very few settlers to opt for Uganda. By hindsight, it was not hard to see why. Uganda slowly and seductively unveiled itself to the writer over the next few years as one of the most beautiful small kingdoms on earth. Perhaps Margach Père had sensed this. He had also correctly assessed the suitability of the soil around Masindi to grow coffee, pawpaws, ginger, pineapples and bananas. The house he built himself in the wilderness might have been designed by Robert the Bruce with a few mod. cons. added. Kinyala was a cross between a border fortress and a Scottish manse. If nothing else, the thickness of the walls kept the heat out.

As a Trustee of the national parks, Chiels knew all about the white rhino operation. The rhinos were up north in an area called Madi District in West Nile Province. If the poachers had their way, they wouldn't be there much longer. While their corpses rotted in the bush, their horns would be on the way to middlemen at the coast. The horn would either be sold for big money as dagger handles to oil-rich Arabs or ground up into powder as an aphrodisiac to perk up old men in China. The parks had hired the rhino catchers to capture and shift as many white rhinos as possible to the comparative safety of Murchison Falls National Park. The catchers were to be paid in baby hippos caught in the Queen Elizabeth National Park in the south of Uganda which they would be free to sell to zoos. There was no conservation contradiction in this as the Queen Elizabeth Park had hippos at pest proportions. Apparently they hadn't caught their quota yet. That's why we were waiting for them. At supper we suggested that Chiels might like to join John Buxton and I, along with his 16mm cine camera, for the rhino catch. He thought, he said, we were never going to ask. Chiels stuck his knife into a freshly picked pineapple, musing in that soft Highland voice: "do you know I've grown these damn things here for twenty years and this is the first one off the plantation I've ever eaten. Even then I had to buy it off some bastard by the side of the road for ten cents." There was nothing resentful in this remark. That was the way things were in Africa and probably always would be.

When you are going rhino-catching for the first and possibly last time in your life, nothing concentrates the mind so much as a great pile of steaming elephant shit in the middle of the road. It announces as clearly as anything is ever likely to do that you are entering a world whose occupants are much larger than you are. It also tells you that an elephant, or more likely a whole lot of elephants, have crossed your path quite recently.

In time, of course, you get a proper sense of proportion about this. Nowadays, when there are possibly more zebra-striped mini buses in the national parks than there are zebras, the wildlife tourists take such things in their stride if, indeed, they notice them at all. But not John Buxton and I as we bounced along the rutted road from Masindi towards the Victoria Nile and the boundaries of Murchison. That pile of dung told us more plainly than anything we had yet encountered that we were in big game country. When you are as green as we were, the thought inevitably occurs to you that, whereas John Blower or Bombo Trimmer would know exactly what to do on meeting an uncooperative wild elephant, you almost certainly do not.

Pretty soon after our encounter with the elephant dropping, we were among the perpetrator, or perpetrators , and in large numbers. There were elephants on both sides and in all directions, all steadily chomping their way through the landscape, occasionally pausing to flatten a large tree whose topmost branches contained some delicacy they could not otherwise have reached. These battleship- grey behemoths reminded me of pictures I had seen as a boy of naval reviews of ironclads at Spithead. You almost expected to see white ensigns fluttering from their considerable grey sterns.

The park proper starts at the Victoria Nile. You cross it at Paraa on a chain ferry among snorting, grunting, wallowing hippos. The hippos struck me at first encounter as rather endearing creatures, flicking water drops off their ear tips and submerging with only eyes, ears and nostrils showing above the surface so that they resembled giant frogs. Very large crocodiles, some twelve feet long, lay companionably on the sandy banks like beached logs or dug-out canoes hauled out for repair. Wrong on both counts. Hippos, I soon learned, are far from endearing. Crocs may look as if they are asleep but they are on permanent red alert. One flick of the tail and they launch themselves like torpedoes. I learned all this— and much more—from John Savidge, warden of Murchison Falls Park. John was to be responsible for the next stage in our crash course in big gameology.

John Savidge dropped us off at Paraa Lodge. In those days, not many tourists came to Murchison. They missed a lot. This was East Africa dreaming of commercial prosperity yet to come but still more or less in its primal state. The old hands half hoped that commercialisation of the wild wouldn't happen but knew it was inevitable. *Uhuru*... Freedom! was just a lion's roar away. Then would come the pressures. Pressures on land. Pressures on farmland. Pressures imposed everywhere by Africanisation. Perhaps, above all, pressures on the wildlife that many African politicians saw as a luxury that the new Africa could not afford. All this would change the parks, maybe even destroy them. The only way out was to develop the parks and their animals as a tourist resource. I heard these fears and hopes echoed and emphasised in every conversation with everyone I met in Uganda.

Paraa Lodge was, in its way, a bastion of the good old colonial times, a rambling building with beams of rough-hewn local timber supporting a thatched roof. Among the rafters, genets hunted birds and small rodents, occasionally missing their footing in the joy of the chase and falling onto the guests' beds or even dining tables. The less nervous accepted this as local colour which indeed it was. More colour was added by the sign outside the main entrance which said: "Elephants use this path after dark." It might well have added: "And in daytime, too."

Wilf and Sue Wolfenden ran the lodge. I do not know why they befriended John and I so readily but they did, offering us a spare room whenever we needed one during the rhino-catching operation. I believe Wilf liked us just because we weren't tourists. Sue liked us because she was too nice to dislike anyone halfway reasonable. Though a genial and friendly man, Wilf couldn't stand the average trickle of tourists who made it as far north as Murchison. He had, however, a pleasing cynicism which the more naive took for a wry sense of humour. I only heard him speak enthusiastically of one guest. This was a formidable American lady who had been landed by the local milk-run Dakota at the park airstrip some five miles from Paraa. Perhaps because she was the only passenger to get off there, no park transport came to meet her. God knows how she found her way, but presumably by following a track more frequented by wild animals than by vehicles. When she finally limped into the bar at Paraa Lodge, Wilf was serving drinks.

"Do you serve blood?" she asked. Wilf took her to his heart immediately.

Above the fireplace in the lodge hung a picture called 'Afternoon, Murchison Falls Park'. Bombo Trimmer had commissioned marine and wildlife artist Keith Shackleton to come up with a suitable painting for the lodge, so Keith painted a huge elephant, more like a mammoth, escorted by lesser members of its herd and backed by the great cauliflower mounds of cumulus cloud that you often see dumped on the African savanna as the day heats up. I asked Wilf if Keith's portrait was of an actual Murchison elephant. Wilf liked elephants almost as much as he liked tourists.

"The Lord Mayor was nearly as big."

"The Lord Mayor?"

"Yes, of Paraa."

"*Was*? You mean he's dead."

"Bombo shot him. He had to. Getting to be a bloody nuisance. The final straw came when he spotted a bunch of bananas on the back seat of a tourist's car and decided he ought to open the can to get at them."

"You mean, he puts his trunk through the window?"

"No. Just turned the car over with his tusks. Pity the tourists weren't in it. It would have taught them not to leave bananas lying around."

It was clear that running a park called for a careful balance between the rights of animals and welfare of humans.

"Then we get the drunks."

"Tourists?"

"Mainly elephants. They toddle into the ranger lines, stick their trunks through the windows and siphon off ten gallons or so of pombe, the local native beer.

Strong stuff. Mostly they sleep it off propped against a tree but sometimes they come down here and lean against one of the tourist rondavels. Usually flattens it."

"What do you do?"

"Not much you can do. Even then they're not as much trouble as the guests. Look at this."

Wilf held out the lodge's visitors book. The last entry said: "Animals magnificent. People terrible." It was signed by the late John Aspinall, gambling casino impresario and later creator of Howletts sanctuary for endangered species where keepers tended to become more endangered than tigers.

Next morning, John Buxton and I reported to John Savidge. Day one of our indoctrination course consisted of a walking safari through the bush in search of black rhino, highly unpredictable and often aggressive creatures. John thought we ought at least to meet a rhino before we tried catching one. As openers, we bumped into a lioness. She was hull-down behind a bank above the dried out river bed of the Namsika River. Mercifully, John saw the tip of her tail and signalled everyone to sit down quickly. Everyone included two rangers carrying John Buxton's camera tripod and our water bottles.

"If you're standing up," Savidge whispered, "you're man-shaped. Lions don't trust men, especially if they are lionesses who've got cubs with them."

This lioness had a single small cub, possibly all she had left of her family. Male lions, I learned later, have a bad habit of eating cubs they consider surplus to the pride's requirements. This lioness didn't intend to lose her baby and announced as much with a roar that sounded like a steam loco, the Flying Scotsman maybe, shouting the odds under a glass—roofed station before charging off northwards. The lioness did a bit of charging on her own account, stopping, along with my heart, about twenty five yards away. I heard the snick of the safety catch on John's rifle coming off. "The last thing I want to do is shoot her," he whispered, "but if she comes she'll be doing all of forty miles per hour." At that point I seriously wondered the wisdom of our sitting position, hardly the best poise for a rapid take-off. But then, I reflected, I couldn't run at anything like forty miles per hour so I might as well stay put.

Just when the situation seemed to be settling down, one of the rangers decided to get up and fetch a water bottle he'd left down the river bank. Standing up was definitely man-shaped. Out she came, all roar, and snarl and dust. Savidge had her over open sights. He may even have taken first pressure on the trigger. At what looked like our last minute, the lioness remembered her cub, turned, gave it a motherly cuff and led off down a gulley into the dry river bed.

To make John Buxton and I feel better, Savidge told us: "That happened to Bombo and I on my first day in the park. We walked into a lioness under a tree. Much closer than today. I didn't even have a rifle."

"What did you do?"

"I didn't but Bombo did. Threw his binoculars at her. She promptly buggered off."

Obviously, there was a lot to learn if you were going to survive on foot in the African bush.

The rhino-catchers arrived three days later. John Blower had described their trucks as looking as though they had been shot up with multiple pom-poms. In fact, the holes, dents and gashes had been caused by close contact with rhinos, hippos, buffaloes, the occasional elephant and the far from occasional tree. One truck, an ex-US Army Jeep didn't turn up at all. It had been flattened by an irritated hippo.

The catchers matched their transport. Francis Parkman who wrote the classic 'The Oregon Trail' about his own trek in the 1860's with the pioneers across the plains to the American West, would have recognised them instantly. The four Kenyans who comprised the animal-catching team, if met on the Oregon Trail, would have been buffalo hunters, Indian fighters, bounty hunters or perhaps civilian scouts for the US cavalry. I still see them as I first saw them, figures transported from the American frontier.

First, the trail boss, Ken Randall, a man of few words and impressive stature with great presence. He would have been the natural boss in any outfit. His features were as battered as his trucks. His partner, Pat O'Connell, good-looking, flash, the dare-devil catching hand. I cast him as the gun-fighter at the peak of his trade. Sure of himself, quick, maybe too quick with his six-gun but a likeable man just the same. Third, Louie Wedd, Ken Randall's son-in-law, a youngster, raw, courageous, anxious to make a name for himself but likely in the end to call out the wrong man. Boot Hill was full of his kind. Lastly, Ken Stewart, small, intelligent, self-contained, maybe the gambler with a Derringer in his sleeve. These were the men with whom we were going to catch rhinos. A tough lot but they left you with the impression that these were professionals who knew what they were doing.

John Buxton and I had hoped that our aged Land Rover would be able to follow the capture truck and that we could film from it. The journey from Kampala had shown that it was definitely not up to this kind of work. So I asked Pat O'Connell if we could film from the catching truck itself. He was not brimming with enthusiasm.

"If you get knocked off, we shan't come back for you."

"That seems quite reasonable."

"And another thing: don't come here with any of your *Daily Mirror* ideas,"

I surmised from this that he meant any radical views about black and white race relationships.

"I don't read the *Mirror*. Well, not regularly."

"Glad to hear it but watch it all the same."

I decidedly definitely to watch it. After that, we got along fine.

Ken Randall said: "Ever met a rhino?" I told him about the foot safari with John Savidge. He didn't seem over-impressed. "There was a black rhino," I told him "about two hundred yards away, under a tree." Ken said: "You'll see them a lot closer than that. A lot of people think that rhinos are stupid bastards. They're not. And blind with it. They're not that either. Put a ginger biscuit on the side of the truck and they can hit it from two hundred yards." I resolved not to take any ginger biscuits with me when we went rhino-catching. The next four days were spent building a boma, a corral of tree trunks lashed together with wire.

The African crew did the work. There was nothing *Daily Mirror* about the catchers' attitude to their African handlers. Nor was there anything paternalistic. They were just a lot of men, black and white, doing a difficult and dangerous job they knew how to do and do well. Whether this easy cameraderie would have worked as well in any other setting I had no way of knowing. Certainly there was respect between the two races within the catching team.

While the boma was being built, I spent four days in a strange state of mental inebriation, previously never experienced. African place names heard in the catchers' conversation swum round in my brain. For some reason, they all seemed to start with K—Kisumu, Kazinga, Kasese, Karamoja. I suppose the K's just sounded more African. One night lying in my tent, I watched a large white rhino, docile as a cow, walk between the guy ropes. It was so close I could almost have stretched out and touched it. Its very nonchalance seemed to be saying: "Here I am. Come and catch me."

Next morning at breakfast of fresh pineapple, beans and scalding coffee, Ken Randall said, as if in casual everyday conversation: "the boma's built so we might as well go and try to catch a few of the bastards... Ever been rhino-catching before?"

I admitted that it was an entirely new experience. "Us too", said Ken. "With white rhinos, anyway. Tried lassoing a black who didn't like it at all. Black rhinos are *kali*—wild—bastards." He said this with obvious affection.

Further speech was obliterated by the arrival of the catching truck, an ex-World War Two Chevrolet 15 cwt that appeared to have survived around 50 fairly serious traffic accidents. Bolted at the rear, one to each side, were stout four foot tree trunks. To the base of each was attached one end of a one inch thick sisal rope. The other end formed a lassoo lightly wired to the tip of a ten foot bamboo pole. The remainder of the rope, about twenty five yards in all, lay neatly coiled on the floor of the truck. The catching technique needed little explaining even to novices like John Buxton and myself. Get alongside the rhino, use the pole to slip the noose over its nose and await results. Results seemed the main area of uncertainty. The two most likely one were (a) that the beast weighing at the minimum a ton would turn on the truck and try to rend it and its occupants apart or (b) put as much distance between itself and its tormentors as possible. In either case the wire securing the noose to the pole would break leaving the Chevvy and its crew to play a very large fish indeed. We were, it seemed, ready to go.

"Only place you can hope to get a few shots," Ken told John, "is right behind the cab. Stay glued to it. Don't move. Don't get in anybody's way."

"Oh righto. Jolly good. Rather!" John said this quite cheerfully in the sort of voice I imagine he might have used if ordered to capture an enemy machine-gun post single-handed.

Ken said: "You sit in front with me." I was flattered by the invitation until I worked out that the front passenger's seat was the position in which I could be the least bloody nuisance to anyone. I'd have felt a lot better about things if there had been a door to the cab on my side. It had occurred to me that the rhino might not be best pleased about what we proposed doing to it. Louie Wedd read my thoughts. "I shouldn't worry," he said. "A rhino can stick its horn through metal just like butter... If it tries to come aboard you can always bail out through the hatch above you."

"But the catching crew may not like that."

"It's possible," he agreed. "It depends whether you'd rather take your chances with them or the rhino."

A minute later, we were off. The catching truck sounded as though it had been specially tuned for the job. In fact it had lost most of its exhaust and all of its silencer. This gave it a healthy, throaty roar. That truck reminded me of one of those old and expendable warships, reinforced for a special mission and not expected to return in recognisable shape if she returned at all—the blockships at Zebrugge in World War One, or the *Campbelltown* packed with explosives to blow up the dock gates at St Nazaire. The Chevvy had that air of indomitable expendability about it.

We started looking for rhino at a reassuringly gentle pace. At this speed it was possible to avoid most of the termite mounds and hyena holes that were as numerous in the Madi District bush as traffic cones on the M1, and far easier to hit. And then someone up top shouted "rhino" and we moved instantly from cruising to battle speed. The rhinos, it appeared, were in tall, dry elephant grass four hundred yards to starboard.

O'Connell's voice: "Female and large calf. They've heard us". Not surprising really. Then: "they're off. Steer right-handed."

Randall: "Can't see a bloody thing". This wasn't surprising either. We were ploughing our way through six foot high elephant grass at thirty mph. Every now and again we hit a thorn tree that disintegrated all over the screen. Tank drivers steer through slits or periscopes. Ken drove by instinct and by hand signals. Every now and again, an arm snaked down through the hatch and a hand indicated the correct course. We came out of the tall grass. There, on the starboard bow, quite miraculously, was a huge female and her one ton offspring. Mum looked as big as a runaway petrol tanker and quite as lethal. Half a minute later, Ken Stewart had slipped a noose over baby's head. Mum backed off looking worried but apparently not about to come to the rescue. Hooray, I thought. John Buxton was calmly rewinding his clockwork camera. "Great stuff. Got most of it". Chiels came up in his own Land Rover. "Some of it may be a wee bit shakey," he said, possibly the film understatement of the year. "I'll just film the loading of the wee fellow onto the truck." The crew wrestled the roped and tied calf onto metal rollers and winched her onto a three tonner to take her to the holding boma.

"That was pretty exciting," I told O'Connell.

"You think so? Well, just hold onto your hat when we go after big momma."

Big momma didn't hang around for long. Once she heard the Chevvy start up, she was off like a runaway train looking for a good collision. The next five minutes were like being shaken in a metal dice box. Once I caught a view of the rhino's backside through the windscreen. A lasso appeared, failed to clear the front horn that was all of three feet long and disappeared over the side along with the bamboo pole. A lot of very bad language from up top while the crew prepared the second lasso. By this time we were submerged in the sea of elephant grass again. Ken shouted: "Lost the bloody rhino!" How I thought, but didn't like to ask, can you lose a thing as big as that?

We were off again. This time the chase was longer and faster. Unbelievably, the rhino suddenly appeared on my side of the cab. This time the noose made it over both horns. I tried to think of something calming like filming a maggot factory or trying to persuade Randolph Churchill not to assault anyone in the studio. It didn't work.

The rhino had crossed our radiator and was taking out rope fast. Ken followed slowly. I've caught some big fish in my time but Ken's rod control was faultless. Never seen anything better. He followed the catch slowly, like the skipper of a boat playing a record marlin. Keep a tight line, put just enough strain on to tire the catch without risking a break. The rhino knew the rules, too— let the catchers recover a little rope then make a wild, sideways run, showing up, horror of horrors, on my side again. We now had a very angry rhino attached to us. The beast showed its irritation by battering our bonnet with a head and jaws about the size and weight of your average upright piano. Much the same shape, too. As an encore, it backed off and stuck its front horn through the metal of the cab about eighteen inches from my left knee-cap... "If the rhino tries to come aboard..." Louie Wedd had said.

At that moment the wrath of the catchers seemed a better bet than being skewered by a rhino. I grabbed the edges of the hatch and ejected like a jet pilot. It wasn't the best of moments but then there probably wasn't a good moment. As I landed on the cab roof, the rope attached to the rhino whipped across it. A second earlier and I would have gone with it. A profusion of well-deserved pleasantries... "Get out of the way, you stupid sod... Serve him bloody right if he goes overboard. I bloody told him to stay put..."

But then O'Connell did one of the bravest things I'd seen in a long time, went over the side and tied the rhino's back legs together. Once the rope was on, the rest of the Lilliputians swarmed over Gulliver and down went three and a half tons of cow rhino on its side.

I felt the least I could do was apologise to O'Connell. "You didn't do badly." he said generously, "but next time keep in the fucking cab. You'll soon get used to it."

Ken Randall looked at the monster lying ridiculously inert and waiting to be winched up onto the three tonner. "I reckon that's the biggest land animal anyone's ever caught."

I believed him. It had felt like it. All told, the team caught twelve white rhinos. Two died from stress after capture. Ten were released into Murchison Falls Park. Back home there were endless technical arguments about the uneven quality of the film but then the technicians had never tried filming from the back of a rhino-catchers' truck.

Years later, the chemists perfected drugs that made rhino capture by darting a routine operation, safer for both man and beast. In South Africa, where mercifully the southern race of the white rhino abounded, the time from darting to loading averaged forty minutes and no one had to bail out through the roof of the cab. I'm told I still hold the record for roof ejection. The sad tailpiece to the film we made called SOS Rhino was that all the white rhinos we caught were later killed by Idi Amin's thugs, their horns ground to powder and sold for exorbitant sums to make aphrodisiacs to give tired old men the horn in China. By the way, there's no proof that it worked.

It's a comforting thought that Viagra may yet save the few rhino, black and white, left in Africa.

A three-ton white rhino attacks Ken Randall's catching truck. Pat O'Connell waits to go over the side to rope the animal's rear legs. The author cowers in the cab.

A white rhino poached for its horns in the Uganda bush. The expedition aimed to rescue the country's remaining white rhino and move them to a national park.

Chiels Margach films perched on boma as a big female is unloaded from the lorry. The rhinos were kept in the boma until they had settled down.

Too Many Hippos

Uganda was inside my head and bubbling away like an overloaded stock pot. Nothing would do until I could get back there. Uganda had seemed to have everything. The country was beautiful beyond belief. It had the largest lakes and the Mountains of the Moon which Ptolemy had thought the source of the Nile. It had the actual source of the Nile in Lake Victoria. It had a forest inhabited by pygmies and known as the Impenetrable Forest. Perhaps most important, just before Independence, it had a black and white community which seemed to have every chance of getting on together. And it had wildlife like the Garden of Eden. As in Eden, there were, of course, snakes, the natural kind you would expect to find there as well as some highly dangerous ones lurking in the political undergrowth. One of these was called Milton Obote, the first President of independent Uganda. As snakes go he was what you might have labelled back- fanged. He was comparatively innocuous, unless, you stuck your own ambitions, financial or political and contrary to his own interests, into the back of his mouth. The bite could then prove fatal.

His successor Idi Amin had every conceivable serpentine talent. He could strangle, and constrict. He could spit or inject venom. He could swallow a whole country, its wealth and many of its people and did just that.

But in the palmy days of 1961, with *Uhuru* about to break out, none of this looked remotely likely. Perhaps if I had studied the bloody history of Uganda before going there I wouldn't have had a whole tropical night-sky of bright stars in my eyes. But I had fallen in love with the place and you know what they say about the eyesight of lovers.

After I got back from the rhino-catching expedition I spent the rest of 1961 in London building up Anglia Television's Natural History Unit with Aubrey Buxton. Between us we made several wildlife films, including SOS Rhino which gave a new direction to the genre. In early 1962, Aubrey invited me to go back to Uganda. He'd just been there himself, more or less as unofficial wildlife equerry to his friend Prince Philip. He'd attended *Uhuru* celebrations and seen some of East Africa's wonders. One of the great things about Aubrey was that he knew all the right people in the world of conservation. He was Treasurer of the Zoological Society of London and had played a large part in the launching of the World Wildlife Fund with Peter Scott and Prince Philip. None of this could do anything but good to a newly formed TV wildlife unit whose only opposition at the time was the considerable one of the BBC.

Where did I fit in? As someone who could make wildlife films that would be accurate as well as exciting and that would attract and hold a wide TV audience. These Survival films might also play a part in persuading the new rulers of the African countries that game animals were worth keeping on the hoof for economic reasons. Most Africans, whether politicians or villagers, saw elephants, buffalo and hippos as dangerous, crop-raiding bloody nuisances. Now they had to be persuaded that they were something that could attract tourists and pull in the hard currency that the new countries desperately needed. But, of course, our main concern as programme makers was to rivet as many million viewers as possible to the box.

And who was I to object to any of that? I lived for and by communicating, previously in newspapers and magazines and now in films. I liked my job so much that, if I could have afforded it, I'd have done it for nothing. But, best of all, I was the lucky man who was regularly going to be required to take walks very much on the wild side.

Since the rhino expedition I had devoured every book I could find on the great explorers. The whole of East Africa was literally only put on the map in the second half of the nineteenth century. I read Burton, Speke and Baker on the search for the Nile source. I travelled with the ruthless American journalist H. M. Stanley on his quasi- military expedition down the Congo River and his search for Dr Livingstone who, despite Stanley's famous one-liner, resolutely refused to admit that he was lost. I took great doses of all the explorers' works—J. W. Gregory who diagnosed and gave his name to the Great Rift Valley; Gustav Fischer, the first man to enter the country of the warlike Masai ; the wonderful Hungarian Count Teleki who, as late as 1887, discovered a huge lake, which he named Rudolf after the Crown Prince who was his sponsor, a lake which no one had previously known was there! I must not forget the Scot J. W. Thompson's *Through Masailand.* Thompson went further north than anyone else and found a lake, Baringo, which was much smaller than any of the early map-makers had supposed which wasn't really surprising since they had never been there. I had also read Alan Moorehead's marvellous *The White Nile.* But of them all, it was Samuel Baker and his remarkable wife who most gripped my imagination. It was plain that Baker was Moorehead's hero, too. Baker was different from all the rest. Although he discovered the second source of the Nile in Lake Albert, he was much more than just an explorer whose aim was to chalk up another first. He and his second wife, a beautiful Austrian blonde fifteen years younger than himself, were interested in everything they met and saw from the wildlife to the local tribal customs. But the thing that mainly bound me to Baker and his wife—later Sir Samuel and Lady Baker—was that their incredible adventures recorded in his books *Albert Nyanza, Great Basin of the Nile* and *Ismalia* took place mainly in the country with which I was currently besotted—Uganda.

Just before I left for Uganda again in 1962, Aubrey Buxton said to me: "would your wife like to go with you? Pay her air fare and you can put the rest down to safari expenses."

Now that is an offer than no woman in her right mind—and some might say wrong mind—could possibly refuse. Needless to say: Joan Willock didn't.

Baker himself might have said it. As he didn't, I'll say if for him. Take a woman with the right stuff. Take her from any background you like. Drop her into the most outlandish situations and if she's the right sort she will go anywhere and do anything.

Sir Samuel himself put it in one deathless phrase after his wife had seized a pistol to deal with a murderous midnight intruder in their tent.

"Lady Baker", he recorded, "was no screamer."

Nor, it has to be said, was Mrs Willock, except on one occasion, and I suppose that any woman transported from a comfortable middle-class home to the heart of darkest Africa is entitled to one scream. Lady Baker herself might have let out a squeak in similar circumstances but you shall judge for yourselves.

I'd had a film idea almost literally floating around in my brain since I first crossed the Nile at Paraa to join the rhino-catchers. Sailing down the river in endless procession were small green succulent plants about the size and shape of a lettuce. Some of these found temporary anchorage in the reeds, only to break away later to join the passing flotillas of similar plants on their voyage down the longest river in the world.

Samuel Baker had observed the same phenomenon and put it to practical use. Whenever he was lost in the swamps of the upper Nile, he took his upstream direction from the main flow of this small green water plant. Though John

Hanning Speke had beaten Baker to the discovery of the Nile source where the river spills out of Lake Victoria at Ripon Falls, Baker was determined to discover whether the river that flowed into his Lake Albert was the same one that flowed out of Speke's Lake Victoria. And though it meant that travelling this hundred or so miles of unexplored river, now known as the Victoria Nile, might delay his and his wife's return to England by three years, the intrepid Bakers decided to press on upstream, guided in parts by the little green water plant. Here was the story I wanted to tell. It had one other great advantage. Because the Victoria Nile flowed through the newly created Murchison Falls National Park, the Nile between Lakes Albert and Victoria was the only stretch of the world's longest river whose banks were thronged with the richness and variety of wildlife that Baker would have witnessed.

I remember asking John Savidge the name of this floating plant when we made that first crossing of the Nile on the chain ferry at Paraa.

"That," he said, "is Nile Cabbage, though if you want to be technical you should call it *Pistia stratiotes*." Nile Cabbage seemed good enough for me though it wasn't until much later that I realised we had the perfect story and the perfect linking device.

Chiels Margach was the obvious man to film the story. He knew the Victoria Nile from Lake Albert to Murchison Falls as if it was his own private waterway which in a sense it was. Apart from the crocodile poachers and the launches of the park rangers who tried to catch them, he was the only person to sail these waters. He did so in a 23 foot ketch called *Kamuji*, Swahili for ground squirrel. *Kamuji* was very much part of Chiels. He'd not only designed her, he'd been into the Budongo Forest, bought a tree, seen it felled, seasoned and cut into the planks from which his boat was to be built. The result was a handy little craft with a minute cuddy and galley in the forepeak, a small cabin and a large cockpit. He told me later that he was so pleased with her that he'd even bought the tree for her successor. Boats, he explained, wear out quickly in a tropical climate.

Long before leaving England, I'd sent Chiels an outline of my story. His reply was that he and *Kamuji* would be ready to sail at a moment's notice. The only snag he could see was that we would need a second cameraman. Handling *Kamuji* in the swamps and fierce currents of the Nile was often a full-time job. Could I persuade John Buxton to sign on again?

But John was once again busy filming marsh harriers and bearded tits for the Royal Society for the Protection of Birds at Horsey. It was then that the third man turned up. I'd been searching for some lion kill sequences for a lash-up conservation epic we were making called 'Tomorrow may be too late'. I'd last heard the name Bill Cowen in connection with the rhino filming. Apparently, he had an optician's practice in Kampala. He also had a 16mm movie camera. After John Buxton and I had returned to England, Chiels had teamed up with Cowen to shoot loose ends of the rhino operation. Now Bill Cowen was here in my London office offering me some of his big game footage. It would be an understatement to say that I found this likeable north countryman pig-headed. It would possibly be no exaggeration to say that he found me awkward and obstinate. We argued and haggled over the sequences I hoped to buy. During these heated but seldom acrimonious exchanges, we developed, I believe, a grudging respect for each other that evolved into something close to affection. Only when the deal was completed—at Cowen's price—did I mention the Nile project. Cowen, I now discovered, had got on extremely well with Chiels. He was about to return to Kampala. It seemed I had no choice . So I signed him on, wondering what might be the result of cooping Willock and Cowen up together in a 23 foot ketch. Surprisingly, it turned out all right. Perhaps it was the presence on board of the latter-day Lady Baker, aka Mrs Joan Willock, that proved the soothing influence.

Chiels kept *Kamuji* on moorings at Butiaba, a small African village on the delta where the Victoria Nile pours into Sam Baker's Albert Nyanza. She was in good company. Right next to her lay the rotting remains of the steam launch *African Queen* in which Bogart and Hepburn had made their remarkable voyage in John Huston's film of the same name. The delta was also the headquarters of the Bugungu, the tribe who made a living by poaching the giant Nile crocs from dug-out canoes. Chiels was in no danger from the Bugungu. I suspect he got on very well with them. Nor was he in the least worried about the crocs. There was, however, a much more dangerous creature in the Nile at Butiaba, a minute flatworm that could penetrate the skin and cause an horrendous disease in the human pelvic region. Bilharzia was one of the few tropical menaces I knew anything about before coming to Uganda. I remember reading how, during World War Two, some gung-ho brigadier had ordered his entire force to swim a West African river as part of a training exercise. Almost to a man they contracted the disease, one of the first symptoms of which is that the victim of the parasite starts peeing blood. Some years before, Chiels had noticed this unpleasant and painful symptom. He had contracted bilharzia simply as the result of hauling up *Kamuji's* anchor chain at her Butiaba moorings with unprotected hands. He took the cure which at the time was prolonged and painful. These days, I believe, the tropical medicine boys have come up with something more tolerable and more effective. When I asked Chiels if there was any danger of becoming infected in the waters where we planned to film, he said there was nothing to worry about. Part of the life cycle of the bilharzia parasite depends on the presence of a certain species of snail. The currents above Paraa were too rapid to suit the snail. It only lived in sluggish waters and the disease was most prevalent around human habitations. There were no villages on the upper Nile.

Kamuji now lay just upstream of Paraa. Next day we would meet Bill Cowen there and board her with all the camera gear. Tonight, my wife's second night in Africa, we were staying with Chiels at his Kinyala plantation near Masindi. Halfway through dinner, Chiels' demonic-looking houseboy arrived at the table in an obvious state of high excitement. In fact he was so excited that he forgot to give a wide enough berth to Chiels' parrot, Koosekoo, a bird of evil nature who hated the houseboy and gave him a fierce peck whenever he got the chance. He availed himself of that chance now. The fact that the parrot fed almost exclusively on a diet of local red peppers may have had something to do with his fiery nature. A few minutes of frantic whispering in the *bwana's* ear and Chiels rose calmly from the table, apologised to his two guests as 'something had come up in the kitchen'. Joan and I assumed that some minor culinary disaster had occurred, the sweet had fallen on the floor or the one pineapple had mysteriously disappeared. Twenty minutes later, Chiels reappeared. "I must apologise," he said, "we've had a wee drama. I had to wait for the police sergeant to come up from Masindi."

"Something been stolen?"

"No. It's a wee bit more serious. The manager killed the cook with a panga while he was preparing the sweet so I'm afraid we'll have to make do with cheese."

"Good God," I said, "what will they do to the killer?"

"Oh, there'll be a trial, I expect. He'll probably get six months. They tend to take a lenient view of such things in these parts. Apparently, the cook had been fooling around with the manager's wife."

What do you say at a dinner party after that? Would you care for an After Eight? I looked at Mrs Baker. Africa had dropped her straight into the deep end. As far as I could tell, my wife appeared to be swimming strongly.

There was a new warden at Murchison, Roger Wheater. John Savidge came with Roger to see us off. John was going back to England for a year's course that would equip him for the post of scientific officer to the Uganda Parks. In the meantime, he'd been gathered up by a lady with the unfortunate name of Miss Remnant. Miss Remnant had come to East Africa to make the long and dangerous walk round Lake Rudolf with the travel writer John Hillaby. One result of the walk was Hillaby's excellent book *Journey to the Jade Sea.* The other was that Miss Remnant had set eyes on John Savidge and decided to marry him and that was that. Roger was equally charismatic though from a different background. John had come literally from the Groves of Academe, from a degree in forestry at Oxford to become warden of a national park. Roger came from the Uganda police where he had made a name for himself by quelling a riot at a copper mine single-handed. Both men had great charm and presence. John had learned instinctively to get on with his African staff. With Roger the knowledge came through experience and training. In an earlier age these young men would have been empire builders. Now they had the even harder task of giving part, an important part, of the empire away.

It was a tight fit aboard *Kamuji.* Apart from our skipper there was Tibamwenda, Chiels safari hand and Zakaia, the ancient cook who made the most superb wholemeal bread by rolling the dough on his sweating and extremely corpulent stomach. Her complement was completed by Bill Cowen with a mound of camera gear, Joan and myself.

We set off upstream under sail among rafts of hippo and hadn't gone far before a hippo showed its resentment at our intrusion by trying to surface under our keel and lifting the ketch and crew a foot out of the water.

Living aboard *Kamuji* was cramped though tolerable provided everyone made the right move at the right time. As skipper, Chiels saw that we did so, though I never heard him raise his voice about anything.

It was on the third night that Mrs Willock gave her one permitted African scream. Bedding down was quite a problem. Joan was given the small cuddy which also served as a galley in which to sleep. As soon as supper had been cooked, the butane stove was heaved on deck leaving behind, however, a temperature of ninety or more degrees. There was no room to rig a mosquito net in this little hell-hole and so it was my task to spray my wife from head to foot with a farm-size aerosol can of bug-killer. Any malarial mosquitoes that penetrated this screen would then have to contend with the anti-malarial drugs in her bloodstream. We could only hope it would all work.

The two African crewmen curled up on the tiny foredeck. We three European men were better off, but not much. We climbed on top of the cabin roof and lay down side by side, like crackers in a box, under a mosquito net roughly draped across the boom. Once in position, there was very little room for movement. The two outside men, of which I was one, had at the most three inches between themselves and a sheer drop into the river.

Before leaving England, my wife had confessed to me that the one thing she was scared of was scorpions. When in the middle of the night something large, leggy and active fell on her face her first instinct was that the scorpions had struck at last.

Her second reaction was to scream. Bill Cowen, who was sleeping heavily in the middle position on the cabin roof, floundered to his feet. With nothing to stop me, I simply rolled off into the Nile. I remember waking with terror as I hit the water. Strangely it wasn't the ten foot croc we had all seen earlier on the bank nearby that got to me. My first thought, despite all Chiels reassurances was: "Oh God! Bilharzia!"

After that, Joan never so much as raised a peep again. It was just that scorpions were too much for her. In the middle of the night, she was certainly in no state to remember that scorpions are not especially common on boats whereas cockroaches, which in some ways are more unpleasant, certainly are.

The Nile Cabbage which provided our story thread begins its long voyage in Lake Victoria. It must be admitted that the plant is quite common and doesn't belong exclusively to the Nile. Nowadays much of Lake Victoria's contribution must be sliced to coleslaw by the turbines of the Ripon Falls hydro-electric plant at Jinja. Those cabbages that survive wander through the swamps and channels of Lake Kyoga. The river speeds up at Karuma Falls. Beyond these huge rapids the river tumbles 1,200 feet in twenty miles in a series of flashing, crashing cataracts. The country hereabouts is some of the wildest and loneliest in this part of Africa. It is hilly, burnt up and most of the trees have been ripped apart by elephants.

Above Murchison Falls, the river fauna is no longer Nilotic for the simple reason that nothing can get up or past the Falls. Crocs, tiger fish, Nile perch are all presented with a barrier, impassable and absolute. The only animal ever to travel the Falls is an occasional unwary hippo, caught in the fierce currents and swirled to the lip of the cataract, there to be squirted into the twenty foot gap through which the whole great river passes onto the rocks one hundred and fifty feet below

One of the fascinating things about this part of Africa is that some of the gigantic upheavals that have created this grandest of landscapes are comparatively recent in geological time. One such earth movement tilted up the western end of Lake Victoria so that it overflowed to create Lake Kyoga and the Victoria Nile. When the newly formed river came to Fajao a mile below the present Falls it was faced with a leap over an escarpment. But the soil was comparatively soft there so that as it leapt, the river started to cut its way back for nearly a mile until it met hard rock. There it was only able to carve itself out a twenty foot gap and went on leaping through that until today. Samuel Baker and his wife were the first Europeans to set eyes on this spectacle and called the huge cataract Murchison Falls, after Sir Roderick Murchison, President of the Royal Society.

All of our wildlife filming in *Kamuji* had been done in the river below the Falls. We'd got shots of the Nile Cabbage in every conceivable situation, except tumbling over Murchison Falls themselves. So we set out to film just that. Even a mile below the Falls, the river currents were too powerful for the ketch to make any progress upstream with her cruising engine. We managed to get as far as the old landing stage at Fajao. There we unloaded the camera gear as well as several sacks of Nile Cabbage. The chance of finding the plant at the top of the Falls themselves seemed very remote.

There is no path from Fajao to the Falls except a mile-long game trail. The grass all around is tall and steep cliffs rise on one side. The bank falls away to the whirlpool on the other. In the confinement of the gorge the heat is stupefying. The low scrub is perfect for tsetse flies which attack in squadrons. At first, the going is gradual but then becomes uncompromisingly brutal as you approach the Falls themselves. The further you press on, the more the Falls possess your senses, first with the continual, almost mechanical roar and then with the sheer vehemence of the water crashing to the last of the three great steps by which the river descends. When you start the climb to the last part of the precipitous footpath the Falls seem almost to suck you in. You are enveloped in a delicious ice-cold vapour. The trees are hung with dense drapings of moss nourished by the spray.

One hundred yards below the Falls, in the centre of the narrow trail, was a large bull elephant. The elephant had found something to his liking and saw no reason to move. In fact, he refused to move for the next two hours. We sat it out—and so did he. In the end we had to content ourselves with shots of Nile Cabbage gyrating in dense rafts in the Hippo Pool at the foot of the Falls. We need not have bothered to bring our own. Filming the wretched weed sliding over the lip of the Falls would have to wait for another day.

When you live crowded into a small sailing boat among crocs and hippos on the upper Nile, you get to know quite a lot about your companions. I even learned things about my wife to whom I had been married for fifteen years. I discovered how incredibly adaptable she was. Though she never took to the African wife's method of washing clothes by pounding them with stones in the river, she kept our clothes clean, never seemed to be thrown by what was going on around her and was always excited by the totally unfamiliar world into which she had been suddenly pitched. She did, however, keep her own contacts with what she had previously known as normality. Mrs Thatcher would have been proud of her. I have a picture of her walking behind a park warden literally on the heels of a pride of lions and clutching a handbag. She also insisted on bringing aboard something she called a beauty box, a small square case, the sort of thing which models carry to touch up their make-up. Before we boarded *Kamuji*, we had a few sharp words about this as husbands and wives sometimes will. I argued that there was little spare room aboard to stow such fripperies. The skipper gently and tactfully overruled this, saying he was sure the beauty box could be stowed somewhere. My wife had no intention other than that it be stowed at all times very close to her person. I silently dismissed this as a typical feminine foible. The beauty box obviously had no practical use other than that of a comforter, the equivalent of a blanket to suck when reassurance was needed. I was hopelessly wrong.

Lady Baker may, for all I know, have had an equivalent item of equipment, a work-box possibly filled with needless, threads and smelling salts. If so, her husband never recorded the fact. However, I will record that the beauty box saved our bacon on a number of occasions and I will briefly list them.

For a start it contained small bottles of detergent for washing our smalls. It also included a spare pair of nylons, not an item you would think much needed in the African bush. Not so. Once, the fan belt of our aged Land Rover broke when we were miles from anywhere off the beaten or any other kind of track. A nylon stocking tied tightly round the pulleys of dynamo and cooling fan makes an excellent substitute and lasted fifteen miles until we made our camp.

Another Land Rover and another emergency, this time a totally blocked main jet which no amount of blowing or sucking will clear. Fortunately the beauty box contains a selection of needles of all diameters one of which does the job. The beauty box to the rescue again. Roger Wheater requires us to bring home for an autopsy the corpse of a very dead civet cat. Even live civet cats have very powerful musk glands. Inside the vehicle, the stench is unbearable. The beauty box has a partial answer. A very expensive spray bottle of *Arpège* perfume partly eases the situation.

Cosmetics to the rescue once more. Frank Poppleton, head warden of the Uganda Parks, is worried about skin cancer. Though he has been exposed to the sun all his life he is acquiring a few unwanted sores on his very fair skin. The beauty box contains sunblock cream. Since when Frank has used no other. After that, I never again scorned the beauty box or my wife for lugging it along with her.

I learned a lot about Bill Cowen, too, and came to admire this pig-headed, brave and utterly obstinate man who refused to be put off by animals, weather or people. Bill was now in his mid-sixties. In many ways he was a typical north countryman, even down to his speech mannerisms. He'd use phrases like 'ready for off?' meaning 'let's go' or 'it's come from together' translated as 'the damn thing's broken'. He'd made his first trip to Africa twelve years previously taking his wife and son Donald on safari in a large and completely unsuitable car. Miles from anywhere in the Rhodesian bush and travelling far too fast—Cowen always drove too fast—he hit a large bump. Ten miles further on, the temperature needle went off the clock and the engine all but seized. The jolt had loosened the fan belt and the radiator had boiled dry. Mrs Cowen didn't have a beauty box and probably wasn't wearing nylon stockings. It was a measure of Bill's greenness at the time that he wasn't carrying any spare water. Not wishing to alarm his family, he sat them down in baking mid-day heat under a thorn tree and told them that someone was bound to come along, realising, in fact, that this was extremely unlikely. While he was telling them this for about the third time a dust cloud appeared on the horizon.

"Spitting cobra," said Roger. I was quite happy to leave it at that but not the intrepid Wheater. "It's a youngster. Should be easy to catch. Want it for the park museum." With that, Roger dived into the undergrowth, grasping his floppy sunhat in his right hand and emerged half a minute later with a three foot serpent gripped tightly in the hat and held just behind the head. The snake looked extremely annoyed and was dribbling more milky venom from two holes in its front teeth with which it would obviously have liked to give Roger a lethal injection.

We emptied a box that had contained sandwiches and bottles of Fanta Orange, punched some holes to give the serpent air and put it in the shade to reflect on its impetuosity. Roger said: "If that had been a full-grown spitting cobra the venom would probably have hit you in the eyes. They aim at anything bright."

"And if it had scored?"

"You're wearing glasses so you'd probably have been okay."

"And if I hadn't been wearing glasses?"

"Might have blinded you for twenty four hours. The best thing is to wash your eyes out with milk or water. Of course if the snake had really taken a dislike to you it could have finished you off with its fangs. They're a sort of double-barrelled weapon. Shoot or bite."

Despite the seductive appearance of the Hippo Pool, that was the nearest we came to a bite all afternoon. Except for the tsetse fly, of course. They didn't bother me much. I have an epidermis that has been known to blunt hyperdermic needles. The latter-day Lady Baker didn't fare so well. My wife's face, neck and arms looked like a map of the moon.

Two days later we made another close acquaintance with a cobra, the black-lipped species this time. Chiels, Joan and I had left Bill filming crocs while we drove back to Masindi for supplies. Bill had built a hide on one of the trails used by these huge reptiles when leaving the water. He hoped to get a head-on close-up of a croc actually entering the hide while he, plus camera, or so he planned, left by the back entrance. He did actually get the shot in slow motion and big close-up of the croc entering the hide. There was no need for Bill to use the back door. The croc was more surprised than the cameraman, spun round, lashed out with its tail and plunged back into the river.

When we reached Masindi we pulled in to its very basic petrol station. I admit that I was surprised to find a petrol station of any sort there at all. It had one of those ancient hand-cranked pumps and a very primitive hand-operated car hoist.

When we drove in, a wide-eyed African attendant was squirting something with an air hose on the underside of a Cadillac more suitable for Miami than Masindi. A powerful American lady was having a tough time dealing with a situation beyond even her obviously extensive knowledge as a world traveller.

Chiels asked politely whether he could help.

"I sure hope so. We seem to have gotten this snake."

The lady's highly nubile teen-age daughter was cooling her legs and feet while dangling them out of one of the back doors of the Caddy. "It's under there," the girl said, gesturing to the underside of the car with one delicate bare foot.

Chiels took a careful look. "Yes," he agreed. "It's certainly under there. It's a black-lipped cobra about six feet long. I think, lassie, I'd move your foot if I were you."

"It bites?"

"It certainly could do."

"Seems kind of dopey to me."

"At the moment, I agree, but not if that laddie goes on squirting it with the air hose." Chiels spoke rather forcibly in Swahili but without raising his voice to the petrol attendant who dropped the air hose and ran for cover.

The American momma naturally wanted to know how she had gotten this snake. By courteous questioning, Chiels established that the couple had travelled up that day over three hundred miles from Queen Elizabeth Park in the south. There had been a torrential rainstorm the night before. Chiels' conclusion, which I have never seen reason to doubt, was that the cobra had taken shelter under their parked car, found the warmth of the exhaust system comforting, had climbed up, tucked itself round the cooling silencer and dozed off.

When mother and daughter set off for Masindi early next morning the cobra had probably still been asleep and saw no reason to dismount. Once the car had hit the road it had had very little chance of dismounting, anyway. So, it found itself a cooler but still sheltered spot on the underside of the chassis, coiled itself safely around a suitable metal support and dozed off again.

Chiels had the answer for most things and he was, of course, a local boy. It just so happened that a friend of his, a charming woman, was a snake *fundi*, an expert, a pupil in fact of the great South African snake man, Ionides. Chiels was sure Mrs Stoneham would be delighted to have the cobra for her collection.

So he went to fetch her and found her indeed delighted. She arrived within half an hour with a long stick with a rope loop at the end and persuaded the cobra to give up its sleeping place under the car, pronounced it to be a beautiful specimen and popped it into a sack.

After that we all went back and had tea at her place. At the back of her bungalow was a corrugated iron drum about three feet wide and six feet deep. It was filled with water.

"Do be a bit careful when you walk past that tank", the snake lady told me. "There's an eighteen foot reticulated python asleep in the bottom of it. He can be a bit unpredictable. He woke up and nearly got the house boy last week."

I gave the tank plenty of margin, recalling as I did so Roger Wheater's words.

"Try to remember," he had said, "that basically snakes don't want any trouble."

Ever since, I've always tried to keep that thought firmly in mind but at times it's been difficult.

Until this trip I'd thought of hippos as rather jolly jumbly sort of animals with an unintentional talent to amuse. Not the case at all, I soon discovered. Every old hand I spoke to assured me that they were deadly dangerous and caused more deaths in Africa than any other large mammal. The reason is quite simple. Hippos like to spend their day in water, snorting a lot, preferably with just their ears, eyes and nostrils above the surface. This is the comedy element. The deadly serious, sometimes tragic part starts when they come ashore to feed, generally at night and occasionally in the day. Most of the fatalities occur when some innocent local, often a village woman taking her washing down to the river, gets between a dry-land hippo and the water to which it urgently wishes to return, to cool off or simply because it feels safer there. If the woman happens to be on one of the narrow hippo trails among the reeds, then there is nowhere to go when one and a half tons of water horse come belting down the track. The hippo's usual reaction is to open its portcullis jaws and chomp. Top and bottom jaws are both armed with long ivory daggers. Needless to say no one caught in this situation emerges in one piece, more likely in several pieces. Being a vegetarian, the hippo shows no further interest in the disjointed and perforated victim and returns to the water as if nothing had happened. The crew of *Kamuji* had already experienced, when hoisted several feet out of the river, one display of a hippo's strength and general disregard for the rights of others. In the next few weeks there were to be many more such displays.

Part of the art of wildlife film-making, as we were beginning to discover, is to set up several projects in the same geographical area. Thus, when a drought stops you filming desert birds nesting, you can move a few hundred miles to the other side of a mountain range where it's snowing and put a some sequences in the can for a previously planned epic about mountain lions. That's the general principle, anyway, though, nature being an essentially feminine and therefore capricious creature, seldom allows it to work out like that. In fact, it very seldom works out at all. The bonus is that just occasionally you get a nugget which you hadn't foreseen or planned. You never tell anyone, particularly your closest colleagues, that this brilliant sequence was a blinding stroke of luck. After all, you deserve a little.

The situation here was that we had to wait for the crocs on the Nile to lay their eggs so that the monitor lizards could unsportingly dig them up to eat so that we could film them doing so. While waiting for the crocs to lay we decided to move south to the Queen Elizabeth Park where the American lady had gotten her black-lipped cobra. Our plan, worked out, I add, before leaving England was to film the problems that arose when running a national park. The Q. E. Park with its enormous surplus of hippos was perfect for the purpose.

At that time, just before *Uhuru*, the East African countries were swarming with scientists. Most of these, the good ones anyway, were funded by bodies like The New York Zoological Society, the Smithsonian Institute, the Fulbright Scholarship or The Nuffield Unit for Tropical Animal Ecology (NUTAE) based at the Q. E. Park. Apart from a scientist's natural lust for finding out, I believe most of these experts were highly motivated by the thought that the Africans were about to be handed their own national parks to run. The scientists felt, rightly I believe, that they had a slim chance of doing so successfully but a far slimmer one if they weren't armed with the right ecological information. Hippos and the problems they presented came pretty near the top of Uganda's wildlife conundrums.

The problem was simply this. Dick Laws, who headed NUTAE and later became Director of the British Antarctic Survey, estimated that there were 12,000 hippos weighing around 11,500 tons in Lakes Edward and George with a further 30,000 weighing 28,000 tons in the neighbouring Congo. Each of these beasts came ashore at night to consume around 430 lb of the grasses that would otherwise have helped to support a whole range of animals from waterbuck to buffalo. If something was not done, the areas stripped of the grasses needed by many other animals would simply grow and grow as the hippos went further and further away from the water to find food each night. Laws' answer, or anyway partial answer, was to shoot up to 2,000 hippos a year, the meat being sold to a local butcher who transported some of it 200 miles to market. So the meat did not go to waste. Laws' real problem was to find out how many hippos the traffic could actually bear and therefore how many should be culled each year. It was to be a ten year study and needed all of it. Our job was to film the problem and attempts to find a solution.

Frank Poppleton, Head Warden of the Uganda Parks, was straight from Central Casting. Good-looking, with blue eyes and fair crinkly hair and a winning sense of humour, he had a general air of non-nonsense, straight-as-a-dye command about him. Central Casting could have put him straight into a Sherman tank racing with Horrocks to try to reach that Bridge Too Far at Arnhem. Frank, of course, would have denied any such heroic connotation. He was too late for Arnhem anyway but he was an ex-tank man. so Central Casting at least got that bit right. His training as an officer in an armoured regiment was no doubt reflected in the speed and skill with which he drove his Land Rover, christened the Bundu-Basher, across country, any type of country, the rougher the better, when catching or rounding up game for marking or research for Dick Laws' scientists at NUTAE.

Dick and Frank were the perfect combination. Like many of the East African park wardens of that time, Frank had been born and brought up as a hunter. Though he was an excellent administrator as well as leader and trainer of his ranger force, nothing pleased him better than this new kind of hunting whose object was to produce specimens, alive or, in the case of the superfluous hippo, dead, in the name of research.

Every week, there was a set quota of hippo to be shot in the areas being studied. Mostly this was done during the day. Early on in our relationship, Frank invited me to go night shooting with him in the Bundu-Basher. It was an experience every bit as unnerving as that first big rhino catch.

I retain a vivid montage-like impression of headlights flaring on the upflung arms of scandalised euphorbia trees; the big eyes of a surprised buffalo; a skulking civet cat; the glimpse of a leopard in the branches of an acacia tree; the roaring and bouncing of the vehicle and the sudden silent pauses when we sat, engine off, and looked and listened. An elephant screaming nearby from the blackness beyond the headlight beams, the tearing jolt of a sudden stop as a target appeared, the sharp pinprick report of the rifle in the night and the taste of powder on the tongue. A great corpse rolling over and over, spinning down a slope towards us like a one and a half ton barrel out of control until it hit the front bumper, pushing us back on our wheels.

Then off again to complete the night's quota. More jarring stops. Nine more shots from the Winchester 30.06. Tearing round and round in the bush until one felt like a spark on the rim of a Catherine wheel. Where had we been and how far? Not a hippo alive or dead remained in sight. I could not have told up from down, east from west or north from south. Frank started the engine and cruised round in a leisurely circle covering perhaps a square mile. He knew where each of the corpses lay and indicated them to the Acholi ranger clinging on in the back of the vehicle. At first light the Acholi would guide the butchers to cut the corpses up and the scientists to take the organs and details they needed for research—the numbers and types of parasites, blood smears, specimens of grasses last eaten, numbers of fight scars. The latter had a bearing on competition for food and territory, fighting being a sure indication of over-population..

My wife came when we filmed a daytime shoot at a place in the study area called Lion Bay on Lake Albert. Bill Cowen suggested that she might find the scenes of dismemberment, blood, guts and disembowelment somewhat distressing. Lady Baker-like, she is made of far sterner stuff having married into a shooting family where entrails, plucking, drawing and skinning are an everyday part of kitchen life. Confident as I was of Joan's resilience, I don't think even I expected to find her eating hippo steak barbecued over some burning twigs off the point of Frank's hunting knife. This, she declared, to be as good as prime pork though it probably needed a pinch of salt or maybe some garlic. A single hippo, incidentally, provides twelve times as much meat as a cow, or anyway, an African cow. After crocodile meat shall we yet see hippo on the supermarket shelves?

We all had our bad moments when filming hippo and none more than Bill Cowen unless it was my wife who, sent to flush some lesser flamingo on the edge of a wallow for the cameras, flushed a badly wounded bull hippo instead. Luckily one of his chums had chewed up a back leg giving the lady sprinter a definite advantage. It taught us all a very sharp lesson about taking risks which, as novices, we certainly weren't qualified to take.

When I told Frank Poppleton of our stupidity he was surprisingly sympathetic. Frank was a bit of a fitness freak. A year or so previously, he had stopped his Land Rover in an open grass area of the Park and decided to go for a run. There was only one thorn bush in sight. What he didn't see was that there was an old buffalo bull under the bush. As he jogged past, the buff came out, caught him with the boss of its horns and bowled him down a slope. The buffalo, as irritable as only old males of his species can be, followed up with a charge.

Frank kept rolling downhill just ahead of the hooking horns and by sheer luck managed to crawl into a shallow erosion crack. The bull then tried to kneel on him but the gully was just too deep. For nearly an hour, the buff attempted to hook the Head Warden out with his horns. He succeeded in sticking one horn tip deep into a calf, realised this was the best he could do, snorted and galloped off. The wound turned septic. It took Frank a week in hospital and a good deal of penicillin to recover. The message was clear. Even the old hands get careless. Greenhorns, don't even think about it!

It was fairly useless to try to get this message over to Bill Cowen. One afternoon we went hippo darting. A bearded Viking-like figure called Dr John Lock had turned up from Makerere College outside Kampala, then the University of East Africa. Lock specialised in developing immoblising drugs with which to dart animals for research. He used a cross-bow powered by an old car spring. His colleague, Dr Cecil Luck, a physiologist, was anxious to make skin and secretion tests on any hippos Dr Lock succeeded in darting. He also wanted to learn something about a hippo's eyesight and had discovered that Bill was an optician.

In the first stages of the operation, Bill was to film the chase. Lacking any steady camera mounting device, he suggested to Frank that he sit in the spare wheel carried on the bonnet of the Land Rover. Ropes lashed across his thighs and round the small of his back would ensure that he didn't fall off.

We set off in three Land Rovers, fanning out among the bushes round the edge of the hippo wallows to get the animals moving. The hippos saw no reason to be chivvied. In fact, they did the chivvying. Lashed all too securely to the spare wheel, Bill watched several animals charge at him only to swerve off at the last moment. Bill kept his eye glued to the view-finder and tried to forget what was happening.

When the inevitable charge was pressed home, the hippo selected Frank's Land Rover. Hemmed in by bushes, he had no chance of bashing his way out. He had just started to back out of the blind alley when a hippo climbed up on the back of the Land Rover. Frank and the ranger bailed out. Roped to the spare wheel, Bill had to sit that one out. Luckily, the hippo backed off. Later that afternoon, another hippo charged the Makerere College Land Rover in which I was riding and bit its way through the side and floor, upper and lower jaws meeting with a crunch like a metal crusher.

All told, John Lock immobilised three hippo. From one, Luck got his skin samples and discovered that hippos have an amazing capacity for exuding a special kind of sweat. This secretion is highly concentrated, alkaline, viscous and apparently pumped through the skin at a rate that would amount to ten gallons in twenty four hours. Purpose at that time unknown,

Cowen had still not had enough. Dr Luck wanted that eye test. So the optician turned cameraman erected his hide used for bird photography over the doped animal's head. I don't know whether he had time to set up the letters on a test chart and ask "better or worse" as he tried different lenses. What I do know is that he made a very hurried exit when the hippo came round and chased him for fifty yards. He had, however, established that this hippo at least was very short-sighted.

Skulls from culled hippo wait examination by scientists of the NUTAE. Age deduced from the skulls enabled the scientists to plan their culling programme.

A shot hippo has been winched ashore. Scientists will take specimens of food as well as organs. The remainder of the one ton animal will be sold to butchers.

A huge surplus of hippo was eating the grazing needed for other animals. The only answer was a hefty cull, but which ages and sex to shoot and how many?

Overcrowded hippo become aggressive, especially bulls. On land, the hippo is perhaps Africa's most dangerous big game animal. Catfish share the wallow.

The Wilder Shores of Norfolk

If hippos were frightening, fronting a wildlife show in the studio was petrifying. In those early days of television, nearly everybody in the game, and quite a few outside it, fancied they were born to appear on the box. Some, usually egged on by their wives, tried it. The casualty rate was enormous. Like everyone else, I had my moment. I'm told that it wasn't by any means a total disaster. On the other hand, my picture was never on the cover of the Radio Times, even the East Anglian edition. I had inherited the modest programme which Aubrey Buxton had started and which had proved the jumping off point for the highly successful *Survival* series. Aubrey, I imagine, had discovered that his true metier was fixing things behind the scenes. In fact, when the Royal Television Society presented him with a well-deserved gold medal some years later, it was 'for outstanding work behind the camera.' The cynical said: "a long way behind the camera" which wasn't entirely true or fair since the whole highly successful *Survival* circus wouldn't have started to roll if he hadn't been there to push. So, when one day after my second safari to Uganda he asked whether I would like to have a shot at presenting *Countryman*. I thought what the hell. Apart from researching, writing and producing every *Survival* programme we made, I hadn't much on my hands! Besides, like every other mug in television, I suppose I thought I might be rather good at it. I had come to realise, too, that I couldn't expect to be out in the wilds all the time. Come to that, there was a great deal of wildlife and not a few really wild characters in East Anglia. So, of course, I said yes. *Countryman* itself gave me a chance to take a walk on the wilder side of life, though, admittedly, nearer home. It also allowed me to indulge my favourite pastimes, namely fishing, shooting, bird-watching and trying to train gun dogs. By pure coincidence, practically every guest I had in the studio was enmeshed in similar pastimes. This was fine by the so-called Sugar Beet Network's audience. A lot of them were also interested in sporting and outdoor pursuits. Whenever I could fix it, the studio guests came from the wilder shores of North Norfolk and the Wash.

I remember being briefed by the Head of News before making my first studio appearance. "Every time I go into the studio," he said reassuringly, "I feel as though I am about to go ten rounds with Sonny Liston." Liston was a well-known and ruthless heavyweight of the period. I suppose he meant to give me confidence. As a former ITN man he had been in hotspots all over the world but it is quite possible he had not made his studio debut with a baboon.

The baboon belonged to a lady, a friend of Aubrey Buxton's, who ran a private zoo. There are possibly more zoos and wildlife parks in Norfolk than there are national parks in Africa. Interviewing this lady with the aid of a minute or two of film shot in her stately zoopark looked like a doddle. It probably would have been had not the baboon sat on my shoulder throughout doing unmentionable things not so much to, as into, my ear. As an encore, towards the end of the programme, the baboon literally brought the house down. The creature had spotted that a strip of 'gaffer' tape that held the flats of the scenery behind us together was loose. The baboon abandoned my right ear, nipped down and unzipped the tape, bringing the flats crashing to the floor. After that initiation, everything that later happened on *Countryman* was a doddle.

I had some great eccentrics on the show, not least Kenzie Thorpe about whom I had previously written a book *Kenzie, the Wild Goose Man*. Kenzie was the classic case of poacher (nearly) turned game-keeper. Half gypsy, he had grown up gunning and had probably played with a rusty muzzle-loader in his cradle. Not a pheasant from Boston Stump to Sandringham was safe. He knew more about the wild geese, the pinkfeet that came from Iceland to the shores of the Wash each winter, than anyone before or since. He could call geese out of the sky and hares from their forms in the cornfield. He could make redshank, golden plover and curlew swerve in flight and come to him as if controlled by radar beams rather than his imitation of their call. Just before World War Two, when Peter Scott was making his first modest wildfowl collection of wildfowl and wading birds at his home at the East Lighthouse, Sutton Bridge, Peter recognised Kenzie's remarkable talents and took him on as his man, a role that included catching and taming wildfowl but did not succeed in excluding Kenzie from his shooting, poaching and wildfowling activities.

Kenzie was a genuine original East Anglian wildman of the type that can almost certainly not exist again. Guiltily, I confess that people like myself, writers and broadcasters, have done much to bring this decline about. We blew these great characters' cover by making them minor stars. And Kenzie, for one, would have had it no other way, he revelled in the fame that had come his way and handled it far better than most pop stars. He thought nothing of imitating his employer, a deception helped by the fact that there was a superficial facial resemblance, the high cranium and a tendency to frontal baldness. It also helped that Kenzie could produce some occasionally quite good but often quite dreadful wildfowl paintings which the gullible sometimes took for Scott originals. In the end, Prince Hal abandoned his Falstaff. Peter's newly formed and flourishing Wildfowl Trust and his growing role as world conservationist did not sit well with Kenzie's past and indeed with his present. Nothing, thank heavens, would completely change the old rogue though about the time I had him on *Countryman*, he had assumed a mantle of semi-respectability. The Wildfowlers Association of Great Britain and Ireland (WAGBI) had appointed him a warden of their fowling reserves on the Wash. They almost certainly did so in self-defence. I've no doubt that he revelled in his title but the Wash sands had always been his kingdom and it's unlikely that his semi-legal status did much to change his ways.

He was at his rumbustious best in the studio that day. But then Kenzie had always been a performer. The film we showed of some of his more respectable activities was shot by the man towards whom I have been gradually working my way, Ted Eales from Morston, next to Blakeney, on the North Norfolk coast. Ted, for me, summed up the whole essential and ancient link between the hunter and his quarry, between naturalist and field sportsman. And Kenzie? He will long be remembered by the Anglia sound engineers. When asked by me to demonstrate how he called pinkfeet out of the moonlit sky, he produced a call so penetrating that he came very close to putting the sound men and their highly technical apparatus, in fact the whole transmission, off the air.

When *Survival* became a household word in television, urban and suburban friends, knowing my shooting and fishing activities, often asked me how I could possibly reconcile making those beautiful wildlife programmes with going out next day and shooting a mallard at evening flight or walking up partridges with a few friends and our dogs.

The simple answer—simple to me at least—was that they were different parts of the same whole. The questioner invariably found this answer obscure and evasive. For a long time I tried to explain. Yes, it was possible to be both a hunter and a naturalist. Sure, you could be a naturalist without being a hunter —I use the word hunter in the American sense rather than giving it the British connotation which invariably means hunting foxes with hounds. It often strikes me, incidentally, that the Americans have got the right word to describe a field sportsman whether he is a fisher or shooter. Hunting one's quarry is surely the essence of the thing and what it is all about.

My questioner might well follow up by asking to be told what is admirable about being a hunter-naturalist? Well, nothing in particular. Did I say that there was? No, my interrogator might persist, but you certainly implied it. Did I? Well that wasn't my intention. What I will say is that the hunter has to understand his quarry and the way it lives and is therefore a long way towards being a practical naturalist. What's more, if only out of self-interest, he is more likely to create the conditions, or if you insist on the jargon word, 'habitat', in which it can best and most numerously exist..

How, I might ask, do you think that Norfolk got all those hedges and copses? God certainly didn't put them there. Nor did any well-intentioned townsman or town-planner. Country land-owners planted them, partly for farming purposes but largely for field sporting ends. And if I get really worked up, I might add that the true hunter actually reveres his quarry as well as wanting to possess it.

Oh, steady on, I say, that's going a bit far isn't it? Well, actually, no, I would try to explain patiently, it isn't. I might even go on to list the number of national park wardens of my acquaintance who were, or still are, hunters, the knowledge gained from hunting considerably helping them in their task of conservation. I might be tempted to add that Peter Scott shot more wild geese than anyone save perhaps Kenzie Thorpe. Yes, but he gave up, didn't he? So he did and I might one day give up though I very much doubt it...and so on and on in ever widening circles.

Long ago, I stopped trying to explain, convert and make myself unpopular by arguing at dinner parties. After a time, when asked how I could make those beautiful wildlife films and go shooting next day, I replied: "because I love doing both."

I've used that answer ever since. It seems to work or at least it shuts people up. Some even move away, perhaps in the fear that I may splash blood on them.

Ted Eales was the perfect example of the hunter-naturalist. His father had been warden of the National Trust Nature Reserve on Blakeney Point, famous for its tern colonies. Ted had naturally succeeded him. Ted had been brought up among boats and mud creeks, samphire and eel grass. He was typical of the longshoremen of that wild north Norfolk coast; men like his friend Stratton Long of Blakeney, punt-gunner, boat chandler and all-round shooting man; men like Ted's fellow warden Billy Bishop, two or three miles along the coast at Cley. Billy was a warden of the Norfolk Naturalist Trust reserve at Cley. All these men had shot from boyhood. All were born and bred naturalists who would have been baffled if you had asked to see the join in their apparently conflicting interests. To them, as to myself in a more modest way, it was all of a piece. They knew more about the birds of their coast - the migrant waxwings, bluethroats, brent geese, wigeon, teal, avocets, ruffs and reeves not to mention four or five species of terns—than has been written in a hundred ornithological tomes. They were all wartime petty officers with all the guile and craft of that species. Any service but the Royal Navy would have been unthinkable to them. Did not Nelson draw many of his crews from their home coast? They were coastguards and netters of sea trout along the shore and cullers of a reasonable number of wildfowl in winter. I would not have been surprised to have been told that all of them had webbed feet.

Aubrey Buxton had grown up among them. He knew their talents and their quality and rightly suspected that Ted had untapped abilities. Early on in *Survival's* story he had armed Ted with a 16mm movie camera in the belief that if he shot birds in flight with a twelve bore he could do the same with a camera. This coupled with Ted's unrivalled knowledge of the wildlife of his own shoreline, and the fact that he spent at least half the year living among it all in the derelict lifeboat house on the Point, suggested that this sportsman-naturalist might come up with something good. This Ted did, even though his camera often lay in the bottom of his boat, coated with sand, along with the anchor and anchor cable. My own close association with Ted came in the first instance from this horribly treated camera. Ted had little time for technicalities or technicians. The executives at Anglia Television, Norwich, where we put out *Countryman*, not to mention the technicians of *Survival* in London, were a mad lot of boogers. Ted was not what you would call an office man. But then he had no need to be. Our friendship sprang from the fact that I asked him to shoot as much wildlife film as possible for the *Countryman* series. Whenever I could, I got him into the studio in person. The Norfolk tongue as spoken by the true native is wonderful to hear. The audience appreciated being talked to in their own language and Ted seldom produced wildlife film that was less than bootiful.

The weatherman at Anglia never did understand why, the moment the programme was over, we dashed up to his met. office demanding to know what the weather was likely to be down on the coast at Blakeney. Even less did he understand why we were both upset if the forecast was fine, still and clear. The fact is that the optimum conditions for coastal wildfowlers at evening flight are a gale of wind, preferably with some sleet or snow in it and a light veiling of cloud to disperse the moonlight and outline the wigeon against the sky. Oh, and a full tide if you can manage it, to push the duck off the sands and muds to flight inland. Fowling clothes, guns, waders and ammunition and Ted's spaniels were already in his car under the eye of the security man in the company park. If we were smart about it, we could make Morston Creek in time to launch the boat Ted used in summer to take bird-watching visitors over to the Point. We never shot more than half dozen duck between us. Wildfowlers seldom make, or wish to make, big bags. Just being out there in the magic darkness is enough.. An hour and a half previously I had probably been chatting in the studio to some worthy with a private wildfowl collection which Ted had filmed. Now here we were, under the moon, trying to shoot a few duck. Neither of us found anything strange or inconsistent about this. If you don't believe me—and I shall quite understand if you don't—I shan't try to explain why!

If you're looking for a walk on the wild side, you couldn't find a better place in England, at least, than the Ouse Washes, sometimes called the Bedford Levels. I found the Ouse Washes largely thanks to Ted Eales. They run for 23 miles between Denver and Earith through Cambridgeshire and Norfolk. Look at the map and you can see their parallel lines drawn straight as a ruler across the fen country. Until the 17th Century this land was perpetually under water, with occasional islands like Eley standing up above the flooded fens. Their status as a former inland sea is perpetuated in the name of some of the fen towns, Littleport for example. From the air you can see the outline of old wharves in villages from which the water has long retreated. In the old days, the fens provided a refuge for outlaws and political refugees like Hereward the Wake. Until quite recently, you could catch malaria in the mists of the untamed fens. The old enmen themselves were as wild as their landscape, living by shooting and trapping wildfowl and catching eels. Then in the 1600s, the landscape or perhaps waterscape, changed. There had been many attempts, some successful, to drain parts of the inland sea that was the fenland.

Then along came the master drainer, a Dutchman called Cornelius Vermuyden, hired by a syndicate of speculators and noblemen, who finally did the job. The main source of flooding was the River Ouse. Vermuyden built two artificial rivers three quarters of a mile apart. One ran between high embankments and was called, and has been known ever since, as the Hundred Foot River. The parallel river three quarters of a mile to the south was at the level of the intervening land. It was named, revealing its Dutch ancestry, the Delph. After Vermuyden had finished his vast enterprise, the Hundred Foot River remained tidal, bringing its flood and ebb all the way up from the mouth of the Ouse towards King's Lynn. The Delph carried most of the Ouse flood water from the Midlands. When this was too much for it, it simply overflowed its low-lying banks and spread out over the three quarters of a mile of rough meadows in the direction of the Hundred Foot. There it came to a full stop against the Hundred Foot's man-made bank, known, for etymological reasons I have never fathomed, as 'the cradge bank'. In doing so, the Delph's overflow created at various depths and extent throughout the winter, and in exceptionally wet periods during the spring and sometimes part of the summer, a miniature inland sea. Vermuyden had created in the Ouse Washes a reservoir and safety valve to contain the Ouse floodwater. A wash in these parts is the local name for any flooded area. Unwittingly, the Dutchman had also created one of the greatest wildfowl wintering areas in Europe. From October until March, the Ouse Washes are home to around 20,000 wigeon, 12,000 mallard, several thousand wild swans, both Whoopers and Bewicks, as well as teal, gadwall, pintail, shoveler and the rest of the European dabbling and some diving ducks. There is no accumulation of wildfowl to match it this side of the Dutch polders and the River Elbe.

The fenmen, of course, had always known this and taken a rich but sustainable harvest from the winter wildfowl. It wasn't discovered by amateur wildfowlers until Peter Scott and a few friends found it and shot the washes regularly while undergraduates at Cambridge. I think it is fair to say that when Ted Eales rediscovered its rich filming possibilities—not to mention wildfowling wonders—and introduced me to them, the washes and the fenmen hadn't changed a great deal.

Ted's contact was Josh Scott and his uncle George Kent. George could have passed for a Duke at White's or Boodles any day. From boyhood these two had punt-gunned, set up huge bank guns to discharge a pound of shot into pools fed with tail grain and rotten potatoes to attract the highly marketable mallard. They'd made a good living netting eels in the drains and dykes that criss-crossed not only the washes but the adjoining fenland. They'd shot their fair share of wild fen pheasants and caught green plover for market in thirty yard long clapnets. Josh remembered the tribal rivalries of the fen villages when it was more than a Welney lad's life was worth to venture into the Littleport barely five miles away. These two were true fen tigers, a race which like the wild tiger of India and the Far East is fast dying out. Perhaps the only fenman to match them was Ernie James who lived beside the Delph at Welney and still made six foot long osier eel-traps in the style no doubt used by the ancient Britons. Some city slicker saw Ernie's traps and suggested they would make marvellous standard lamps which posh shops like Heals would buy for a lot of money. Ernie really wasn't interested. He made one and then decided it was better put to its proper purpose, stuck rotten meat in it and lowered it into the Delph to catch eels.

Ted Eales, of course, spoke the same language as the fenmen though in a different dialect. So George and Josh would do anything for him and, because I was Ted's friend and colleague, for me, too. For *Countryman* we recreated at least some of the old fen tigers' way of life. Because, green plover were protected in 1954 we could not, of course, catch them in clapnets, even for filming purposes, without breaking the law. We could, however, catch these beautiful birds for ringing, or as Ted said 'to be wrung'. Ted, as warden of a National Trust nature reserve, had a ringing permit. So we set up the thirty yards of netting on a carefully prepared 'ground', the term for a strip of grass just awash with flood water. We could no longer use tethered live plover as Josh and George would have done in earlier days, so we put out some old carved wooden plover decoys. Then we crouched, camera at the ready, in a hide thirty yards away while George and Josh called the wild birds down out of the sky with an imitation of their plaintive call. The wooden decoys were only convincing enough to fool half a dozen birds who landed confidently with a whoosh of their rounded wings. George pulled the cord. Two old car springs at either end flew out of the notch in the hazel twig that held them down and the net flashed over, trapping six astonished lapwing. In the old days their necks would have been quickly wrung. Now their legs were 'wrung' with numbered British Museum rings and the plover released into the sky. In a modest way we had captured on film for *Countryman* something that will never be seen again in the Ouse Washes.

And, of course, we went shooting on the Washes when the filming was done and sometimes when there was no filming to do. In those days, you could roam where you liked without anyone saying you nay. It's not like that now. But even today, the washes are a magical place. To get onto them, you must either drive three miles up a precarious, muddy, rutted bank in a four-wheel drive vehicle or cross the Hundred Foot River. Crossing that river, especially in the dark, in a small rubber boat, against a six knot current tide at full flood, or landing on sloping twelve foot banks of mud at low tide, is a commando experience full of hazard. Once onto the wash and you are in a world that few people except the odd fowlers ever visit. Horizons in the fens are limitless. So, if you are fortunate and conditions of wind and water are right, are the wildfowl. Wild swans—protected of course— cross your portable hide with a few feet to spare. Snipe zither about the sky. Shoot those if you wish and can. They're hard to hit and delicious to eat! Parties of duck travel the line of the washes at dawn and dusk, mainly wigeon, sometimes in packs of a hundred or more, the drakes whistling and the hens growling. Occasionally you get a shot at a small party flying fast and low and fooled by your decoys, but a dozen duck for a dawn or dusk's flight would be something to put in the book. But, as Ted once said to me, "being there is the thing, boy" and being there is all of it.

It was through Ted, of course, that I met Josh Scott. Josh took his name from the fact that his ancestors came to the Ouse Washes as Scots prisoners after the defeat of Prince Charlie at Culloden in 1745. The prisoners were brought to the fen country as labourers, to throw up the banks, notably the banks of the Hundred Foot River, for Vermuyden's great drainage plan. Josh swore that if you dug in the mud of the embankment, you would find fragments of clay pipes which the Scots smoked as they worked.

The washes began to change several years after we started filming and shooting there. The conservationist organisations, notably Peter Scott's Wildfowl and Wetland Trust and the Nature Conservancy, had rightly decided that this 23 mile long inland sea was so important to wintering wildfowl that it must be partly protected. The Wildfowl Trust bought land on the Denver side of Welney suspension bridge and village and set up a 500 acre reserve there for the ducks but mainly for the Bewicks and Whoopers, the wild swans. Peter rightly saw in Josh the ideal poacher turned game-keeper. Josh took the job as the Warden of the Wildfowl Trust reserve and made a fine job of it. Unlike Kenzie, he could give up shooting wildfowl but that didn't mean that he was anti- wildfowler. Far from it. Josh soon found Ted and myself and some kindred spirits a half wash. We bought it just in time, before the big numbers game started. We paid £627 for 22 acres of precious washland! The big numbers buy-up of washland started when the Royal Society for the Protection of Birds began acquiring washes as reserves. With a million pound a year income, the RSPB could afford to pay several thousand pounds an acre and readily did so. The hard -core local wildfowlers saw this as a disaster. I happened not to agree with them— entirely. Without protection, there's little doubt the washes would have been shot to hell and gone. It was the ducks that would have gone—elsewhere. As it was, the fowl couldn't sit on the reserves for ever, no matter how much artificial feed they were given. Sooner or later a good proportion of birds, both from the Wildfowl Trust and the increasing number of RSPB reserves, would have to flight out to feed elsewhere, notably on the rich fen farmland. In doing so, some of their flight-lines would cross wildfowlers' land, including our own modest but often quite productive wash. The Wildfowl Trust, perhaps due to Josh's influence in the early days, appreciated this and took a liberal and sensible attitude. The RSPB on the other hand never has and probably never will see that it is in its interest to make common cause with the wildfowling and shooting community in general. After all, they both want the same thing, if partly for different reasons, that is to say, more birds.

Anyway, the wash worked for us. It worked so well back in the sixties and seventies that we decided that we must have a permanent dwelling place on our wash in which we could sleep the night, totter out before dawn without the drama of the drive up the bank or the even worse drama of ferrying ourselves across the Hundred Foot River. What we needed was a hut.

Before I leave the subject of the washes. I must tell the story of that hut, particularly since its central figure is that great shooting man and conservationist, Ted Eales.

One stormy morning, Ted is in the look-out of the old lighthouse on Blakeney Point where he fulfilled the job of part-time coastguard in severe weather. This morning the weather has been exceptionally severe. He sweeps the horizon with his binoculars and observes that it is afloat with large planks of prepared timber. A local radio bulletin confirms that a Swedish timber ship has shed its deck cargo in the Wash during the night. No longshoreman could overlook such an opportunity. At the next favourable tide he sets out in his motor launch to perform some salvage work. Out on the storm-tossed sea he finds he is not alone. But then on this coast he could hardly expect to be. His friend Stratton Long, former punt-gunner, wartime gunnery officer in an MTB flotilla, is afloat early, too.

"What you doing out here at this hour, Ted?"

"Same as you, Stratton."

So they combine forces and tow in as much of the timber as their two boats can handle. Back in the sandhills of the Point, they wrap the best of it in canvas and bury it. Being law-abiding citizens, they naturally have to report the cargo spillage—eventually—to the Customs and Excise who tell them that they must appoint an agent to sell any flotsam or possibly jetsam. So they appoint their good friend, fellow former petty officer and wildlife warden Billy Bishop to do the job in the certain knowledge that Billy will charge locals and friends a very fair price for the planks regardless of type of wood or size.

So, when the subject of building ourselves a hut in which to sleep when wildfowling on the Ouse Washes came up, Ted admitted that he knew where he might find some suitable timber. The canvas-wrapped planks emerged from the dry sands of the Blakeney dunes in mint condition.

The hut designed and constructed by Ted was built out on Blakeney Point. The central feature around which everything else was designed was an old Land Rover windscreen, later destined to be the kitchen window. When the hut was complete in four separate sections, Ted contacted a friend with a furniture van and told him to wait at Morston Creek at the next spring tide.

The plan was to tow the sections of the hut lashed together to form a raft across the mile of water between the Point and Morston Creek, load them onto the van which would then be driven seventy five miles to Welney. The van driver can have had no idea what was in store for him. The three miles of Hundred Foot Bank between Welney Suspension Bridge and our wash are only just navigable by a four wheel drive vehicle in winter. I doubt whether a furniture van has ever before attempted this nightmare drive even in the comparatively dry ruts of high summer.

It was a close-run thing whether the van would even be called upon to make the attempt. Ted's experience on minesweepers during World War Two should have suggested what happens when you tow a paravane, a finned apparatus designed for cutting mine mooring cables. It dives. That is exactly what the sections of the hut did when towed at more than three knots. With the tide on the turn and dropping fast, it seemed that by the time they reached Morston Creek and the waiting van, the water would have drained out. In this situation, Ted ordered Ron Downing, a partner in our wash and assistant at the hut building, to nip over the gunn'l and sit on the stern of the raft to keep its nose up.

With Ron's aid as stern ballast, they made Morston Creek while there was still some water in it but with the tide ebbing fast. Never a man to admit defeat, Ted rushed off to a friendly boat yard and borrowed some boat jacks. With their aid, and with all concerned coated in marine ooze from the creek bottom, they somehow hauled the hut onto the van.

The hut stands on the wash to this day. I have not slept in it for sometime.

In our wildfowling heyday I shared it most weeks with three men and at least three dogs. We never got a lot of sleep despite the amount of vintage claret shipped across the Hundred Foot. The sound of wigeon whistling in the darkness outside kept one awake in anticipation of the morrow. And the labradors tended to wake us all up, wagging their tails among the aluminium saucepans in which the previous night's sumptuous meal had been cooked on the Calor Gas stove. The mice gave us a lot of trouble. They breed tiger mice in the fens. They were extremely active in our absence. Ted thought he had got the answer by hanging the frying pan from the ceiling by two feet of string. Not so! Fen mice can apparently abseil.

One other treasured memory of the hut on the marshes. One of the planks Ted and Stratton salvaged was, I think, sandalwood. It was known as the aromatic plank. Whenever I could, I put my sleeping bag next to it. It fought well against the smell of wet labrador. Ted Eales has been gone, alas, several years now. If I could tell him that every time I hear the word sandalwood mentioned I think of him he would probably look at me and say: "lovely bit of timber that, boy. *Bootiful*!"

Ted Eales, all-round Norfolk countryman, broadcaster, wildlife cameraman and warden of the National Trust Nature Reserve at Blakeney Point.

Kenzie Thorpe, wildfowler, goose guide and poacher supreme, not to mention self-taught painter. Kenzie liked to be mistaken for his boss, Peter Scott.

The north Norfolk coast produces great characters and none greater than the late Billy Bishop, warden of the Norfolk Naturalists' Trust reserve at Cley.

A Right Royal Rudolf

How Lake Rudolf contrived to hide itself for so long is a mystery to me. At a time when British and German explorers were swanning all over East Africa, it managed to get overlooked until a Hungarian nobleman, Count Teleki, with his artist companion, Von Hohnel, put it on the map in 1887.

Rudolf is long and thin. Like most African lakes, since independence, it has been renamed. It is now Lake Turkana after the pastoralist tribe who inhabit its western shore. The lake is never much more than twenty miles wide, and stretches from Ethiopia in the north where a river with a name like a patent washing powder, the Omo, flows into it. It continues 200 miles almost due south until it ends in a volcanic wilderness complete with a minor volcano which, at least, has been allowed to keep the discoverer's name, Teleki's Volcano. Even today, Lake Rudolf—I'm afraid I still think of it under that name—is a wild place, especially the eastern shore which is often visited by raiding bands of *shifta* from Somalia. *Shifta* is another word for bandit. Somalis are rather good at producing bandits and elephant poachers. George Adamson was, incidentally, killed by a band of *shifta* though not on the shores of Lake Rudolf. The eastern shore at Koobi Fora is the scene of the astonishing discoveries of some of the earliest hominid remains by the heroic and highly individual Richard Leakey and his international team of palaeontologists perhaps the most brilliant of whom is a native Kenyan. It was while Richard was flying his Cessna to his camp at Koobi Fora that the engine stopped. The forced landing that followed resulted in the amputation of both Richard Leakey's lower legs. Why the engine stopped has never to my knowledge been properly explained. Water in the fuel? Just wild supposition, naturally. Once you declare opposing views to those of the ruling powers in an African country almost anything can happen. And Richard at the time was doing rather a lot of that. For instance, you may get beaten up. Richard did. It is also just possible that you may not get the purest aviation petrol at the pumps. Who knows ? What is certain is that the crash didn't stop that indomitable man. He is still stumping around making his voice heard whenever it seems politically necessary.

Apart from the Turkana, the shore is virtually uninhabited except for the El Molo, a tribe so small in numbers that they are practically an endangered human sub-species.

Naturally, I was delighted to be told I was going back to Kenya—I'd been in and out of East Africa quite a lot since the Uganda days. I am not sure that I was so delighted when I was told with whom I would be going. This time, Lady Baker, aka Mrs Willock, was *not* coming along. Prince Philip, however, was.

I'd worked on a couple of *Survivals* earlier with the great man. It can be hard going. In a way I sympathise. The Royals get shown so many things and places by so-called and even actual experts that at times they must want to scream: "Why? Why, in God's name, why? Just because you tell me so, I don't have to just smile and believe every damn word you're telling me."

Most Royals are far too well trained and polite to do any such thing. Prince Philip is not, or, at least, not always. If he wasn't the Queen's husband he would probably be chairman of ICI or British Airways, in which case, both or either, would have to buck their ideas up.

I hope I betray no confidences since I have no wish to book a bedsit in the Tower. Risking that, I will give you a case in point. Quite early in *Survival's* career we made a fine one-hour programme about the Galapagos islands. It was shot by Alan Root, of whom you will hear a good deal more. *The Enchanted Isles* was a landmark for our team because it was the first wildlife programme to sell to network television in America. Prince Philip, who had been to the Galapagos with Aubrey Buxton in attendance kindly agreed to speak part of the narration. I went along to rehearse him, or rather for him to nitpick my commentary. The session took place very informally in Windsor Castle in a room hung with royal ancestors. The ornithological adviser on the programme was Dr Bryan Nelson of Aberdeen University. PP had met him in the Galapagos and knew that he was the acknowledged world expert on the fish-catching birds called gannets and their close allies the boobies. They are wonderful film material. They dive often from a great height on shoals of fish, folding their wings at the last moment before they hit the water like a bomb. One of the Galapagos species of booby is the blue-footed. Alan Root had shot some great material of the blue-footed boobies landing in their nesting colony. Just before touching down, they turned up their blue feet as if to display them. Bryan Nelson had assured me that this was exactly what it was—display, in fact mating display, possibly reinforcement of the pair bond. Birds go in for that kind of courtship display and who was I to question the word of a world expert ? If I wasn't, Prince Philip, was. To hell with world experts. He was, after all, an aviator and knew an air-brake when he saw one. We discussed, no, argued would be more the word, amiably for quite a while until it became obvious that the royal patience was being sorely tried and the royal view about air brakes intended to prevail.

I played my last card. But Bryan Nelson is a world expert, sir.

PP pushed his chair a trifle closer and gave me a hard stare at close range. It was a little like looking down the muzzles of a double-barrelled shotgun. "Look," he said. "I meet a lot of experts. Only last week a chap took me round a ruined castle. All that remained above ground were a few fragments of the walls. That's the great hall, he said. Fair enough. He showed me a smaller rectangle and declared it to be the dining-room. Just off it was a far smaller square of brickwork. That, the chap told me, is the kitchen. I asked him how he knew. Its smaller than the rest, he said, so it just has to be. Experts! Don't give me bloody experts."

I salvaged something from the wreck. As far as I remember he agreed to say: "it may be a kind of display but it looks to me very like it is using its blue feet as air brakes."

Roll on, Lake Rudolf, I thought. With luck I may just get eaten by a crocodile.

The Lake Rudolf expedition was a direct outcome of Aubrey Buxton's close and genuine friendship with the eminence he sometimes referred to as You-Know-Who. Little wonder that the Queen's husband was sometimes irreverently referred to within the *Survival* unit as 'The Chinese Prince'. You-Know-Who was an easily deciphered social code name that fooled no one and wasn't intended to. Another of Aubrey's social verbal gambits which I, for one, always greatly enjoyed was: "I had dinner last night with someone called Lord Mountbatten." Did this suggest that the lower orders might never have heard of El Supremo? I never quite decided but enjoyed the verbal ploy as a rare example of top-drawer-speak.

There is no doubt that Aubrey, later Lord, Buxton and the once and future Prince enjoyed a great rapport. The Prince was without doubt vitally and genuinely interested in conservation, witness his total involvement in the World Wildlife Fund, now the Worldwide Fund for Nature. I have little doubt that Aubrey helped this valuable interest to blossom. From where I modestly stand, Prince Philip has a proper and balanced attitude to both conservation and field sports. He is in many respects the hunter-naturalist, albeit a privileged one, to whom I referred in the last chapter. He rightly ducked out of a ceremonial tiger shoot in India. You may recall that diplomatic whitlow that suddenly developed on his trigger finger. How, after all, could the Chairman of the British Appeal of the World Wildlife Fund shoot a magnificent creature of an endangered species? But he shot regularly with Aubrey both at driven game and when flighting wildfowl on the Cley Marshes on the North Norfolk Coast. Aubrey without any doubt fostered his interest both in birds and in bird photography, not that Aubrey could take a good picture of a bearded tit if it sat on the end of his telephoto lens. Nor did he pretend that he could. But our *Survival* chairman and mentor and sometimes executive producer was, ornithologically speaking, greatly knowledgeable.

With this kind of expertise at hand, You-Know-Who decided to take up bird photography and bought himself a Hasselblad camera. He produced a book of rather smudgy — by professional standards but not by yours or mine— bird photographs called 'Birds from Britannia', the latter being the name of the now decommisioned royal yacht. Now we are coming to it— the royal safari to Lake Rudolf. Prince Philip had been invited by the Emperor of Ethiopia to visit informally in order to, amongst, other things, take some pictures of birds. Aubrey Buxton made the perfectly proper suggestion that his royal friend extend his birding tour to Lake Rudolf in Kenya.

Survival, which is to say Anglia Television, would pick up the tab. As an appreciative gesture, the royal guest might care to appear before the cameras to give his views on the most important conservation issues of the day a chore entirely in keeping with his world role in the conservation scene and one which would form the authoritative backbone of a *Survival* Special to be called 'Now or Never'. In other words he would be filmed doing, what in the business, are known as 'the links'.

Union rules being what they were in those days, this wasn't something we could shoot with a couple of wildlife cameramen. To put our star on film, we required fully paid-up members of the ACCT, the film technicians union. We managed to cut this down to a crew of three, a camera and sound man, and a director. The director was that same Ron Downing who had acted as stern ballast on our hut when towed by Ted Eales across Blakeney Harbour. And, of course, myself as interviewer, producer and general dogsbody. It was all going to be very informal.

It would have been fine if it had stopped there but, of course, it didn't. We took over a fishing camp halfway down the west shore of the great lake. There it would have been perfectly possible to live a simple and enjoyable life and, to give him full credit, I think our royal guest would have preferred it that way. But once you get into these television circuses, especially ones that involve heads of state, nothing is allowed to be simple. Every eventuality must be catered for.

At that time *Survival* had just recruited a new wildlife cameraman, John Pearson, who was also a pilot for East African Airways. John was asked to hire a twin Navajo which is quite a lot of aeroplane. In this, John would daily fly food from Wilson airfield, Nairobi, to the camp strip. The plane would also be useful if, for example, our star was bitten by a cobra. Not that this was likely, since the entire area of the camp was scoured for any nasties it might be harbouring, such as scorpions and gaboon vipers that would in the ordinary way have been left to their own devices. But no way was this an ordinary way.

The Kenya government apparently felt an equally heavy responsibility. They sent an aged Bren gun carrier, an officer of the Kenyan army and a small detachment to sit unobtrusively in the sandhills behind the camp.

So I flew out with the film crew. We established ourselves several days before the royal plane, an Avro Andover of the Queen's Flight and piloted by Prince Philip and carrying the originator of the expedition, Aubrey Buxton, flew in to Lodwar, the nearest airfield able to accommodate it. There was a pleasant irony in this. It later turned out that during the Mau Mau rebellion, when Jomo Kenyatta was the arch villain of the piece, we incarcerated him in a small hut at the end of Lodwar runway. But then there is a well-established precedent for locking up future heads of state and the Brits have been better at it than most. Now, here was Mzee Jomo Kenyatta, revered President of the independent Kenya, sending his troops to welcome a British Royal. Splendid stuff! And it was certainly appreciated. I recall Prince Philip after greeting the small and very smart guard of honour which met him at the aircraft steps saying with total sincerity words to the effect that it was wonderful to see that we had handed something on to these chaps.

I won't pretend that filming our star was a whole bundle of fun. In fact, I soon began to sympathise with the poor fellow who had shown him round that ruined castle and pointed out where the kitchen was. I think it may have been the influence of the Hasselblad and his new-found interest in photography, but the star had more than a marked tendency to question the requirements of the camera and sound man.

"I should have thought the sun was bright enough without having to put a reflector on my face."

"Well, sir" —-the crew had been told to treat the Prince as if he was the colonel of their regiment. Poor lads, very few camera and sound men of the time had been in a regiment let alone had a chance of addressing its colonel. Quite correctly, however, they addressed him as sir as I did myself, but then I had had the advantage of five wartime years in the Royal Marines. "Well, sir," the cameraman said respectfully. "If I don't put a reflector on your face we won't see your features at all under that floppy hat...." But the hat never came off and the reflector was only grudgingly accepted. It was all a bit like that.

On one or two days Aubrey took his royal friend bird-watching. He couldn't have had a better mentor. Aubrey knew every wading bird on that lake in every phase of its plumage. On these days I went fishing, usually for tiger fish with bright flashy flies and once for Nile Perch with Philip's detective, a large amiable man called Jumbo Thorning. Jumbo was crazy on catching big fish and Nile perch in Lake Rudolf can easily top the hundred pound mark.

I confess that these days, I'm somewhat of a purist fly-fisherman—though if I want a fish badly enough, say, to eat, I'm prepared to use a hand grenade to catch it. But trailing big plug baits from heavy rods behind a motor launch is not my favourite form of sport. Jumbo Thorning was quite happy with this. He wanted big fish and plenty of them. Now, even a thirty pound Nile Perch on a rod more suited to catching shark can't give much of a fight. But put the same fish on the end of ten pound breaking strain nylon fished from a light salmon or sea trout spinning rod and you may be in for a surprise. I'd brought just such tackle with me with the idea of giving the theory a trial. I'd met these perch before in the Nile itself and didn't have too much respect for their fighting ability, at least on heavy tackle. So being a fishing know-all, I set up my light rod alongside Jumbo's heavy tackle, streamed exactly the same plugs and spoons that he was using. And what happened? The great detective landed fifteen or more fish up to thirty and forty pounds. Me? Using the same lures, at precisely the same speed and depth, I never caught a fish over six pounds all day and mighty few of them. Jumbo was very nice about it and suggested I must be doing something wrong. Undoubtedly, but what? Angling success had relaxed this extremely nice man. Towards the end of the day I summoned up courage to ask him what it was like working for his boss.

"Great," he said, "So long as I remember to say good morning sir, to him first thing in the morning and good night sir, last thing at night, I can say almost any damn thing I like in between." Not quite the way to treat the colonel of your regiment, maybe, but it obviously worked. I'd say Jumbo was happy in his work, even when not catching immense Nile Perch.

When not filming or recording the star, we made one or two expeditions. The most adventurous of these was to Central Island. Lake Rudolf has three uninhabited islands, North, South and the one in between to which we were now headed in the fishing camp's moderately unseaworthy motor launch. I suppose our guest was taking a bit of a chance out in mid-Rudolf in this tub without even a life jacket. If so, it didn't trouble him in the least. Central Island lay eleven nautical miles, north-east of the fishing camp. The waters of Rudolf can blow up with alarming speed when a wind comes roaring out of the Ethiopian mountains to the north or the desert to the east. A boatload of scientists had been lost in such a storm a few years previously when trying to make South Island from the western shore.

I thought of this when we were about halfway there. The wind began to get up, nothing serious, but it was putting up a nasty short sea, full of lop and slop and slowing up our heavily laden launch considerably. Our sailor Prince was obviously enjoying this enormously and demanded to be given the helm and throttle. You may possibly argue the toss with the colonel of your regiment but certainly not with an Admiral of the Fleet. The Admiral's response to this situation was full speed ahead and damn the passengers. The launch's response was to wallow like a harpooned whale, corkscrew between the increasingly shortening sea and to chuck enormous amounts of water over our captain's head—he was largely sheltered behind a glass screen —onto the unfortunates crouching in the stern. It was all jolly good fun, though the fun ran out a bit during the last three or four miles.

I'm glad I went all the same. At that time, not many people had landed on Central Island. It consists in the main of three extinct volcanic craters. The surprising thing about them is that the water in each one is of a distinctly different colour, red, green and blue, the result, perhaps, of some volcanic residue in the soil and the algae that this has encouraged. For the gigantic crocodiles of Rudolf, Central Island provides the perfect nursery. A gently sloping beach makes landing there easy. The warm grey volcanic ash around the crater lakes is soft and easily excavated, a perfect incubator for their eggs. Comparatively few predators reach the island. There were no crocs at home when we made our intrepid landfall. It wasn't the breeding season. I wasn't entirely sorry about this. A few days earlier, on a tributary of the Omo River, one of the larger Rudolf crocodiles had engulfed a missionary. When someone shot the beast two days later, only the legs of the victim were found in its stomach. A croc's digestive juices are formidable and had disposed of the rest of its victim in just two days.

We obviously weren't the first to set foot on Central Island recently. On the first crater lake we came to was one of the loneliest jokes in the world, the equivalent, perhaps, of an astronaut leaving a grafitti funny on the moon. Nailed to a post driven into the volcanic ash was a sign saying: "Lake A. No fishing. No shooting." I discovered later that it had been put there by a laconic character called Bob McConnell, the Fisheries Officer whose job was to teach the Turkana, normally a cattle people, how to make a living by catching tilapia and Nile Perch. I don't suppose Bob cared whether anyone ever saw his joke. Central Island is a fairly grim place. Bob probably just thought it could do with a bit of cheering up.

There were always relaxations after the chores of the filming day. At night a long table was set out on the shore at the fishing camp, complete with cutlery, glasses, though not, as I recollect, candelabra. A half moon pendant and a tiara of tropical stars provided all the light we could possibly need. John Pearson regularly flew in the goodies for dinner in the Aztec, making a tricky landing between the doum palms on a sand strip a mile or so inland.

Our guest naturally sat at the head of the table. Each night the film team was directed to rotate so that everyone got a chance to sit next to the star. The star was, I am pretty sure, greatly enjoying himself. I am equally certain that he would have enjoyed himself just as much if we had been dining off iron rations, seated on wooden crates outside our tents. He was off the hook and relaxing in a way and a place that he greatly enjoyed.

Not for the first time I discovered that it is not easy to make light dinner party conversation with a royal personage. To put it in radio terms they are usually set to send rather than to receive. This makes for a fairly one-way conversational traffic. There is, after all, absolutely no reason why they should be interested in your minimal affairs. They spend enough time in public life obliged to look as though they have a burning interest in the everyday lives of everyday people. So it wasn't easy to talk to our guest though when in the mood and set to send he did come up with some rather splendidly indiscrete stuff on his own account. I particularly treasure his description of how, on his recent informal visit to the Emperor and his court, the Ethiopians had set up a huge and ornate tent, the sort of thing Kubla Khan might have required had he been a bird-watcher. The tent was hung internally with rich and ornate draperies and many ancient inconveniences but few, if any, modern ones. The latter included the total absence of a loo. However, his hosts did dig a discretely hidden hole in the sand at the far end of the tent and provided their camper with a cardboard shovel.

One moment stands out all from those somewhat strained banquets beneath the stars. John Pearson's cargo in the Aztec invariably included a crate of ripe mangoes. This was long before the days when supermarket shelves groaned under loads of exotic fruits and everyone knew how to deal with them.

PP was obviously a dab hand at mangoes. He had tackled them all over the tropical world. Our cameraman, Geoff Holsgrove, was, like many of us, having trouble extracting the large stone at the centre of the fruit. It was Geoff's turn to sit next to our guest. He watched in undisguised admiration as HRH made a surgical incision around the whole length of the mango, deftly flipped it open and almost in one movement flicked the stone into the darkness far out on the sand.

"I reckon," Geoff told him, "that if you sat inside the railings at Buck House and did that you could get five bucks a go from the tourists."

The royal mango surgeon was thrown, but only for a second. "Hm," he said, as if seriously considering the proposition, "you may well be right. I've never thought of that."

One rather nice domestic touch on the part of the royal camper. On a wooden crate that served as a dressing table, I noticed that our royal guest had displayed a picture of his wife in a silver frame.

After five days we had everything in the can we could possibly get or need. I confess that I had serious doubts about how it was all going to tie together. Prince Philip, Jumbo Thorning and Aubrey Buxton packed their holdalls. We saw them aboard the Andover at Lodwar. And then we went back to camp and drank rather a lot. I can't pretend that the safari had been the most fun I've ever had on location, but it was certainly a right royal experience.

When next morning, the lads who ran the fishing camp took the Prince's tent down and lifted the floorboards, they found several scorpions and two rather nasty looking night-adders sheltering there. But I am quite sure our guest wouldn't have taken a damn bit of notice even if he'd known who was sleeping with him.

We did make a one-hour Special featuring Prince Philip at Lake Rudolf. It was called 'Now or Never' and it had a royal premiere at the National Film Theatre putting over a solid conservation message. If nothing else, it contained some marvellous wildlife footage shot by *Survival* wildlife cameramen, none of it at Lake Rudolf. As with all lash-ups of this kind, however worthy, you can unfortunately, see the joins. If they showed up too badly then I gladly take the blame for them.

The fishing camp on the western shore of lake Rudolf. Prince Philip's hut is on the right. After he left, several poisonous snakes were found beneath the floor.

Prince Philip and Aubrey Buxton relax between film 'takes'. Our star was not always the easiest subject to film. He had just taken up photography himself!

Picnic on Central Island, Lake Rudolf. Left to right, Aubrey Buxton, Geoff Holsgrove (cameraman), the author, film director Ron Downing and Prince Philip.

Central Island, Lake Rudolf consists of several extinct volcanic craters. Prince Philip and camera team look for a film location beside one of these.

I recorded one hour of Prince Philip's knowledgeable and always forthright views. He seemed more at ease with a tape recorder than with a film camera.

Some Really Wild People

My life on the wild side wouldn't have been nearly so wild but for the people with whom I worked, the wildlife cameramen and women. I was lucky if I spent two months of the year in the field. The other ten months I was back at base editing, writing, researching, recording, in fact doing all the things creatively exciting in themselves that go into the process of film-making. The wildlife cameramen spent practically every minute of their lives in lonely and outlandish places. Sometimes it took a whole year, sometimes more, to shoot the film for one one-hour programme. You had to be slightly crazy, or anyway a monomaniac, to want to live like that. To a man, and to a woman, they were a breed apart. And since many of my own fairly modest experiences depended on my close relationship with these brilliant eccentrics perhaps this is the moment to introduce them.

We'd come a long way since those early programmes. *Survival* had collected round itself something akin to those private armies that brought off incredible feats and irritated the General Staff so much during World War Two. I often thought of our wildlife cameramen as a sort of miniature Foreign Legion. No discourtesy to those amateur pioneers like Chiels Margach and Bill Cowen. We owed our start in life to them. But by the end of the first ten years we had a team of professionals, armed with the latest photographic and specialist equipment. They had their own cross-country vehicles. Most owned or flew their own light aircraft. Some were brilliant naturalists. All of us, including myself, depended for much of our knowledge on the experts and scientists with whom we worked. After all nobody could know everything about the natural world. To make films that were accurate as well as entertaining we all, camera people and myself, had to decode what the scientists and experts had to tell us and convert it into film and commentary. It wasn't all that easy, at least not always. Understandably, our scientific advisors wanted every 'i' dotted and every 't' crossed. They weren't interested in generalisations or broad statements. For cameramen working with scientists looking over their shoulder in the field it was sometimes even harder. Every now and again, you met a scientist who realised where you as a film-maker were coming from. Roger Payne, the expert on hump-backed whales, was one of these. So was Shirley Strum who studied the famous Pumphouse Gang of baboons at Gilgil, near Nairobi. Such scientists were a pleasure to work with. They rightly wanted the fruits of their research correctly presented, but they also knew that we were in the business of entertaining millions. If we gained their interest and got the viewer involved with our wildlife films, then it was greatly to everyone's advantage, including the scientists.

But now for the camera teams. I use that word though it is something of a misnomer. Often, as in the case of Alan and Joan Root, Des and Jen Bartlett, Dieter and Mary Plage, Richard and Julia Kemp, John and Jenny Pearson, the team consisted of husband and wife. The female half of the combination had to be quite as crazy, or maybe dedicated, as her husband. Most of the wives were accomplished stills photographers or sound recordists. And, of course, they also ran the logistics, the accounts, the camp, the catering and coped with the fair amount of paperwork involved in filming, possibly the hardest chore of all when, say, living in a tent on the tundra.

The daddy of all wildlife cameramen is without doubt the Australian Des Bartlett. He is probably the best all-round naturalist of them all. Des was taking stills photographs of weddings and babies in Sydney when Armand Denis of the early BBC series 'On Safari' fame came to Australia looking for a cameraman to join him and his wife Michaela in Nairobi for a few weeks filming. Des had just met and married a stunning and budding Wimbledon tennis star, Jen. So they went to Nairobi and have never returned to Australia, except on family visits, since.

I first met Des and Jen when my wife, Joan, came with me to Uganda on her first trip into the wild. Aubrey Buxton had asked me to find Des and try to persuade him to film for the infant *Survival.* I eventually tracked Des down in a dense tropical forest where he was filming a caterpillar that built a case for its chrysalis out of lengths of twig which it cut and glued together. It was the sort of esoteric subject about which Des Bartlett could be expected to know.

Joan, I remember, wanted to spend a penny and was still a little wary about what might be lurking in the undergrowth. Julie, then aged three, Des and Jen's only daughter, took my wife by the hand assuring her there was nothing to worry about. Julie should have known. The day before she had been grabbed by a semi-tame lioness and carried two hundred yards before the lion had dropped her.

Des, then working for Armand Denis, assured me that he'd like to work for *Survival*, but that as long as Armand was in business he couldn't think of it. True to his word, when Armand retired, Des phoned me from God knows where (when Des phones it can be from the nearest call-box or Honolulu. He is one of those people who board planes as other people board buses).

Since that meeting, my wife and I have worked with Des in the Antarctic, Arizona, Monument Valley, Tombstone, the Petrified Forest, the Grand Canyon, Alaska, the Skeleton Coast of Namibia, the Namib Desert and the Caprivi Strip. Over the years we watched Jen educate her daughter at the end of a hard day's filming in the back of a Land Rover via a correspondence course intended for the Australian outback. When Julie, now married with a son, went to boarding school in Australia, aged fourteen, she was a year ahead of her grade. Des, now in his early seventies, sports a patriarchal beard. Despite a serious flying accident in Namibia he is as spry as ever. After two operations and two years on crutches he is back in the field filming.

Alan Root is in a class of his own. In my view he is the best wildlife film-maker of his time. Though I successfully wrote and produced his early *Survivals*, his best film-making has always been conceived, filmed, and written by himself. The project starts in Alan's head and ends that way. It has a unity that only a real film-maker can produce working to his own script and shooting every foot of his own material.

Where the talent came from I don't know. Does anyone ever know that about any creative person? Alan's father was in the meat trade. He migrated to Kenya after World War Two to see if there was any future there for him. When he wrote to the family to follow him out, he told Alan that from one window he could see the snows of Kilimanjaro and from the other the snows of Mount Kenya. So when he went out to Africa, Alan took his toboggan with him. For all I know he is planning at this very moment to make a film about tobogganing down the snows of both mountains.

Alan is not only a born film-maker, he is a born light aircraft pilot. I have had more excitement flying with Alan—more of that in a later chapter—than you would wish to find this side of the Battle of Britain. He is also a human collection of spare parts and surgical patches. An index finger is missing as a result of a puff-adder bite from which he nearly died. The lack of this finger is no small handicap for a cameraman when focussing. He was bitten in the backside by a leopard when honeymooning on the Serengeti. A hippo put one tusk through his leg when he was filming underwater, by a miracle missing main artery, bone and muscle but making a hole, in Alan's words, big enough to put a Coca-Cola bottle in. With his then wife, Joan, he flew over Kilimanjaro in a hot air balloon and was imprisoned as a spy when they landed on the Tanzanian side of the mountain. But everything that has happened to Alan Root is of his own making, including such remarkable films as 'The Year of the Wildebeeste' and 'Castles of Clay' the incredible story of what goes on inside a termite mound. To look at Alan is mild and blinks occasionally behind his glasses. These days he looks almost ambassadorial with his well-kempt beard. Alan stays outside Kenyan politics. Unlike many wildlife cameramen he is an all-round man aware of current tastes in films and music, neither of which art-forms would fascinate Des Bartlett.

Dieter Plage, since killed while filming in Sumatra, was in many ways the opposite of Alan, though he, too, was fascinated by the world of cinema and books. A West German, Dieter was possibly the most cosmopolitan man I have ever met. I have seen him sit in a jungle clearing devouring the latest issue of *Der Spiegel*. Wherever he was on location he would tune his radio to the BBC World Service to keep up with the international news. Unlike any other wildlife cameraman I have known or worked with, Dieter was interested in a wide spectrum that ranged from the latest feature film to world politics, perhaps particularly the latter. Dieter had first-hand experience of what distorted politics could do to the world, and especially to the country of his birth.

He was born at a time that made him eligible for the Hitler *Jugend*. As a result he had less tolerance of dictators, black or white, than most people I have met. His father had been radio officer aboard Germany's flagship luxury Atlantic liner, the *Bremen*. During the war *Vati* Plage served as a radio officer with the Luftwaffe. Dieter himself had had a hard wartime childhood. He owed his survival to his mother who had escaped ahead of the advancing Russians by fleeing with her son at night across frozen rivers. No wonder Dieter was devoted to his *mutti*. Before he came to *Survival*, he had worked in the American film industry where he acquired a wide knowledge and worship of film technology and an appalling imitation of an American accent. His English was excellent with an occasional lapse into German syntax. Though miles apart temperamentally, both Des Bartlett and Dieter Plage were what I would describe as camera nuts. I once said to them that I would not be surprised if once a day they spread their prayer mats in the direction of Munich where the great god of movie cameras, Arriflex, dwells. The faithful who have made the pilgrimage to Mecca wear a green chord in their head dress. Dieter and Des made the pilgrimage to Munich so often that Arriflex gave them each a golden camera badge in recognition of their loyalty and possibly of the fortune each had spent on cameras at the Arriflex factory. I have a photograph of the two ace cameramen, taken on a sandbank in the middle of wild river in Nepal, kneeling in homage on a prayer mat at sundown, the mat oriented in the direction of Munich.

Flying with Dieter was like flying with Luft Hansa. Even my wife, when flying up a horrendous valley approaching Everest with Dieter, felt that she would live to see tomorrow, and light aircraft flying, which she braved time and again, is definitely not her favourite occupation.

Dieter was impossibly good-looking and knew it. During his early days with *Survival* he was always surrounded by dolly-birds, as he called them. He even married one and took her to Namibia to sleep in a tent on top of a one thousand foot sand dune, heaven to Dieter but not to his bride. The lady discovered that the safari life was not for her and the marriage came apart.

All wildlife cameramen and women are obsessive. They couldn't possible do the job otherwise. But Dieter carried obsession to a level of magnifence that was barely tolerable. In the middle of a dinner party, he would say things like: "Ach!"—yes I discovered that Germans really do say Ach—"Ach, Colin, I have been thinking of shot 56 on roll 349" when it was the last thing anyone else wanted to think of at that particular moment. So when he stayed with us on visits to England I would wake him in the morning with: "Ach, Dieter, I have been thinking of shot 56 on roll 349". In time this cured him—up to a point.

Thank God, he had one of the most highly tuned senses of humour it has been my good luck ever to meet. Don't let anyone tell you that the Krauts haven't got a laugh in them. On the downside, he was capable of fits of deep depression when filming or film equipment went wrong. Despite these occasional blacks Dieter was the greatest fun to be with on location. You could laugh him out of most things. The best thing that happened to Dieter was when Des Bartlett found him his second wife—Mary. Des was a great procurer of wives and girlfriends for fellow workers in the field. Sometimes his suggested liaisons took, but not always. The second Mrs Plage, a dental nurse when Bartlett met her, was perfect for Dieter. I think at first she was dazzled by him, or at least by his largely unfounded reputation as a sweeper of dolly-birds off their perches, but she soon sorted all that out, sorted him out, cut him down to size, adored him and took to the safari life as if she'd longed to live in a leaking tent all her life. A remarkable story with a tragic end.

Nor must I forget the ladies. Cindy Buxton, Aubrey's daughter, was never a great camera woman but she had the guts and endurance of any ten men. An extraordinarily attractive petite blonde, she treated elephants, hippos and Argentine invaders as something that could be dealt with by the exercise of pertinacity and a show of confidence which perhaps she did not always feel. She often worked on her own, as in the Luangua Valley of Zambia or the remoter islands of the Falklands. Argentine invaders? She and her assistant Annie Price were filming king penguins and elephant seals in a remote bay on South Georgia when the Argentines invaded the island as an opening gambit in the Falklands war. So what did the girls do? Well what was a girl to do in such a situation? Carry on filming, of course. Which is exactly what they did although from time to time they could hear a shooting war taking place not far away across the ice fields at Grytviken. In the event they sat it out until the Royal Navy got there. But by then they had all the film they needed. Game girls and a pleasure to work with.

And lastly, Lee Lyon, the lovely and talented Californian girl, who claimed Cherokee blood. Lee—another Des Bartlett 'find', worked for a time as Dieter Plage's assistant and was killed by an elephant while making her first solo wildlife film. But much more of Lee to come later in this story. There were other wildlife cameramen on the team, of course, but these were the principals with whom I most frequently took walks on the wild side.

Des Barlett built this dummy termite mound as a hide to film elephants drinking from waterline level. The steel shutter was to repel rising water, not elephants!

Cindy Buxton waves the Union Flag with her film partner Annie Price. The pair continued filming on south Georgia throughout the Argentine invasion.

Alan and Joan Root more than 20,000 feet up during the first hot-air balloon crossing of Mount Kilimanjaro. On landing in Tanzania, they were arrested.

Dieter Plage and Des Bartlett with a new camera. Legend had it that at sundown they faced their prayer mats towards the Arriflex camera factory in Germany..

Alan Root handles a spitting cobra used in his one hour film about a termite mound. The snake that spat at the author was fortunately much smaller.

Boadicea and some other Wild Women

Perhaps the best introduction to Oria Douglas-Hamilton would have been first to meet her father and mother. Both were small in stature, about knee-high to a dikdik. But what they lacked in height they more than made up for in spirit, a characteristic which their offspring inherited in vast measure. Kenyan folklore had it—and I see no reason to doubt the legend—that they had trekked across from the Congo, set eyes upon the glories of Lake Naivasha fifty miles north of Nairobi in the Great Rift Valley, and said, one in Italian and the other in French: "This is it!" On the shores of the lake they build an italianate palazzo, widely patronised by bats, and settled down to raise two girls, Oria and Mirella and a son, Dorian, who distinguished himself during the Mau Mau troubles.

Perhaps it was not surprising that the man Oria married, Iain Douglas Hamilton, was crazy on flying, a hobby he managed to combine with becoming a world authority on elephants. Iain's father had been killed flying a Mosquito in World War Two. Rudolf Hess had crash-landed his Me 110 on the estate of the Duke of Hamilton, Iain's uncle, so the aeronautic tradition was strong, but it went back further than that. Oria's father had flown a single-seater fighter, a Spad, on the Italian front in World War One. A German pilot had shot the tail off the Spad and watched it crash into a pine forest. Chivalry was then part of the game in air combat. So the Germans flew over and dropped a wreath on the Italian airfield. However, though the subject of these tributes may have fallen, he was certainly not dead. In the words of Oria's father: "The Spad fluttered down just like a sycamore seed and settled in the top of a pine tree." So he borrowed another fighter, flew over the German field and returned the wreath with thanks and a note to the effect that the tribute was much appreciated but premature.

Oria's mother must have been one of the first French women to take to the air. At a Paris airshow several years before the Great War she had flown with the pioneer French aviator, Maurice Farman, in an improvised seat lashed above the skid of one of his pusher-engined 'box kites'. Such parents can hardly have produced anything but a remarkable brood. As Oria's and Mirella's mother remarked to my wife: "some mothers have daughters. I have dynamites." Or to put it another way, as did Oria in a later conversation. "If my mother had known what

I have done she would have died, but if she had known what Mirella had done, she would have committed suicide." It was possibly no exaggeration that I would have rated mama as being of far tougher stuff. However, it was common knowledge that Mirella had had a love affair with Shaibu, a Bajuni fisherman. But then you should surely make allowances for the artistic temperament in such a wild setting. And both Oria and Mirella were certainly artistic if not actually untamed. Oria showed her creative abilities in the film we were about to make together and in the Masai jewellery she designed for fashionable boutiques. Mirella produced three books of brilliant photographs 'Vanishing Africa', 'African Saga' and 'African Visions'.

The way we all came together was like this. *Survival* had a very friendly relationship with the publishers, then known as William Collins, and particularly with their creative and eccentric boss Sir William, Billy, Collins. Collins was the publishing house which recognised the possibilities of Joy Adamson and Elsa the lioness after nineteen other houses had turned down Joy's random notes and dog-eared pictures After Elsa, Collins were deeply into wildlife. Billy now proposed to publish a book about the work of a bright young scientist called Iain Douglas-Hamilton who was studying the problems of behaviour and population dynamics of elephants, and of one particular herd, in Lake Manyara National Park, Tanzania. The remarkable thing about this study was that Iain did most of his work on foot among the herds. Moreover, his camp, and indeed his study, was shared by his wife Oria accompanied by their two small daughters, Saba (The Swahili seven; she was born on the seventh day of the week) and Dudu (Swahili for insect). It was obviously a story with all the elements of a hit. Some film had already been shot by a French cameraman Christian Zuber. It contained some exciting scenes but didn't add up to more than ten minutes screen time. Obviously, if we wanted to make an epic of the Douglas-Hamiltons' work we had to put our own wildlife team into the field for as long as it took. Dieter Plage and his new assistant, the beautiful Californian girl Lee Lyon, were chosen for the job. Collins aimed to do a book which was eventually called 'Among the Elephants' an understatement if ever I heard one! The *Survival* Special which emerged was more accurately called 'The Family that Lives with Elephants.'

After some hard bargaining we had a deal. Iain was no simple scientist and Oria no mean negotiator.

Iain was at that moment just returning to Manyara. He had been away from his study for a year obtaining his D Phil at Oxford. So, in a sense, he was making a fresh start, an ideal and interesting point for us to join the safari and start filming. The big question was: would the individuals in his study herd remember Iain or would he have to start building up relationships all over again?

Our chairman and producer, Aubrey Buxton, was all for Joan going along, not that you could have stopped her. I think he believed she might have a calming influence if such a thing were needed. Myself, I had some heavy doubts about the personality mix. I don't say that Italians, or perhaps Franco-Italians and the Welsh, or perhaps the Anglo-Welsh, (my wife is only half Welsh: the other half, thank heavens, is Yorkshire) have much in common except temperament. It was the temperament side of the affair that worried me. The close proximity of the two ladies in confined and perhaps occasionally hazardous circumstances might, I thought, be compared to putting TNT next to nitro-glycerine and BOOM. In the event, I couldn't have been more wrong. My wife likes people who are what she often refers to as warm not to say out-going and even outrageous, provided they have charisma and charm. Oria had all of that and a bit to spare and my own Mrs Baker wasn't far behind. That we had a meeting of like minds or anyway psyches was evident from day one. Against what had seemed in London fairly long odds, it was plainly going to be a swinging safari.

But there was other business, if you can call it that, to be done in Africa first. Future plans had to be discussed with Alan Root. Alan had a camp at Lake Lagaja on the Serengeti where he was filming scenes for his now classic 'The Year of the Wildbeeste'. Lagaja plays a tragic part in the year-long story of the wildebeeste migration. It is here that that thousands of calves become separated from their mothers while crossing the lake and either eventually drown, starve to death or become prey for lions, hyenas or wild dogs. No female wildebeeste will adopt an orphaned calf, even if she has lost her own. A brutal part of the story, maybe, but essential if you intend to give a true picture of nature at work. Alan suggested that he fly up to Nairobi and pick up Joan and myself. We could then spend a few days at his camp. Then he'd fly us on to join Dieter and the Douglas-Hamiltons at Manyara.

Alan was an hour or two late arriving in Nairobi. He had, he explained, had a brief encounter with a stork. Nothing serious. Just a small dent in the leading edge of one wing. The dent was caused by a mild birdstrike with a migrating stork of which there were hundreds thermalling their way up the Rift Valley on migration. The delay in calling for us had been caused by the need to clean up the dent in the wing and remove any remaining blood and feathers. For a nervous light aircraft traveller, and my otherwise intrepid wife freely admits she is that, this was not perhaps the best way to start the journey.

At Wilson, Nairobi's light plane airport, Alan showed us the dent. There were two surprises. First, and reassuringly, it wasn't very large and didn't appear life-threatening. Second, the stork hadn't struck the high wing of Alan's familiar Cessna but the low wing of a small, compact French monoplane called, a Minerva Rallye. His Cessna had suffered an unfortunate accident, not, for once, with Alan at the controls. A mechanic had started up another machine without applying the brakes or chocking the wheels with the result that it had taxied, unmanned, across the apron and badly mauled Alan's Cessna with its propeller. The insurers had supplied Alan with the Minerva while his own aircraft was being repaired. Alan had many good things to say about the little machine, perhaps to reassure my wife though I doubt it since Alan doesn't believe much in reassurance. You take life as it comes and like it or lump it. The Minerva, Alan explained, had automatic flaps that enabled it to leap off the ground after a very short take-off run, or wallow along in the air at a safe and prudent fifty miles per hour. However ideal low wing monoplanes may be for getting places they are not much good for aerial photography. The wing gets in the way. However, for the moment we are just concerned with getting there.

Alan's then wife, Joan, a slim charming girl with glasses and the gentlest nature and the best legs south of the Sahara, joined us at Wilson. We loaded our meagre baggage and provisions for the camp and the four of us climbed aboard. "She doesn't have all that much power to spare with a full load on," Alan said cheerfully. But when he opened the throttle I was glad to see that she leapt off the ground like a little gazelle.

The one hundred and forty miles between the volcanoes Longonot and Ol Doinyo Lengai are possibly the most spectacular in Africa. We were now flying over a landscape torn apart by huge earth forces over two hundred million years ago. The Great Rift Valley, they say, is one of the few, possibly the only, earth feature that you can see from the moon. It stretches 6,000 miles from the Jordan Valley to the mouth of the Zambezi. It is still tearing itself apart. In perhaps another 20 million years, everything east of the main Rift may have said goodbye to Africa and set up on its own in the Indian Ocean, just as Madagascar has already done.

Ahead of the little monoplane now, and not all that far beneath its wings, were scarps, steps and green crests which Alan appeared to be keen on clearing with fifty feet or so to spare. This is the way Alan likes to fly a lot of the time. Fortunately, he is very good at it.

Beneath us now was the white slash, decorated with obscene scarlet rashes, of Lake Magadi. Magadi in Swahili means coarse soda. Lake Magadi produces soda faster that the modern machinery of the Magadi Soda Company can dig it out. A few years before we made this flight, one million lesser flamingoes, about a third of the Rift's population of this lovely bird species, had made the mistake of nesting there. Perhaps it wasn't a mistake but a calculated risk. Their traditional nesting ground on the next lake we were to fly over, Natron, had been flooded. What they didn't, or couldn't, allow for was that the water in Magadi was so saturated with soda that every time their chicks waded through it they coated their legs with soda. In time, anklets of soda built up so that the young were immobilised and died of hunger or exhaustion. Alan and Joan Root, together with John Pearson, our airline pilot wildlife cameraman, had filmed this calamity and organised international help to drive the chicks out of the worst affected areas. The result had been a dramatic film we had called 'Death Trap Lake'.

Twenty miles further on we approached the lake that has always been a death trap for many creatures. The lake is called Natron, the chemist's word for sodium carbonate of which it is mostly formed. I noticed with some relief that as we approached, Alan eased the nose of the Minerva marginally upwards until we were flying at the unusually high altitude of one hundred feet.

"Gotta watch your rate of climb indicator here," Alan said. "Make sure you're maintaining your altitude or even climbing. Too easy to descend instead. Don't want to end up in that lot. Look ahead and you'll see what I mean."

Natron shimmered brilliantly pink. Its surface was glassy. Sheltered by the steep wall of the Nguruman Escarpment on one side and the extinct volcanoes Gelai and Shombole on the other, it lay like a mirror in which Ol Doinyo Lengai, the Masai's Mountain of God at the far end of the lake, reproduced itself as a perfect mirror image. Add to this the effect of the mirage created by a mid-day surface temperature of one hundred and fifty degrees and it became impossible to tell up from down.

The mistake was made, Alan said, by hundreds of birds and insects. At migration time the shorelines were littered with the corpses of birds that had failed to watch their rate of climb indicators and had crashed into the soda. Even at one hundred feet, the heat from the pink soda flats could be felt beating up through the cabin floor. Alan slid back the canopy so that we could get a better view. What we got was a choking stench of soda.

"Like to fly over Lengai and look down into the crater?" Alan asked. "Sure," I said, though I was by no means sure that I answered for everyone. Lengai is over 9,000 feet. Alan had been right about the Minerva when fully loaded. She didn't have much power to spare. At around 8,000 feet, the gallant little aircraft let us know that she really didn't think she could climb much higher. Did I hear a sigh of relief somewhere? Did I give one myself?

Below, though at a safe distance, were some very nasty ribs of sharp lava from Lengai's last big eruption when it coated the surrounding landscape with thick layers of washing soda! Alan reluctantly banked away to the west. Half an hour later we put our wheels down on a short, comparatively level piece of grass dotted with termite mounds. Below a small cliff were the tents of the Root's camp at Lake Lagaja.

Down on the lake shore, and in the shallows, hundreds of young wildebeeste calves were wandering aimlessly about. They had lost their mothers or failed to follow them when they had waded out to cross the lake. Now they would become easy prey for the predators. Perhaps this was nature's way of weeding out the unfit. If they were not smart enough to stick to their mothers, then what chance would they have on the merciless plains when they grew up? Many thousands more, young, old and sick animals, would die before the migration was over. But it didn't matter. Many thousands would be born to replace them during the migration. This was the system by which the wildebeeste migration worked. You couldn't help feeling for the lost calves, but sentimentality has no place in good wildlife film-making. Compassion and a sense of marvel at the workings of nature, yes, but sentimentality most definitely not.

For me, to be and see was everything. You can be told about, read scientific papers about, talk to the greatest experts about, but there is no substitute for being on the ground with someone who knows what is happening when it happens. Alan was just such a guide. Alan Root was possibly unique among wildlife film-makers in that he thought his story through from the beginning. He knew what he wanted and how he wanted it before a single foot of film rolled through his camera. And the results were usually reflected in the finished product.

When I went back to London and viewed the rushes that came in from the field, it was a tremendous advantage to have been in the field, seen the sights, heard the sounds, even to have smelled the smells. Without this field experience, it would have been impossible, to shape, alter, make suggestions to the cameramen, produce the film and write the commentary.

It was tempting to believe that all the stresses were back at base, in the cutting rooms, recording studios and management meetings and that the wildlife cameraman in the field lived a carefree, idyllic life. It was not by any means true. Stresses in the field took a different form, that's all. The rains came a month early, or they didn't come at all. As a result, the migration, or whatever event was planned for filming, was a month early, or a month late, or just didn't happen. Mechanical problems were perhaps more easily resolved than natural ones. But not always. Take the case of the hot-air balloon.

Alan had pioneered the use of hot-air balloons on the Serengeti for photographic purposes. An assistant bringing the balloon envelope back to camp in a trailer after a successful photographic flight had forgotten to tuck in two or three feet of the envelope. The plains of Serengeti are generously supplied with thorn bushes. A bush had seized the flapping three feet of envelope as the trailer passed. When the Land Rover and trailer arrived back at camp, the balloon had vanished. Alan bitterly described himself as the owner of the most expensive set of nylon handkerchiefs on the Serengeti.

At Lagaja he had just taken delivery of a new balloon in which he invited Joan and I to fly at first light next morning. Strange creatures women. She was as keen on flying in a balloon as she had been unenthusiastic about soda-hopping over Lake Natron.

Round the fire at night, with hyenas giggling and yapping just beyond the circle of light, we discussed Alan's next epic. It was to be about life in and around a termite mound. One of the stars of this film shared our camp at Lagaja. She was known as Millions. If you were unwise enough to ask why, which you were almost certain to do, Alan would fall on one knee and give a fair imitation (which almost anyone can do) of Al Jolson singing "Aardvark a million miles for one of your smiles".... Aardvarks are a one-off animal. There is only one family and one species. They are long on almost everything—long on ear, muzzle, claws for digging out their favourite food, termites and ants, and they have a long sticky tongue for getting hold of them. They are pretty common on the savannas and in the woodlands of Africa, but not, I suppose, when you actually want to film them. In the circumstances, all you can do is to keep one handy and then film it doing what it would do naturally. It is known as controlled filming and in some circumstances is perfectly permissible. Millions' favourite toy was a Land Rover spare wheel which she tirelessly buried and dug up. In the normal course of events, wildlife camera people do not go in for pets, although Joan Root had a semi-tame caracal (the African lynx) which slept on the end of her bed. At various times Alan has owned a baby hippo, clawless otters, and a striped hyena called Auntie Minnie who was almost as affectionate and house-trained as a dog. But all these animal familiars had played walk-on parts in his films. I doubt whether the Roots thought of them as pets but rather as animal wildlife extras with whom they couldn't bear to part until, like the hippo, they outgrew themselves.

We did go ballooning soon after dawn one morning. Nowadays, largely thanks to Alan (he and Joan flew over Kilimanjaro in a hot-air balloon), ballooning is a common tourist attraction on the Serengeti. But in the early days it was an adventure Alan couldn't resist playing one trick on Mrs Baker Willock. She jumped enthusiastically into the basket when the balloon had just attained take-off buoyancy. It might have floated off with her in it, had not Alan stood with one apparently careless finger holding the edge of the basket.

There are two things I most remember about balloon flying with Alan. The first was how the wildebeeste herds reacted to the shadow of the envelope on the savanna. Nothing would persuade them to run through the shadow. They ran round its circumference. The other was Alan's offer to take the morani, the proud warriors of the Masai, aloft. The Masai are not easily impressed. When it suits them they are prepared to adjust to their fellow white citizens' strange ways. Two morani accepted Alan's offer. To the Masai, ownership of cattle is everything. Cattle are their God. They were thrilled in a childlike way to enjoy the aerial view of their kingdom but what they really wanted was to count their cattle from the air!

To reach the Douglas-Hamiltons at Manyara, we flew over the Crater Highlands. Now that these vast uplands have been greened by time, it is hard to imagine the volcanic upheavals that created them. The huge green shoulder of Lemagrut. The caldera, the collapsed volcano of Ngorongoro, into which you could drop the whole of Paris with room to spare. I remembered the first time I stood on the rim of Ngorongoro and said to Joan—it was on her second filming safari to Africa— look over the edge and in the bottom of the crater you will see huge herds of animals. In my ignorance and enthusiasm I had overlooked the fact that the crater's walls are over two thousand feet high.

In those days it was a hair-raising drive by Land Rover on the edge of precipices to reach the bottom of this enormous soup plate. But when you made it you were among wildebeeste herds which some game wardens said kept themselves aloof from the Serengeti herds just over the rim. We saw black rhino mating, a prolonged ritual which gave you some idea of what sex must have been like in the time of the dinosaurs. There were flocks of flamingoes on their own miniature soda lakes as well as prides of lions and packs of hunting dogs, in fact a whole Ngorongoro eco-system, a lost world, apparently in balance and existing independently, though other experts, as experts always will, disputed this simple theory and claimed that the wildlife interacted with that of the Serengeti Plains just next door. Maybe they were right. What I do know is that we made an early *Survival* called 'The Eighth Wonder of the World' which the Ngorongoro Crater was and, despite the influx of tourism, I hope still is.

As the cloud shadows chased each other over the immensity of the Crater Highlands, tinting their slopes a deeper green before moving on to rinse them into a vivid emerald, Alan banked to avoid a storm and lost height towards Eyeasi, yet another soda lake at the tail end of the East African Rift. It was an idyllic, uneventful flight until we reached the wall of the Rift where it drops away a sheer six hundred feet to the narrow strip of forest and savanna which is Tanzania's Lake Manyara National Park. The Park, never more than four miles wide, runs for some twenty miles between the Rift wall and Lake Manyara itself.

All we knew about the Douglas-Hamilton's camp was that it was at the end of one of the narrow water-cut ravines that run down from the rim of the Rift towards the lake shore. Alan now announced that he would fly along the top of the Rift until he found the right ravine and then fly down it. Predictably, all the ravines look alike. If there are detailed aerial maps then we certainly did not have one. The ravine Alan chose got narrower and narrower and more winding. Alan announced calmly that he guessed he had got the wrong ravine. He'd never been down this gorge before. Some Sonjo tribesmen living in a hut whose roof was at ground level—a method of construction originally intended as a defence against the warlike Masai—dived for cover as we side-slipped over them. Perhaps they thought the Masai were once again intending to blood their spears. Now the slow-flying abilities of the Minerva really came into their own. After Alan had performed some wing-tip grazing evolutions the ravine eventually opened up as Alan had undoubtedly known it would. We then set out along the lake shore to find the camp. Finally we spotted the tents on the bank of the dried-out Ndala river bed. Alan buzzed the camp in the time-honoured manner not entirely suited to those whose heads and stomachs are not accustomed to the effects of even quite moderate G-forces. To make sure they'd got the message we dropped them one in a streamered metal container and flew off, more or less sedately, to the Manyara strip eleven miles away on top of the Rift. My wife dismounted, gallant as always but undeniably a little white about the gills. The dropped message had suggested that the Douglas-Hamiltons meet us at the Manyara lodge.

Lodge transport was a long time coming. Perhaps, suggested Alan, we had better buzz them, the acknowledged way in these parts of waking up tardy suppliers of expected services. Leaving the two Joans on the strip we took off and literally dropped over the edge of the Rift Valley. So abruptly did the Minerva disappear that anyone watching would have been justified in supposing we had crashed. Alan made a tight turn and zoomed up over the rim of the Valley at such low altitude that a man poised on the diving board of the Manyara Lodge swimming pool fell in with his drink in his hand. We repeated the evolution to ensure the lodge had got the message, our wheels clearing the roof by a matter of feet. Alan observed wickedly: Joan wouldn't have cared for that. He spoke the literal truth and I am not sure that I did either. But it did get the lodge transport moving. It was on the strip almost before we had finished taxying.

Iain, Oria, the children Saba and Dudu, Dieter Plage and Lee Lyon met us at the lodge. I remember thinking that whatever we were about to face with elephants, it couldn't be quite as nerve-wracking as bush-flying with Alan Root. I was wrong

In the back of the Land Rover, TNT and nitro-glycerine were reacting one to the other as if this was the chemical juxaposition they had been waiting for all their lives. Which once again proves that the last person to know anything at all about women, especially if he is the husband of one of them, is a man. Oria and Joan were plainly tuned to the same wave-length.

The tented camp was pitched on a sandy bluff above the nearly dried-out Ndala sand river. Apart from the three tents, there was a rough shelter with a corrugated iron roof which served as a social centre and dining rom. We dumped our stuff in one of the tents, had a quick mug of tea and then Iain said: "Like to meet some elephants?"

Now Iain and Alan are built of much the same material. Though both are quiet-spoken and give the appearance at times of being almost reserved, both, in the right circumstances, enjoy playing to the gallery. What one does, the other has to do more extravagantly. For example, one afternoon at Manyara, they had a contest which involved creeping up behind an elephant and pulling out one of its wire-like tail hairs. Whoever got the most in a specified time won, provided he survived which both, knowing their elephants, naturally did. Iain did not require us to remove any hairs from the rear end of his elephants. He did, however, want to see how his guests would react when confronted, perhaps menacingly, with the front end.

The problem at Manyara was that affecting elephants in practically every other part of Africa. There were simply too many—in this case around 500—occupying too small a space. With the protection that national parks give them, the herds multiply. Because they cannot move outside the parks without being shot as crop-raiders, they have to make do with the food that the park provides. In the case of Manyara, their favourite food was the pod-bearing *Acacia tortilis*. Elephants shake down the pods when they are in season. When they're not in season, they eat the rest of the tree, stripping off the bark with their tusks or ring-barking the trunks so that the trees die. Sometimes they just push the tree over to get at the best bits. When the trees die, the entire eco-system changes. Grassland replaces woodland. Woodland species like giraffe, impala and bushbuck start to disappear.

One immediate and drastic solution is to shoot a lot of elephants, not just single animals but whole herds. Strangely, it is kinder to do this. Elephants live in close-knit family groups. Fracture those groups by shooting individual animals and the whole social system falls apart. Iain's objective, faithfully carried out, was to complete his study without shooting a single elephant to obtain the data he needed. Data included how rapidly the Manyara elephants bred, their food preferences at different seasons, their migration patterns around the park, the composition of family groups and the age and sex of family members. Only when he had acquired all this information could he begin to propose a management plan which might solve some of the Park's and the elephants' problems.

So, that first evening, we set out to meet some of Iain's elephants. We weren't required to make the first sortie on foot. Iain's working Land Rover, however, did not give a marked feeling of protection. It had, during the early part of his study, been substantially modified by a cross-tusked matriarch called Sarah, named after an ex-girlfriend. Iain knew all his elephants by christian names, often taken from Biblical or classical mythology. Unlike most of the great beasts who became his familiars, Sarah had not got a close rapport with Iain. I knew the story. It had formed the most remarkable sequence captured by the French cameraman Christian Zuber during the first period of Iain's study. In fact, it was probably this sequence by the Frenchman that had persuaded us to put our own team into the field. It happened like this.

Iain had darted a young bull and placed a radio tracking collar on him. After a few weeks the young bull had supplied all the information Iain needed about his movements. Because he was short of radio collars, he decided to dart the youngster again and get his instrument back. All went well until the all-important moment came when Iain had to inject the unconscious animal with the antidote to bring him round again. At this moment, cross-tusked Sarah decided to intervene in an extremely aggressive and protective manner. Iain tried to dash in on foot several times and give the antidote. Each time, Sarah charged screaming and thrashing the foliage with her trunk. Iain knew that if he didn't get the antidote injected soon, the young bull might die. Eventually, Iain charged himself—in the Land Rover. He reached the bull safely, leaned over the side and stuck the hyperdermic needle in. This was too much for Sarah who now made a charge that was no longer a threat. She partly demolished the front of the vehicle and converting the round steering wheel into a rectangle. Sarah pushed the Land Rover back twenty five yards until it hit a tree when, mercifully, she backed off. Little had been done to repair the vehicle since. Moreover it showed a marked reluctance to start and a perverse inclination to stop.

So we set out in this badly treated vehicle to look for some elephants. We had both been in close proximity to elephants many times. I am always aware that, if they are so minded, they can reach into your vehicle and pull you out with their trunks, or even tap you on the head with a trunk, a blow that is almost certain to push your head down into your shoulders.

I found my palms sweating slightly as we drove quietly into the middle of the first herd, especially when Iain shut off the engine. It was like being becalmed among a fleet of drifting battleships. Great grey hulls brushed against the side of the Land Rover.

Meantime, Iain quietly consulted his card index system while Oria took down notes. Calypso had a fresh tear in one ear since he had last seen her a year ago. A teenage elephant nursemaid had been given a new calf to look after. In between observations, Iain gave Dieter, perched on the tailboard like a rear-gunner, instructions to film some interesting piece of behaviour. The elephants plainly recognised Iain and accepted him. Gradually, Joan and I began to relax, realising that we were with a man who really did know and could communicate his own sense of security to these great animals.

We visited three herds, spending half an hour with each. Something in the purposeful way Iain was searching the area told me that we weren't through yet. Nor were we.

"Ah," said Iain at last. "I want you to meet someone."

In a small clearing in front of her herd of female relatives and young stood the most impressive elephant I have ever seen. She didn't stand there for long. She came in a headlong, horrifying charge, shaking the dust off her huge ears, flailing the bushes to splinters with her trunk and trumpeting at the top of her very considerable voice.

When scared out of my mind in a wildlife situation I need a displacement activity. Mine is dementedly taking photographs. Somehow, looking at the scene from a viewfinder makes it seem as if it is happening to someone else, somewhere else. Behind me the cine camera was whirring away and I heard the shutter of Lee Lyon's Nikon clicking. In the forty yards it took the great elephant to reach us I took four shots. All were okay as mementos of a terrifying occasion, but none was memorable. Only one was superb—Lee Lyon's. She had taken what is probably the finest still of a charging elephant ever made. It has been used in newspapers and

John Owen who was not noted as the most accomplished aviator on the Serengeti and had a penchant for taking off cross-wind, loaded the labouring Oria into the small cockpit of his Cessna and flew her to the nearest good hospital in Nairobi one and a half hours away.

Oria did a fine job of bringing up her two small girls in the wilderness. I recall that she was great on what she called tactile touching. Come to think of it, it is pretty hard to imagine any touching that isn't tactile. She derived this theory from the way the elephant mothers continually caress their calves. We filmed some delightful scenes of Oria tactile touching the children on the sand flats of the Ndala River while elephants did likewise with their calves in the water. As a theory it was perfectly reasonable. After all everyone including elephants, children and adults enjoys a bit of tactile touching. But as expounded in Oria's charming slightly foreign accented English on the soundtrack it had an exotic freshness.

We lived in great though simple style with a cuisine that might be best described as Afro-Italian, Oria's safari cook conjuring up *cordon noir* meals out of tins and local vegetables including wild watercress that grew in the streams running down from the Rift. If there were tensions, they were between Dieter and his able apprentice camerawoman Lee Lyon. It was quite clear that this obviously talented, immensely determined and highly attractive Californian meant to make it on her own as soon as she could learn enough. Dieter, already deeply experienced both technically and in wildlife film-making, very reasonably insisted that she do things his way. To be fair, I think the delightful Lee saw that this was what she must do. As a team in the field, they worked excellently together which was just as well in view of projects that lay in the future in which they would both be involved. However, some nights, their tent shook with the sound of what might charitably be described as friendly persuasion that occasionally overspilled into a flaming row. Oh well, creative people are like that. To their credit, by morning the atmosphere had usually cleared.

There were moments of far higher drama in the camp. One night, while we were eating supper, a noise like a buffalo stampede in a western movie roared out of the night. In a few minutes it became clear that this was exactly what was happening. No western film has ever accurately portrayed an actual buffalo stampede since the animals that once roamed the American prairies, 60 million strong, were, in fact, not buffalo but bison. Approaching the camp now were around two hundred of the genuine article, the African Cape buffalo, weighing up to half a ton apiece. For several anxious moments it looked as though the camp was about to be over-run. But buffalo have sharp noses and a sharper sense of fear. At the last moment they caught the deadly scent of humans and split in two streams round the bluff on which we sat, leaving us with the thunder of their hooves and the dust clouds of their passing.

Another night it was lions. Dieter could never resist showing his films to anyone, anywhere, who was willing to watch. He particularly enjoyed showing them to African rangers and game guards who reacted with wild excitement to the moving images of animals with which they were not always familiar. To this end he carried a sixteen millimetre projector in his gear.

I forget what the film was that night. To view it we had moved several hundred yards up the valley to a clearing where a make-shift screen could be rigged between trees. The show was a great success the game guards whooping with delight and yelling in mock fear when rhinos charged or crocodiles slithered off the river bank.

When we returned to camp, all the camp beds and sleeping bags had been dragged out of the tents. Our own were torn with tooth marks and wet with fresh saliva. All round in the sand was a pattern of pug marks made by an inquisitive pride of lions.

Joan and I had had some experience of wild animals in our tent. Two years before, when filming with another of our wildlife cameramen, Bob Campbell, in Amboseli Park under Kilimanjaro, we had woken to the sound of a large amount of water being drunk at very high speed. The previous night we had all had a stand-up bath and had left the galvanised tub on the bonnet of Bob's Land Rover. A female elephant with a very young calf had just drunk it all. Not content with that, the mother brought her baby under the fly sheet of our tent and had begun to inspect with her trunk everything inside from the cooking stove to the occupants. Never having entertained an elephant before, neither Joan nor I quite knew what the next step should be. Luckily, Bob had crawled under the brailing at the rear of the tent and admonished the elephant with a sharp slap—she probably thought it was a mosquito alighting—on her trunk. She then very politely withdrew, taking her baby with her. At that time, Amboseli elephants were known to be peaceful and seldom aggressive, for the very good reason that there was then no poaching in the park and no one had shot at them when they wandered outside its boundaries. This is Masai country and the Masai do not hunt elephants and have, quite rightly, a vested financial interest in the welfare of Amboseli National Park.

But the situation we now faced with the lions was slightly different. Lions are supposed to be scared of things like tents simply because they not only carry man-smell but are unfamiliar. Despite this, Hugo Van Lawick, the film-maker, and his then wife Jane Goodall, the chimpanzee expert, had watched Serengeti lions demolish their unoccupied tent.

Even Iain and Oria were concerned, but mainly for the children. He was pretty certain the lions wouldn't return but there are no certainties in such situations. He ordered our splendid park ranger Mahoja Burengo to sit outside the children's tent all night with loaded rifle.

Our own tent was possibly the most vulnerable. It was nearest to the bank of the Ndala river. One could just imagine a hungry lion springing up the three foot vertical slope and crashing through the back of the tent to devour the sleeping occupants. Before I turned in I took what seemed to be a ludicrously ineffectual precaution, I placed a spare safari bed against the back of the tent to act as a lion obstacle. Lord knows what good I thought it would do.

Before we retired to our lion-salivated bedding, Iain handed both Dieter and I a very large tyre lever. "What am I supposed to do with that?"

"It's better than nothing," he said. "Try hitting the lion on the nose with it." The disturbing thing was that he was quite serious.

The lions didn't come back. When I got up to pee in the middle of the night the excellent Mahoja was sound asleep. Naturally, I didn't mention this to Iain in the morning. Anyway, I'm quite sure that would have been what he expected. And when I told him, somewhat sheepishly, about the bed I had put out as an anti-lion barrier, he didn't laugh but said it wasn't a bad idea at all. Lions, he said, are often wary of strange objects. We found the lions next day. They were sound asleep in a tree, having killed and eaten a buffalo. Manyara lions are well-known for sleeping off binges in trees. And a small piece of lion fieldcraft I learned years before from Frank Poppleton, Head Warden of the Uganda Parks. "Do you know how to look for lions sleeping in trees?" "No" "You look for bell-ropes hanging down."

The one-tusked elephant Virgo brings her calves out of the forest to greet Iain Douglas-Hamilton after a year's absence in England obtaining his doctorate.

Boadicea's charge on the front cover of this book. Elephants, Iain claimed, had spent more than a million years perfecting their threat charges.

The pride of lions that took the bedding out of our tents. We found them in a nearby tree next day sleeping off a meal of buffalo.

Manyana bull elephants were usually non-aggressive. Four sisters called the Torone girls changed on sight. One had to be shot in self-defence by a park ranger.

Joan Root and my wife bottle-feed Millions, the young aardvark. Why call the creature Millions? Aardvark a million miles for one of your smiles.

Joan looks as apprehensive as I felt. This elephant brought her small calf into our tent at Amboseli. Elephants in this park are notoriously friendly.

Our Land Rover comes to a dead halt on the Semliki Flats, Uganda. A blocked main jet is cleaned by a needle from my wife's beauty box.

Chiels' Margach's ketch *Kamuji* on the Nile below Murchison Falls. Chiels built her from local timber. Joan slept in the cuddy beneath the forward hatch.

A River Runs Through Them All

When the fishing bug first bit me, oh, about sixty years ago, I realised I was going to be seriously ill for the rest of my life. In the first stages of the disease I would stop and look into puddles in case they had fish in them. Nowadays, the symptoms are milder, but not much. The only sure treatment for a lightning attack is to ensure that I always have a rod of some sort within casting distance. For this reason, I have always managed to smuggle tackle with me when setting out for a wildlife film location.

As I have already admitted, I am a hunter-naturalist. Such people are full of illogicalities and inconsistencies which they would do well not to try to justify or explain. Here is one of mine. Once on foreign soil, I have no wish to shoot with either a shotgun or rifle. I suppose I would shoot for the pot if it was strictly necessary but so far we have never been that hard up for food. Many times I have been offered a shotgun to flight duck on an African lake. But I have always politely declined. At home, wildfowling is a passion as all-consuming as fishing. Why, then, the blockage? The only conclusion I can come to is that flighting duck under a blazing sun in a cloud of mosquitoes just doesn't seem right. At heart, I'm a four seasons man. Winter gales, winter frosts, scudding black clouds, rain, sleet or snow are the side dishes with which wild duck should be served. Nothing else will do. It is the atmosphere that counts and tropics just do not have the right ingredients. I told you it was illogical!

But fishing? Water is water everywhere on earth. What creatures does it hide? Water, fresh, brackish or salt covers two thirds of the globe, thank God. The seasons, or lack of them do not seem to matter. That's the way it works for me, at least. And so I have taken my rod on every possible wildlife location. And here, for fellow addicts, are some of them.

SWEDEN

We took the Midnight Sun Express from Stockholm to Kiruna. The midnight sun refuses to set well before you reach that Arctic town. During World War Two, the Germans dug up a lot of the countryside surrounding Kiruna and shipped the result south to build tanks and guns. Kiruna, an otherwise undistinguished city, is built on a mountain of iron. It might not be wise to try finding your way about in those parts using a compass. I imagine the needle would spin like a top.

I don't think that the veteran Swedish bush pilot and his even more veteran Norseman float-plane ever thought of using a compass. He used the sort of instincts common to the Atlantic salmon and lemmings on migration when it came to finding his way about in the look-all-alike countryside of the far north. Two Swedish friends, a cameraman and myself squeezed ourselves in among the drums of oil to be delivered to Lapp herdsman somewhere out on the tundra. My reason for the expedition was to bring back footage of Arctic angling for my *Countryman* programme, as good an excuse as any to go fishing. Knud, our pilot—they're nearly all called Knud possibly for the convenience of visiting idiots like myself who can't cope with the glottal stop—wore a cap like an American Civil War infantryman with the peak turned up at the front. I was a bit worried about the door of the Norseman. It was held shut by a piece of string. When I asked Knud whether the floatplane could cope with its load in the very short space of water that lay between us and the fir trees, he smiled charmingly and said: "Pleez. I have very good book on *fleyging*." So we bumped down the lake on floats the shape of coffins— a thought which in itself disturbed me— and soared over the conifers with inches to spare. Knud had, it seemed, been flying since birds got wings. The taiga, the last of the sparse northern forests, disappeared beneath our tail. I believe the word *taiga* means 'little sticks' in Russian. Ahead now lay the tundra, that vast northern desert of marsh and moss, frozen solid in winter and briefly carpeted with wildflowers and covered with clouds of midges, mossies and other biting insects in the short Arctic summer. Knud was peering with apparent concern through the oil-specked windscreen for the first sight of our destination, a lake called Rastojaure. I was pretty certain at the time that the concern was put on for my benefit, to pay me back for worrying about our apparently overloaded take-off and the door closed with string. In retrospect, I am not so sure. After we had found Rastojaure and made a faultless landing on its shallow, glassy surface, Knud confided to me that he had flown up here in winter to go ice-fishing, that form of angling peculiar to the earth's frozen regions in which you drill down through several feet of ice and dangle a bait in the chilly waters beneath. The Americans are great on ice-fishing and even have special huts towed out onto frozen lakes in which they can sit in comparative comfort while bait dangling. But not Knud. Knud had arrived at what he thought was Rastojaure in his faithful Norseman floatplane armed with rod, bait and ice drill.

Experienced bush pilots think nothing of landing float-planes on level snow. This is what Knud did. But after he had drilled a number of deep holes in the surrounding landscape he had contacted three feet of permafrost and frozen gravel but not a drop of water. He had, apparently, missed Rastojaure by several miles. It was, he said, quite easy to do. I believed him. In summer, the tundra was a uniform green broken by endless lakes. In winter, everything is snow white. Perhaps a compass would have helped him. We were far enough from Kiruna now to escape the confusing effects of a city sitting on a pile of iron ore.

The lake was full of gigantic Arctic grayling. It was possible to fish for them during the day but decidedly uncomfortable. The larvae of every kind of biting chironomid, the fancy name for midges and mosquitoes, spend the winter tucked up in the mosses of the permafrost. The moment the midnight sun peeps above the horizon they pop out of their larval husks and prepare to pester any living target that comes in range. They are not quite so active during the hours between midnight and three in the morning. This, then, is the time to fish if you wish to remain sane. It wasn't hard to discover what the fish wanted to eat. Midges and mossies are basically black. So any black fly was welcome on the end of your cast—black gnats, black buzzers, black Pennells, even Zulus with their red tails which, presumably, reminded the fish of the blood, mostly ours, with which the mossies were gorged. Anything, as they say in the fashion mags, goes with black. So a little black number was the thing to put on.

The big fish of three pounds and upwards were not all that easy. They, in the manner of lesser grayling with which I was familiar in Britain, were erratic and clumsy risers, missing the fly as often as you missed them. The monsters were usually to be found rising close to the shore where, obviously, they found the food most plentiful. Catching fish anywhere, with anything, really comes down to offering them what they want, where and when and how they want it.

By four a.m., with the sun well above the tundra horizon, it was time to call it a night. Every midge in Sweden was now humming and pinging to get at you. You could see one of the other fishermen making for camp when he was half a mile distant. A column of black insects travelled with him, towering from the crown of his hat to a height of ten feet or so above his head.

Ordinary insect repellents acted as insect attractors. One of the Swedes had a revolting grease used by the Lapps and made from some unmentionable part of the reindeer. It kept midges away but the smell didn't go too well with the hasty bacon and eggs snatched before diving into our tents and zipping ourselves in. By ten in the morning it got so hot in your tent that you were forced to unzip and beg the Swedes to lend you some of their foul-smelling Lapp grease. The Swedes constantly murmured something which sound like *jabla, jabla mig.* I never found exactly what it meant but it did partly relieve the feelings.

The day before Knud flew in to pick us up, we yomped miles across the tundra to a point at which the lake at Rastojaure drained out through a small river into another lake. In twenty four hours I caught over a hundred grayling and brown trout to three pounds. After a time I didn't bother to fish any more. Even with fishing you can have too much of a good thing. In fact, it's no good if it's too easy. But it made a good *Countryman* programme.

DENMARK.

Rune Sternberg, one of the Swedes with whom I fished at Rastojaure, had told me a story that I just had to investigate. I had four days left in which to do it. Four days but no cameraman. He had to return to another job in Stockholm. The story was this. On the Danish island of Bjornholm lying about one hundred miles east of Copenhagen between Poland and Sweden, you could catch freshwater river fish in the sea. Rune even gave me the name of the man who could take me fishing for pike, perch and carp in the ocean. Not surprisingly, his name was Knud, Knud Kure. Knud was the editor of the island's newspaper.

So, directly the Norseman piloted by the first Knud dropped me at Kiruna, I caught a plane to Copenhagen. There, with great good luck, I got one of the sporadic Dakota flights to Bjornholm. The schedule is an occasional one at the best of times. Even if you can get there quickly there is no guarantee of a rapid return. Fog often closes Bjornholm's airport. I didn't have a cameraman but if the story was true and as good as it sounded I could always make another trip.

I phoned the island's newspaper from Jantzens Hotel at Gudhjem, a kind of Danish Polperro without tourists. Knud answered. He was putting the paper to bed. I gathered that he was not only editor, but chief reporter, sub-editor, features editor, compositor and occasional type-setter. Yes, he would like to take me fishing. Was it true there were coarse fish? Though Knud spoke excellent English the term defeated him. I explained: "river fish in the sea." "Of course," he said. "Big river fish in the sea but tomorrow we will go fishing in the sea for sea trout." Where did the freshwater fish come from? From the rivers of Bornholm? He laughed politely. The island was barely thirty miles long and at the most ten miles wide. There wasn't enough water in its four small streams to cover a fish's back. The fish came, he said, from the rivers of eastern Europe. But tomorrow, he would show me. In the neurotic manner of all fishermen I asked him what flies I would need for his sea trout. Flies? Not to worry about flies. Tomorrow he would bring baits. I didn't like the word baits. It smacked too much of worms and preserved sand eels. Sea trout deserved something more noble.

Knud turned up as I was finishing breakfast of local smoked herring eaten with a raw egg. Delicious! Knud could have passed for Kirk Douglas's brother or anyway his cousin. A genuine Viking. Good casting as it turned out. Though Knud naturally didn't raise the subject—I found it out later from the lady who ran the hotel—Knud had been a hero of the Danish resistance. Peenemunde, the German rocket research station on the mainland, was barely half an hour's V 1 flight from Bjornholm. One of the earliest V 1's had gone off course and crashed on the island. It must have disappeared from the German radar screens so the Germans almost certainly assumed that it had crashed in the sea. Knud and his friends reached the V weapon before the occupying German force stumbled on the truth. They photographed its vital parts. The Danish underground somehow got the pictures back to Britain.

Now all that Knud was interested in was living a peaceful life and catching big fish. For a start, he showed me what he had meant by baits. They were the most beautifully crafted fishing objects I have ever seen. Shaped like a willow leaf, they consisted of a slim sliver of the brass used for separating lines of newspaper type. Riveted to this was melted type metal, lightly tapped with a hammer to imply the presence of scales and stippled with colours that gave the impression of a shimmering food item that a hungry sea trout must have been thinking of all its life. They were good enough to caress and admire but far too good to use for fishing. They belonged in a show-case. But, of course, we gratefully used them for their proper purpose, catching fish.

As a rule, I do not much enjoy spinning. This was different. We balanced in our bare feet on rocks slippery with fronds of bladder wrack swaying in the gentle Baltic tide. The weed stetched out thirty yards from the shore. Beyond was deep blue clear water where family flotillas of eider ducks cruised led by the drakes in their black and white dazzle camouflage. The sea trout patrolled the outer edge of the weed, searching for food or perhaps trying to detect the presence of the river in which they had been born, sampling the sea water with their taste-smell organs. I have learned that sea trout do this in the most unexpected places, off the North Norfolk Coast, for example, where there are certainly no sea trout rivers. They are simply searching for home and they were doing it again in this unlikely setting. My first fish hit Knud's post-impressionist lure two yards out from the weed edge. It now had two choices, to bury itself in the bladder wrack, in which case I would have little chance of landing it, or to take off for open water. Luckily it did just that, stripping line and leaping like a tarpon. When it was finally exhausted I was able to fool it into sliding over the top of the weed. I had it in the net, four pounds of gleaming sea silver, dotted with the blue-black hall marks of its race. Wonderful, but it wasn't what I had come for,

An hour later something hit the lure with a flash of red gills. It certainly wasn't another sea trout. The fish leapt once breaking out the battle colours of a piratical sea-pike of around six pounds. Some freshwater pike fight, some sulk. This did both. It appeared to have twice the guile and guts of its river relatives. When I finally netted the fish, it glowed with a silvery sheen gained, I suppose, from sea feeding. Was it fancy, or were its primrose spots more delicately shaded than those of pike I had caught in British lakes and rivers? I like to think so. A sea pike is given to very few anglers to catch and therefore must be allowed some magical characters.

By the end of the day, Knud had four sea trout between two and a half and four pounds. I had my pike. That was what mattered. Knud understood my delight. A pity, he said, we hadn't had time to catch a carp or even one of the huge perch that cruised the weed beds.

Next day I was supposed to fly out. But the Baltic fog came down and blotted out Bjornholm. Maybe the Dakota would come tomorrow. There was an element of *manana* about the people of the island. I phoned Knud. No day for fishing, he said. Why didn't I walk out on the stone mole of Ronne harbour and look for some sea perch. So I did just that. After half a mile of stumbling over the giant rock pile that constitutes the harbour wall I came to a gap. Knud said this was the place the perch haunted. And there half hidden by the swirling mist was a shoal of striped perch whose leader weighed all of four pounds.

Next day, the Dakota made it in. Knud saw me off. I told him about the perch. I had been lucky, he said. Every now and again, a great salt water surge from the North Sea came through the Kattegat. One was forecast soon. When the North Sea surge took place, the walls of Ronne harbour were piled high with dead carp, perch and pike who couldn't handle the strong salt water. But in six months, he assured me, the population would build up again. I swore that when they did, I would come back to film them. But by then I was busy with other wilder projects. I never did return.

HUNGARY

I only fished once behind the Iron Curtain. This time my wife came with me. For once this turned out to be a bit of a disadvantage. To tell the truth the trip hadn't much to do with wildlife film-making except that everything was in a sense a recce for possible future programmes. The event had such a very Iron Curtain flavour to it that I can't very well leave it out. The way it happened was this. We had two very good Hungarian friends who had taken English nationality. George Frank and his wife Kato had fled, pre-war, to escape Hitler. George had done his bit for his new country by broadcasting for the BBC during the war years. As a travel agent with friendly connections in Hungary he was gradually persuading the Communist regime there that they could develop a tourist industry. The revolution which so nearly succeeded was ten years past. The Berlin wall was still a long way from tumbling. The Red Army was still in Hungary though most of it was discretely tucked away in Dracula country in Transylvania.

To persuade the Communist regime still running Hungary that they were ripe for tourism from the West, George organised a small party of leading tourist agency bosses to visit Hungary and chat up the government. For some reason he invited me. The pretext was that Hungary had some notable freshwater fishing, particularly in Lake Balaton, where giant coarse fish, unfamiliar to British anglers, lurked, notably a predatory creature called the asp. I was, I should add, in addition to making and appearing in TV wildlife shows, writing a fishing column in a national newspaper.

A typical Iron Curtain drama started at London Airport. My friend George Frank, met me in the departure lounge where my wife and I were waiting to board the Russian Ilyushin jet and literally seized my rods. This was most un-Frank like behaviour. I couldn't take them, he said. An urgent message from the Hungarian government had forbidden me to fish. For God's sake, why? George took me into a private part of the departure lounge. Lake Balaton had been poisoned, he told me. What, all of it? The bloody thing was about ninety miles long. Apparently, said George, some farmer had tipped something into it. The Hungarian government didn't wish such inefficiency to be publicised in the West. I told him it must have been bloody strong stuff whatever it was to poison a lake that size. I had visions of the wretched farmer in chains on his way to the salt mines.

After a lot of discussion, it was agreed that George should confiscate my rods until he could talk to the authorities in Budapest. We arrived after dark in Budapest to be met by a tall, thin elderly man in the sort of black leather coat the Gestapo favours in war films. It was all very much Harry Lime. My wife was very gallant about it but I could tell she was uneasy. So, to tell the truth, was I. We drove through dark, wet, badly lit, glistening streets straight out of a Le Carré spy novel. Occasionally we passed barracks where unmistakeably Russian soldiers stood on guard. Was this the road to the salt mines?

After about two hours we arrived at a workers holiday hotel on the poisoned shores of Lake Balaton. It was, to be honest, a pretty good hotel in which any package holidayer would have been happy to stay.

In the morning, another tall man in another leather coat, in yet another Volga saloon, turned up with my rods and announced he was going to take me fishing. He liked to be called 'Easy' since his initials were E. Z. Easy and I spent two very agreeable days fishing for small crucian carp, but not in Lake Balaton. We got on very well. Personally, he said, he couldn't wait for the Russians to leave. Things had been very tough. His daughter had even had to sell any spare mother's milk her baby couldn't handle to raise cash. But things were improving.

While I was busy watching a float bob to announce the arrival at the bait of yet another small carp, the tourist bosses in our party were being shown Budapest. One of them knew it very well from a previous visit in 1957, when, along with a party of fellow students, he had flown in to give aid and succour to the Hungarians who were trying to, and nearly succeeded in, throwing out the Russians. One afternoon, he broke away from the conducted tour to revisit a hospital where he had aided wounded revolutionaries. As proof that the Communist fascination with spies and espionage had not yet departed, the secret police put a not very skilful tail on their guest. He was not particularly alarmed but confessed that it gave him a creepy feeling. It certainly didn't boost his confidence about promoting western tourism when he returned to Britain.

There was a further and more disconcerting display of Communist espionage paranoia at the farewell dinner given by the Foreign Minister for our party.

Possibly it was not entirely tactful of my wife to tell the Minister for Tourism that she had known, the British spy, Greville Wynne, and that none of his friends could imagine where he was getting his money from. My wife likes to keep the conversation going in sticky social situations and is extremely good at it. This time, as she freely admits, she chose the wrong topic. Wynne, you may remember, spied for Britain while posing as an international salesman and was arrested in Budapest while visiting with an apparently innocent convoy of display caravans.

The Minister didn't make a lot of it at the time but next day our passports were taken away on some pretext and showed no signs of returning. I remember spending a sticky two hours at the airport, behind a strangely ominous brown curtain. The Ilyushin was warming up its engines and the rest of the party had boarded before a civil servant appeared with a murmured apology and handed our passports back without explanation. Perhaps they thought I was going to blow the story about the poisoning of Lake Balaton. I never did find out the truth about that. Come to think of it, I'd like to have caught an asp but I doubt whether I'll ever wish to catch another crucian carp.

AFRICA. Lake Rudolf

I've never thought much of tiger fish. Catch one and you've caught the lot. They strike me as pike without the pike's brain and that's not saying a lot. I admit that they look good with their silvery yellow torpedo build. And they have a most impressive set of pointed, sharp-edged teeth. I was never desperate enough to want to eat one. But because they were there I had to fish for them.

There was Lake Turkana, née Lake Rudolf. Tiger fish are widely distributed throughout Africa, from the Gold Coast to Botswana. Every writer on the subject has described them as 'a great game fish' so, the second time I went filming on

Lake Rudolf, I decided to see how tiger fish would react to a fly. After all, pike will take a fly. There is even a legend that the biggest pike ever caught in the British Isles, from Loch Ken, was caught on a fly that resembled a water vole. The skull of this fish exists but its alleged 75 lb weight has never been authenticated and I don't suppose it ever will be. It's fairly certain that a monster pike was caught from this loch. Personally, I'm happy to leave it there in the never-never land of pike mythology.

The one thing I did know about tiger fish was that they had teeth like tin-snips. Before leaving the UK, I hunted down some fine wire trace called Elasticum from a tackle merchant in North Wales. As for flies: I was told that anything bright would do. This turned out to be dead right. The only trouble is that you need an awful lot of anything bright. It's one fly per tiger. After a tiger has taken your fly, you can forget it. There's not much left except the hook.

By the early hours of the morning on Lake Rudolf it was too hot to stay in one's tent. If you took your bedding out onto the sand, the mosquitoes slaughtered you. So I usually went fishing. The mosquitoes still slaughtered you but at least you could hit back. Fishing took your mind off them, as it does with most aggravations in life.

Rudolf is full of crocs but I never worried about them snatching me for breakfast. The beach was gradually shelving, the inshore water shallow so that you could see a croc coming a mile off. In fact, croc attacks were infrequent in the lake. I suppose they have so many large Nile perch to eat that they don't bother about people. At that hour, the water was cool and had an agreeably slidey, slippery feeling on the bare feet. Rudolf is sodary but fresh by comparison with many of the central African lakes. The wonder of the moment was just being there. With the sun about to come thundering up over the far shore, the faint outline of doum palms just along the beach, it was easy to imagine you were Alan Quartermain. I imagined that I knew something of what Rudolf's discoverer, Count Teleki, had felt when he first set eyes on this immense lake. There was also the certain knowledge that I was the only angler within perhaps five hundred miles in either direction. As it turned out, I was wrong about that.

The tiger fish were feeding about twenty yards out, within easy casting distance. The flotilla leader seemed to be a decent sized specimen. I tied on an imitation stickleback with a tin foil body and plopped it down in front of his nose with a horrid splash. The commotion didn't worry him as it would have done a more intelligent fish. He ignored the stickle but the fish behind him took it. Two pounds and the fighting quality of an out of condition rainbow. I released the fish, taking care to dislodge the fly from those rat trap jaws with a pair of pliers The fly itself wasn't worth recovering. He'd shredded it. None of this had put the shoal of tigers off. This time I offered a bright sea trout fly to the leader. He was nearly killed by the rest of the shoal in the rush to grab it. Another two pounder, and another fly slashed to pieces.

So now, I thought, for something completely different. I moved along the beach to a little headland cradling a deep pool. I had been wrong. I was not alone. Two hundred yards away, a dim light was slowly approaching. Surely, not one of my colleagues. Unless on an early call, documentary film crews (this was not a wildlife camera team) are not known for unnecessary pre-dawn rising. I'd no idea what fish, if any fish, lived in that pool and didn't much mind so long as it wasn't a tiger. I'd just decided to plumb the silent depths with a wet-fly when the bearer of the light came into view. He carried a large basket-like contraption and a torch of slowly burning reeds, a Turkana fisherman about six feet tall, wearing a coloured clay head dress and straight out of Rider Haggard. Holding the torch over the reed margins, he stood as still as a Goliath heron for maybe five minutes and then suddenly clapped the reed basket down onto the surface. Sliding his arm through the ribs of the basket he removed two small fish of about half a pound. My guess was that they were tilapia, that splendid African freshwater food fish that tastes as though it has lived in the sea.

Not to be outdone, I started stripping line, cast and put the wet fly down on the far edge of the pool, allowing it to sink slowly. The Turkana, who hadn't acknowledged my presence in any way, was standing on one leg supporting himself with his staff. The tribesman stood like this for ten minutes, while I cast and cast again. At about the fortieth cast I felt a pluck and struck. This was no tiger fish but something with the dogged determination of a carp or tench. When I landed it two or three minutes later I was looking at a tilapia of at least a pound As far as I can tell no one has ever caught one of these fish on a wet fly before. I looked round to offer it to the Turkana but he had vanished as silently as he had arrived. I'm sure he thought mine was a hell of a strange way to catch fish. And, of course, he was right.

AFRICA, Lake Naivasha.

On the shores of Lake Naivasha in the Rift Valley fifty miles north of Nairobi is a strange dwelling called the Djinn Palace. It is a hang-over and former hang-out of the wild set of thirties bright young settlers and remission men known as the Happy Valley lot.

I mentioned this because close to the Djinn Palace is a quiet pool frequented by Naivasha's comparatively few and secretive hippos. It is also frequented by a number of small-mouthed black bass. Black bass, as any angler knows, are not native to Africa. They are American fish. In one of those control operations that somehow always seem to go out of control, someone introduced these highly sporting and immensely edible fish to Naivasha as part of a complicated campaign to control mosquitoes. Don't ask me now who was supposed to eat whom. Suffice it to say that in the manner of most introductions of non-native species, the black bass throve much better than the local aquatic fauna.

Alan Root, who then had an idyllic bungalow (not far from the Douglas-Hamiltons) on Naivasha had, among many other wild creatures, a pair of African clawless otters. Even Alan would not describe himself as a competent angler. But his otters thrived on black bass. Occasionally he would trawl the lake with outboard and dinghy. Trailing over the stern and attached to rod and line was a dreadful contraption resembling a miniature mobile and consisting of several small spoons on metal outriggers. This was called by the American bait company that made it a Hula-Popper. According to Alan, the bottom of Lake Naivasha was carpeted with his lost Hula-Poppers as well as the rods to which they had been attached. The rods had simply disappeared over the stern when the Hula-Popper became attached to one of Naivasha lotus water lilies. So Alan was very happy that I should volunteer to fish for black bass to feed his otters, and, if there were any over, ourselves. He showed me the hippo pool and its inhabitants.

That evening I went black bass fishing with a fly-rod and box of lake wet flies. I did very well and had around twelve nice bass in the boat before a hippo surfaced nearby. Now a foul-hooked hippo takes a lot of stopping. It took all the fly-line and a lot of backing. But do you know anyone else who has played a one ton hippo on a three-pound cast?

AFRICA, Tongaland.

Sometimes on safari you fish for the pot. Success or failure doesn't stand between life and death. It does, however, mark the boundary between dietary boredom and something new and possibly exciting in the cook pot. On one occasion it very nearly did mark the boundary between life and death.

We were filming leatherback and loggerhead turtles on a remote beach in Tongaland, north of Natal and on the Mozambique border. To get there had been something of a saga in itself. Mozambique was then destroying itself in a civil war in which South Africa was involved. We wouldn't have made it all but for Carl Erasmus. Carl had close relations with the Natal Parks. Carl, then well into his seventies, had held one of the first private pilot's licences in South Africa. He flew his own Cessna 206 from Durban airport. After a good deal of negotiation, he was able to get Joan and I, along with his wife Morag, a special visa to fly into what was virtually a war zone. Even the landing in Tongaland was slightly problematical. There was, the maps said, an old strip used in World War Two by anti-submarine patrol aircraft. No one could tell us who had last landed there, or when, or for that matter whether the strip still existed.

From one thousand feet. Carl spotted the concrete strip, now vastly overgrown. My own unpractised eye couldn't at first pick out the landing ground from the surrounding brown bushland. Carl made one pass, very fast over the strip, declared it useable, went round again and coming in at high speed in case he had to abort at the last instant put us down with a bump or two and a large cloud of dust. A radio call to Rod and Monica Borland, the South African married couple filming the giant turtles, and their Land Rover was on the strip within half an hour.

This time I hadn't brought my rods. But Carl, like many South Africans, was a keen beach caster and had loaded his fishing gear into the luggage pod beneath the Cessna.

I'd better fill in a little about the turtles. Leatherbacks are the largest turtles in the world. They grow to a length of eleven feet and are increasingly rare. This remote beach was one of their few remaining nesting places. With a civil war on their doorstep its chances of remaining untouched were remote. The leatherbacks, along with the smaller loggerheads, travel vast distances, perhaps from mid-Indian Ocean, or even further, to find the beach on which they themselves emerged from the egg. Like salmon and sea trout, they have this amazing ability to smell, or perhaps taste, or a combination of both senses, their way home. The female flails her way with her flippers far up the beach, excavates a hole and lays hundreds of eggs. There is something even more marvellous about this process. The depth at which she lays the eggs decides whether the offspring will hatch as males or females.

South Africans Rod and Moira Borland had spent many weeks on this beach filming the egg-laying sequences as well as underwater shots of the turtles courting and mating out on the offshore reef. Now the time had come for the eggs to hatch.

The young break out of the soft-shelled eggs and fight their way up through the sand at night. Those that leave the break-out until dawn have the odds heavily stacked against them. Ghost crabs scuttle across the sand and seize them. Frigate birds swoop down without missing a wing-beat and snatch them in their long hooked beaks. How do the young know in which direction the safety of the ocean lies? They are programmed to head for the white gleam of the surf, so the most favourable nights for hatching are therefore nights of bright moonlight.

Rod and Moira were pleased to see us on that lonely beach for a number of reasons, not the least of which was that their diet had got extremely monotonous. We would therefore surf-cast with Carl's rods for kingfish.

Rod, of all people, should have had rods with him—no pun intended. He was a keen and skilful angler. He was also a keen and skilful wildlife cameraman but baggage space had been limited. Essentials like cameras, film, tents, sound recorders had had priority. At the last moment he had forgotten his rods. His wife was an incredible girl. Moira had a figure that would stop traffic. She was utterly committed to life in the bush which as far as she was concerned began and ended in the Okavango swamps in Botswana. If Moira had had her choice she would never have left the swamps. But here she was on a beach, just short of a raging civil war and as happy as she could be, failing enjoying a permanent home amid Okavango's papyrus, hippos, crocodiles and fish eagles. Despite her total addiction to bush life, Moira insisted on touches of femininity and civilisation in her camp. There were always fresh wildflowers on the table when we sat down to eat, a tape of Mozart, or maybe Glen Miller, to accompany supper in camp. All that she and Rod lacked was fish to put on the table beside the wildflowers and to accompany *Eine Kleine Nachtmusik*.

So the first night we hit the beach, rods were rigged. The kingfish, Rod, said, were in. Now, of course, many of the fish of the world have different names in different countries and even in different parts of the same country. There are lots of so-called kingfish. My own guess is that these kingfish were *Rexea solandri,* a close relative of the barracuda.

I might as well get it over quickly. My wife, who would never claim to be an angler, caught the only kingfish, a slim silvery barracuda - like creature about two feet long which Carl declared would make excellent eating. We professional anglers tried to look pleased for her. But this is not the point of the story. When we waded out into shallow water, I noticed the sand was littered with what looked very like small Portugese Men O War. These are not, as many suppose, a single jellyfish-like object—but a colony of different organisms, highly poisonous to the touch. Rod called them 'bluebottles' and said the east wind had brought a whole raft of them in from the Indian Ocean. Moira, he said, had been stung by one a couple of days previously and had been extremely sick. She was obviously allergic to the venom in their purple tentacles. He added that he hoped to God she was being sensible and had stayed in camp getting the supper. But she hadn't done any such sensible thing. For such a bush-wise girl it was a strangely rash action to take. She came wading out to meet us, touched a bluebottle with her leg and almost immediately keeled over.

Rod got the Land Rover and drove her up to her tent. By then she was in a very bad way. Rod had an antivenin snake-bite kit but to try the antivenins in this case might prove disastrous. She was shivering and very cold. We piled blankets on her. Nobody thought of eating, let alone cooking the kingfish. Rod sat by her most of the night, forcing her to take hot drinks. By morning, she had got through the worst. We all gave the kingfish a miss after that.

THE GALAPAGOS.

Fishing for the pot again, or rather for the boat. The boat, a schooner, was the *Cachalote* which is Spanish, or maybe Portugese, for sperm whale, though no one now seems to know the origin or derivation of the word. The *Cachalote* belonged to Fiddy Angermeyer. He'd bought her in Florida and sailed her to the Galapagos with his wife as crew. They had had a brief run-in with pirates off Columbia but had shaken off their attentions with a few bursts of tommy-gun at long range. Neither Fiddy nor his wife seemed to find anything very unusual in this.

Before I get around to the subject of fishing, the Angermeyers really deserve a chapter to themselves. To escape the attentions of Adolf Hitler, the three brothers

Angermeyer bought themselves a trawler in the late thirties and sailed it from Hamburg to Cornwall. They were all fair singers and musicians. They spent the summer singing for their supper in Cornish pubs, or rather for a new suit of sails for the trawler. Then they set sail for the islands six hundred miles off the coast of Ecuador in which Darwin, during the voyage of *HMS Beagle*, formulated his theories about the origin of species. Carl Angermeyer built himself a house overlooking the harbour on Santa Cruz island which he shared with boobies, pelicans and marine iguanas. Ernst was a boat builder. He was now building what he reckoned would be his last boat on a makeshift slipway behind Carl's house It seemed to me to be part boat, part shrine, the culmination of a life's work in which perfection was all. The boat, which no doubt could safely have sailed across the Pacific, if she ever actually got launched, was a thing of great beauty. I doubt if there were any plans. She just grew out of Ernst's mind and heart. There wasn't a nail in her sleek seal-like hull. She was joined with wooden screws, each one individually turned by Ernst. To tell the truth, I don't think Ernst minded if his boat never felt the waves under her keel. To see her grow day by day under his loving hands was enough.

The third brother? I never actually met him. He was said to be a guru, something of a mystic who was occasionally seen about the streets of the small capital of Santa Cruz.

These remarkable men were uncles to our captain, Fiddy Angermeyer. Fiddy knew the islands as well as any sailor there. When we came to make five one hour films about the islands, their unique wildlife and how it arrived and evolved in the aptly named Enchanted Isles, Fiddy was the obvious skipper to commission and the *Cachalote* the obvious boat to carry us all to the remotest parts of the archipelago. She was roomy enough for a crew of four plus two cameramen and all their gear, two wives, a German diving expert, a scientific advisor, and myself.

What has all this got to do with my own passion for fishing? When you're afloat on waters crammed island to island with fish, including great shoals of hammerhead sharks, someone has to keep the cook happy and busy.

So I volunteered and got the job. I won't pretend it was difficult fishing but it would be hard to get bored with catching yellow fin tuna on a spinning rod. We used the *Cachalote's* rubber dinghy with a 50 hp outboard, trailing big spoons and Heddon Bait Company plugs. The yellowfins hit with a blow you could feel all the way up your arm and leapt at once and kept leaping. At least half got off by the third leap and good luck to them. I'd have preferred them fried or grilled, but our Ecuadorian cook went for civiche, raw fish marinated in lime juice or soy sauce.

There was only one thing I liked less. At anchor in deep water I'd be detailed to catch grouper on dead bait. Sometimes I'd haul up—it really wasn't more skilful than that— a golden grouper. You could see something shining like an amber light when the fish was still two or three fathoms deep. The goldens were so beautiful if I'd been on my own I'd have released them. But it probably wouldn't have done them any good. They'd come up from a fair depth so I suppose their swim bladders would have burst, the fishy equivalent of a diver who has surfaced too quickly getting the bends.

Unfortunately, moray eels liked the dead baits, too. The Romans,. it is said, found moray eels a great delicacy though I suspect they confused them with congers. Morays can grow to ten feet in length and have a very disagreeable set of sharp, pointed chewing teeth. They have, when provoked, been known to pursue spear fishermen. I didn't propose to give them the chance to chase me round the deck of the schooner. I've seen the havoc a mere six foot conger can cause in limited deck space. Every now and again, I would stare in horror over the rail of the 'Cachalote' at the long writhing dark shape I had hoped would be a grouper, if not a golden one. Instead I had lured six or eight feet of murderous moray eel out of a hole in the reef. In this situation, there is only one thing to do. Shout for someone with a pair of wire cutters to sever the thick wire trace and watch the lashing monster crash back into the depths from which it emerged.

This stretch of Lake Rudolf's shore-line was thought to be free of crocodiles so I went fly-fishing for tiger fish. They went greedily for any bright and flashy fly.

A two pound tiger fish displaying its lovely lines and horrendous dental equipment. Those razor teeth ripped the fly dressing to pieces.

Jumbo Thorning, Prince Philip's detective, spent all his off-duty time trailing large spoons on stout tackle for Nile perch. He caught twenty and thirty pounders.

The Skeleton Coast

South-West Africa, now Namibia, was the obvious place for Dieter Plage to start filming when he joined *Survival* in the seventies. South-West was one of the African colonies that Germany forfeited after the First World War. Not that you would notice it. Windhoek, the capital, has a Göering Strasse, named not after the fat oaf of the Nazi party but after his far more distinguished father. Three quarters of the books in Windhoek's bookshops are in German. Most of the native population of Hereros speak German. When my wife and I first went there to join Dieter in the field, the travel agency in Windhoek was run by a charming and helpful chap who had been a U-boat captain, a fact that poignantly reminded one that U-boat is only another name for submarine. To complete the Germanic picture, the warden of the Skeleton Coast National Park, Ernst Korlova, had been a Luftwaffe ace, flying everything from Me 109's to Stukas to Ju 88's. I asked him if he was the bastard who had dropped a 500lb bomb on me in Sicily. It landed 30 yards away and failed to explode. It couldn't have been him, Ernst said, he'd been too busy on the Russian front at the time. I discovered later that he had volunteered to fight on for a fortnight after the war was officially over to try to keep the Russians in check.

So Namibia seemed just the right place for a West German cameraman. The natives were not only friendly but spoke better German than he did.

For my money, Namibia can't compete with Uganda or Kenya in scenic beauty and variety. But then, East Africa can't compete with Namibia when it comes to undiluted, desolate wilderness. To begin with, Namibia has the Namib Desert. There is no other desert quite like it. For five hundred miles from the Kuiseb River—usually a bone-dry, narrow, rugged gorge—the Namib marches south in ranks of red dunes, many over 1,200 feet high. Between the dunes lie what are known as streets, narrow, more or less level valleys carpeted with rocks and gravel. The Namib, said to be the oldest desert in the world, collected its sands as they were washed out of the heart of Africa by the Orange River at its southern boundary. The sand was then carried north by wind and ocean current to be deposited ashore in rank upon rank of huge dunes aligned north and south. There are said to be millions of gallons of water buried deep under those dunes. There is certainly little surface water for the creatures that live in this desert, animals mostly specially adapted for life there, but which include some large mammals such as the gemsbok, the southern race of the oryx.

At the southern end of the Namib is the restricted diamond area. The story goes that when the German miners first came here at the turn of the century, they walked towards the dawn at break of day and towards the sunset in the evening. Gemstones were so plentiful that they glittered in the sun's rays and could be picked up for the looking. The remains of the old miners' huts, wind-battered and sand-filled, are still there at Luderitz.

The Skeleton Coast runs the whole length of the Namib, and indeed of Namibia itself, from the Orange River in the south to the Kunene River at the border with Angola in the north. The Coast is littered with wrecks, perhaps the most famous of which is that of the *Dunedin Star*, a Union Castle liner with a party of nurses aboard bound round the Cape for Egypt in World War Two. She ran into one of the many shifting shoals fifteen miles off the Coast and ripped her bottom open. The Captain managed to beach her several hundred yards offshore. Most shipwrecked crews who get ashore on the Coast die of thirst. The *Dunedin Star's* passengers and crew survived after a rescue that took many weeks, cost several lives, not to mention a tugboat and an aircraft. Best of all wreck legends, never yet confirmed alas, is that of a Portugese galleon said to sail on, buried in the sands, several miles inland.

North of the Kuiseb Canyon, the nature of the Namib desert changes. The march of the giant dunes is stopped by the Kuiseb river or rather its gorge. The river itself only flows perhaps once in ten years when rains are exceptional and even then its waters rarely reach the sea. The northern part of the Namib is flatter and rockier, its dunes smaller. Strange formations of gypsum, called 'desert roses', litter the surface. Practically every stone you pick up is an agate asking to be cut and polished. Broken geodes of rock crystal and poor quality amethyst litter old mine shafts. Welwitschia grows here, the strange ground-hugging plant with two leaves like fronds of seaweed that is said to be an early ancestor of modern trees.

Hidden among the gorges cut out by rivers that have ceased to flow, and may only flow again once in the next half century, are lagoons and reed beds. They are rare and hard to find. Quite unbelievably in such an arid landscape, small herds of desert elephants move between these waterholes. Gemsbok and parties of springbok, too, manage to eke out a living in the apparently waterless desert.

Nearer to the coast itself, occasional prides of lions hunt seals and scavenge off carcases washed up on the shore. And this cast of the larger Namib characters takes no account of the true desert dwellers, the snakes, lizards and insects that make the Namib their home.

There has to be a life-support system in such a hostile place. In the Namib it is the cold Benguela Current that surges north just offshore. The Benguela originates in the Antarctic bringing with it sea riches in the form of planktonic life for seals, seabirds and fish. But the Benguela does far more than that. It produces the moisture that makes life in the desert possible. When the warm air from the land meets the cold Benguela, dense mist forms. Each morning the mist builds up and each day it envelopes the Namib for twenty and often many more miles inland. As the mist evaporates, it deposits enough water on the surface of the desert to keep its wonderfully adapted inhabitants alive. What more promising scenario could any wildlife film-maker demand? Not surprisingly, we were to be fully occupied in Namibia for the next twenty years!

Dieter, working with his then assistant, the young South African, Rod Borland, had acquired a special vehicle for dealing with the dunes of the Namib. Not only were many of these sand mountains over one thousand feet high, but their slopes were frequently as steep as one-in-three. The Unimog had been designed for the German Army to cope with almost any terrain on earth including this one. It had twenty three gears, though I forget how many took you forward and how many put you in reverse. In the Namib, whether proceeding backward or forward, you needed them all.

The only snag of this model Unimog was that there wasn't much room in it once the camera duo and their incredible amount of equipment were aboard. The rest of us had, therefore, to travel across the desert in a vehicle to which I have given some of the best years of my life, the stalwart short-wheel base Land Rover. I've travelled over some reasonably rugged and slushy surface in the one I own in Britain but I had never asked a Land Rover to tackle anything like this.

The Unimog would confidently face a one thousand foot direct descent down a one-in-three sand dune. But the first time I was required to do so in a Land Rover driven by Mary Seeley, the American Director of the the Namib's Desert Research Station, I paled noticeably beneath my suntan. Mary suggested that if I was nervous, perhaps I would like to walk down. A few minutes later I was sorry

I had taken up her suggestion. The sand was so hot it grilled the feet through the soles of my desert boots. Meantime, the gallant Land Rover, in low ratio four-wheel drive, was happily inching its way down the slope. I ran after it and clambered aboard, not the easiest feat when a vehicle is practically standing on its radiator. When we reached the bottom, Mary suggested that I might like to try it myself next time. So I did. Provided you started off with the vehicle at right angles to the face of the dune and kept things that way, you had a fair chance of making it. The other thing was to try to avoid standing on any of the pedals, especially the accelerator.

Mary Seeley taught the team more than basic driving skills. The best wildlife cameraman in the world cannot hope to unravel the secrets of such a desert unless he persuades the scientists who are working on the ecology of the area to instruct him. This requires not only tact and diplomacy but also the ability to convince the scientists concerned that you are deadly serious in your determination to give an accurate portrait of the their work no matter how long it takes and how much determination and effort is required to put it accurately on film. Dieter had these qualities in abundance. He also had charm and a great gift for gentle persuasion. As for dedication, I think it would be fair to say he was a driven man. Dieter also knew the basic truth of the trade, namely that all good wildlife cameramen want to be asked back. It is essential that they earn the trust of not only scientists, but heads of national parks, wardens and rangers, too. Mary Seeley recognised straight away that the Dieter Plage, Rod Borland team meant business.

By the time Joan and I joined Dieter and Rod in Namibia they already had a number of films under their belt. Like the pioneer German miners on the Skeleton Coast, they had found the wildlife film gems practically lying on the surface. At the time, South-West Africa, as it then was, was almost virgin territory. There had been some filming on the great salt pan at Etosha, in what became Etosha National Park, but precious little else. The riches were lying there to be picked up. And what nuggets they were. Dieter and Rod filled a sack with them. Seldom in the history of wildlife filming can there have been such a productive time.

One film sticks in the memory, not solely because it was Dieter's first but because it proved once again that big countries produce big, not to say eccentric characters. The story was set in the area known as the Pro-Namib, the desert before you get to the real desert. It concerned one of those smash-and-grab conservation operations that involve moving wild animals to a reserve from an area where they clash with or are likely to be shot by humans.

The creature concerned was the gemsbok. There is a story that this pony-sized antelope gave rise to the legend of the unicorn. It is true that when you view it from the flank, and get its two four foot long straight horns in line, they do look as though the animal has one horn. But that's about as far as it goes. The gemsbok were interfering with the very profitable business of rearing karakul sheep, a small black variety whose fleece poses as Persian Lamb. They were eating the grazing which the karakul needed. The only possible solution was to move them to an area well out of the range of the karakul where they could live wild. The capture officer picked for the job was Peter Flanagan, a man after Dieter's heart.

Flanagan refused to dart his captures. A large animal anaesthetised by a tranquilising dart will often run several hundred yards before collapsing. If a darted gemsbok made for the nearby Namib dunes, there was every chance of losing it. If this happened, the antelope would probably collapse and die before it could be given the vital antidote. So Flanagan, a wild man of the sort Africa so lovingly produces, devised an effective but lunatic method of catching his gemsbok. He built onto the front of his capture vehicles a platform to which an intrepid man might precariously cling while the Land Rover, driven by Flanagan, roared at 40 mph across country. When the vehicle eventually closed with its target, the intrepid man, a Bushman or Ovambo tribesman from the National Parks staff, seized the gemsbok by the tail and clung on, bringing the quarry to a halt. Surprisingly, it worked.

When Dieter approached Flanagan with a request to film the operation, Flanagan suggested that both Dieter and Rod might like to have a go on the catching platform just to get the feel of things. It was the sort of test to which wildlife cameramen become accustomed. When neither fell off and both succeeded in catching their gemsbok by the tail, Flanagan decided they were acceptable.

If the gemsbok capture operation was a gift to a wildlife cameraman, filming its chief character was a nightmare. But then what would Africa be without such lunatics? Flanagan must come high on any list of African nut-cases.

For example: one night Flanagan decided that the only place to have a bath was at the top of one of the larger dunes. His devoted catching crew—and it is no small measure of their devotion— had to carry a tin bath and jerricans of hot water to the crest of a very large heap of sand.

If a fly or any other pestilential insect intruded at meal times, Flanagan was quite liable to discourage it by drawing his .44 Smith and Wesson and blowing it to hell and gone along with the cups and cutlery.

Perversely, he would appear each morning in different gear. One moment he would be there in a crash helmet and bush jacket, the next in a national parks beret and a camouflaged shirt. Continuity meant nothing to Peter Flanagan. If he was a nightmare to the cameramen, he was hell on film to the editors back in London who had to cut the action together. Fortunately the chase was so exciting and Dieter's eye for the scene so lyrical that a quick change or two in mid-pursuit and capture was barely noticeable. Thank God for a few maniacs like Flanagan.

That first trip to Namibia I spent a lot of time in the field with Dieter's assistant cameraman, Rod Borland. It was plain that he had the stuff that was going to produce quality wildlife films. He later proved this by winning the major prize at the Monte Carlo Film Festival with his film about the Namib, 'The Empty Desert'. In fact, of course, the Namib was far from empty, provided you knew how and where to look. Mary Seeley had taught both Rod and Dieter well.

Rod needed what he called 'goodies' for this film. 'Goodies' were the strange creatures that had adapted to the seemingly impossible living conditions of the Namib. The best time to collect these for filming later under controlled conditions was at night. It was an eerie feeling standing in the small circle of bright light shed by a Tilley lamp on top of a thousand foot sand mountain at dead of night and knowing that only two or three people in the whole world at that moment were crazy enough to do such a thing. I, and sometimes my wife, were part of this select group.

On the crest of a giant dune at night, you discover that there are some very strange characters who inhabit this beautiful and frightening wilderness. What would Darwin have given to have met a Tok-tokky beetle, or *tenebrionid* to give it its high-falutin' scientific name. Tok-tokkies have solved the problem of getting a drink in the Namib by evolving a gutter that runs round their wing cases to catch the condensing droplets from the Namib mist. Their evolutionary cunning does not stop there. Their back legs are much longer than their front ones. When they stand upright, the gutter tilts forward so that any moisture it has caught runs into their mouths.

At night on the dunes you may be lucky enough to meet a considerable rarity, a golden mole, a mammal that resembles a fur-covered apple dumpling. It burrows through the soft sand—the grain of its coat assisting its forward progress—in the search for beetle larvae. Then there's a trap-door spider known as the white lady which lies in wait in a tunnel whose miniature manhole cover is made of sand impregnated with silk. When a meal walks by, it whips open the trap door and seizes it. You may meet palmatto geckos and dune crickets, beetle larvae and side-winding vipers. These snakes have worked out a sideways looping movement that enables them to travel over soft sand in exactly the same way that side-winder rattlesnakes progress in the deserts of the American south-west. Darwin would have liked that, too, a vivid example of what scientists call convergent evolution. But anyone's favourite character has to be a small lizard called *Aporosaurus*. I wish it had a friendlier name. It deserves one but if it exists then I don't know it.

Aporosaurus has to cope with the fact that the Namib dunes run north to south. There is therefore a hot side (east) and a slightly colder side (west). The hot side of the crest has usually been made concave by the prevailing wind and is packed down hard by the sun. Known to scientists as the slip-face, it is the most productive place for finding food. Seed gets blown here, often from hundreds of miles away. *Aporosaurus* likes to hunt and eat on the slip face. However, there is a price to pay. Being cold-blooded, the little lizard heats up very quickly. Soon after sun-up he nips over from the western side of the dune where he has spent the night buried in the sand to keep warm. He starts to look for breakfast. The 'kitchen' soon becomes uncomfortably hot. However, *Aporosaurus* has no intention of getting out of the kitchen just because he can't stand the heat. He has several tricks in reserve that help him to keep his cool. First, he jacks his tail up off the hot sand. This enables him to lose a little body heat to the surrounding air. He catches a beetle or two and gets even hotter. So he goes to stage two, and lifts his entire body off the sand. Two seeds later and a degree or two hotter, he raises first one foot and then the other, He has only one shot left. This involves lifting body, tail and opposing front and rear feet off the sand. After that there is only one course left open if he doesn't want to fry, to nip over the crest to the cooler side of the dune where, if he cools down too quickly, he simply lets everything collapse on the sand and warms himself up again.

After that first safari with Dieter and Rod, it was to be nine years before we returned to the field in Namibia. Perhaps I had better again explain that word 'we'.

What, the reader may well ask, was my wife doing all the time sharing my wild life with me? Well, to begin with she was being a very lucky woman. Few wives and mothers, not to say housewives living in Surrey, can have had the chance to see and experience wildlife and wild places at the sharp end as she did for close on thirty years. But *you* know women. At least I assume you do, particularly if you happen to be one. Once invited along for the ride, it is very hard to persuade them to get off the bus. We were lucky in that when the three children were small there was always a devoted granny to keep the home fires burning. For my part, I was thrilled to have my wife along. The same goes for the camera persons. We were all close friends, a family almost. I doubt whether there has ever been, or ever will be, anything in the ephemeral world of television like the bonds that held that private army together. Joan had had her one scream in Uganda. After that, nothing ever threw her. Quite the contrary. Amazingly she took on the trappings of Lady Baker at the first snap of a crocodile's jaws. At home, in Surrey, I doubt whether she would have spotted a roe deer if it was standing fifty yards from the edge of the road. In the wild, someone had lent her a new pair of eyes and set of senses. She often saw birds and beasts in bush, desert and woodland before I did and identified them, usually correctly. I can't explain this. It is part of the amazingly complex brain that steers the human female through the most unfamiliar and sometimes alarming situations. Nor would it be right to say that Mrs W. was simply along for the wild ride. She kept notes and diaries, a thing I never do, believing myself to have total recall and a photographic memory. These notes were invaluable to me when recall proved to be not quite total and photographic memory slightly out of focus. She added one other valuable contribution to our work. Apart from that one blip in Budapest when she let slip her acquaintance with a well-known British spy, she is extremely good at handling people and chatting up and listening to boring officials to whom it is important to be polite and to whom someone must lend an apparently fascinated ear. Mrs latter-day Baker was, as she constantly tells me, a fortunate woman to have done all this. She also says that today it seems like a dream. Me, too, sweetheart.

By the time we got back to Namibia, Dieter had moved on to Ethiopia. Rod was operating on his own. Namibia had been annexed by the father and mother of all wildlife camera teams, the Australians, Des and Jen Bartlett. Des had been as good as the word he had given me when I went head-hunting him eighteen years previously in the forests of Uganda. He had said that the moment Armand Denis retired, and the Armand and Michaela Denis pioneer series 'On Safari' closed down, he would join us. He and his wife Jen had done exactly that.

In the years since the Bartletts came aboard, we had worked together in the American South-West, in Alaska, the Falkand Islands and the Antarctic. Now Des was back where he had always wanted to be, in Africa. He saw Namibia, as Dieter had done, as a bottomless mine of wildlife nuggets. The difference was that Dieter saw enticing projects in other parts of the globe. He wanted to move on. Des, I swear, wanted, and indeed wants, to stay in Namibia for ever filming everything that moves and some things that don't. As I will recount: he damn nearly got his wish—about staying there for ever, I mean.

South-West hadn't changed a great deal in nine years. Independence was still a fair way off. A very nasty war was being fought up beyond the Kunene River in Angola, in the north. No one could forecast how independence would work out and in particular how South Africa would react to having to let go the reins. One thing was certain, the desert hadn't changed. The Namib was, after all, the oldest desert in the world. Nor had those entrusted with protecting and studying it. Mary Seeley was still in charge at the Desert Research Station, pursuing an admirably liberal research programme and encouraging scientists with what, to a layman like me, seemed the most esoteric and peripheral of studies. A young American with a grant from some learned body back home was studying how far and fast the dunes of the Namib moved in a given period. A tall angular lady scientist who flew her own aeroplane and whose favourite expletive was *Jeez.... shit!* had set up a programme designed to find out how fast a carcass would decay in the desert if shielded from major scavengers such as vultures, jackals and hyenas. To this end she had various mammal carcases up to the size of gemsbok pegged down under fine wire netting. This ensured that only the insects and their larvae and possibly very small rodents could get a meal off them. What was proved at the end of it I am by no means certain but then I am not a scientist.

Like Dieter, Des was infinitely patient in his enquiries and instantly won the trust and respect of dune-studiers and carcass-watchers and all manner of experts and scientists in between those two extremes. Where Dieter was the mercurial action-man, Des moved at the pace of the seasons. For someone of my own somewhat impatient temperament this takes a bit of getting used to. When driving across the desert a small black mark might appear on the shimmering horizon, rather in the manner of that great scene in David Lean's 'Lawrence of Arabia' when Anthony Quinn starts as a mirage and takes an age to ride into close-shot and materialise as a man on horseback. In this case the black dot eventually solidified at our approach into a snake expert called 'Slang', what else since slang means 'snake'. Slang is out in the desert studying side-winding vipers. We pull up alongside. Des takes out a little black notebook. One hour later, with the temperature inside the vehicle well off the clock, we are still talking to Slang. When we eventually move on I ask Des whether he learned much from Slang. "Not as such," he says. It is his favourite expression. "But you never know when it may come in useful". In his small neat hand-writing, in his small neat notebook, Des will have recorded the names of other snake experts in other parts of Africa, and, for all I know, other parts of the world. Des is perfectly right. It is typical of his painstaking approach. He can now be certain that if he ever wants the ultimate expert on green mambas in Botswana, he now knows, thanks to his hour-long chat with Slang, where to find one.

This trip Des and Jen want us to see the real Skeleton Coast. As guide we have dive-bomber ace Ernst Korlova. Not too many tourists at that time visited the Coast. Even then most seldom ventured further than the recreation area and the fur seal colony at Cape Cross. We are bound in a four-wheel drive Toyota truck to Ernst's base at Mowe Bay. Anyone who thinks the Outer Hebrides are off the beaten track should try Mowe Bay. It consists of two very basic sand-blasted huts containing an interesting collection of sand-blasted relics. The prize of the collection, gathered by Ernst when beach-combing one of the loneliest and most treacherous shorelines in the world, is a carved head from maybe the stern post or quarter-deck rail of a Portugese galleon. The waves have slightly softened the features of this turbaned head but it speaks across the centuries of Vasco da Gama and the captains who followed in his wake.

That night when we sit round the fire a jackal approaches and takes a bone from Ernst's hand. I ask him whether he isn't afraid of a bite that might be loaded with rabies. These jackals are his friends, he says. I ask him how he knows that they're safe to feed by hand. Ernst says: "I put out water for them. If they drink I know they're all right. Hydrophobia? Morbid fear of water. Sure symptom of rabies".

Next morning we push up the coast towards the Hoarusib River, which, of course, isn't a river at all, at least not at this moment. About ten miles north of Mowe Bay we come to a strange monument on top of a low coastal dune. It is what remains of an aero engine, a Pratt and Whitney Wasp, I guess, World War Two vintage. The sand and mist have done their best to deface it. The cowling has long since blown away but the cylinders and propeller shaft have been fused until they resemble a metallic sculpture. We are close to the spot at which the captain of the *Dunedin Star* beached his badly holed liner forty years before. The engine is one belonging to the Lockheed Ventura which the South African Air Force pilot Captain Naude landed here in an attempt to rescue the stranded nurses and crew of the beached liner. Naude himself as well as his aircraft became prisoners of the Namib when the soft sand clamped the wheels of his bomber and refused to let it go. Of the *Dunedin Star* herself there is little to see except maybe the top of a boiler. The Skeleton Coast is renowned as a ship-breaker. It dismembers luxury liners as easily as fishing trawlers. The relic is so much a piece of South African history that I cannot imagine why someone, perhaps the Air Force, has not performed the comparatively simple task of salvaging this lonely engine and placing it in a museum.

Des and Jen are not particularly excited by this relic. What excites them is the prospect of spending the next ten years, and more if necessary, telling the story of this extraordinary piece of desert real estate and its wild inhabitants. They see a whole series of films for television, hours and half hours. Knowing their thoroughness and determination, not to mention naturalist knowledge, I have little doubt that they can and will do it. Whether television will have an appetite for the output they plan I have no way of knowing. Business conditions and audience demands in the shadow world of the box change so fast that the Bartletts may be simply performing an act of faith.

The canyon of the Hoarusib has been carved out by flash floods over centuries. Sometimes the flood, which is by no means an annual event, dies long before it reaches the coast and disappears into the sand. But the wildlife of the Namib knows that the water is down below somewhere and will search until it finds it either in permanent springs or by digging for it. Amazingly there are elephants in this burned-out wilderness and their story is one that the Bartletts plan to tell. We do not find elephants but we do see giraffe, springbok and gemsbok and that is amazement enough.

It isn't perhaps so strange that we see occasional large mammals. Until 1970, this northern region was a game reserve. Then the South African government took away its protective status to create ethnic homelands with the not entirely unexpected result that Himba herdsmen and poachers shot out many of the lions and elephants. A coastal strip only twenty five miles, the Skeleton Coast National Park was all that was left to give protection to wildlife. Des and Jen have an almost missionary zeal when it comes to saving wildlife and wild places. I have little doubt that a strong motive for spending the rest of his life filming in Namibia is to make a visual argument that helps persuade the government to save what is left while there is time left. How much time left? For the national parks anywhere in Africa, I confess I do not know. For Des, my old friend has always seemed indestructible. But as I write this in the year 2000, Des is 73 years old.

Before this trip is over, we all have two more calls to make. The first is to Etosha National Park which lies around one hundred miles to the east of the Skeleton Coast. Together, since the Bartlett's first came to Namibia we have already made eight films in Etosha. One of these, 'The Lions of Etosha', was nominated for an Emmy in the United States.

The stars were the members of a pride of lions that dominated the Ombika waterhole. The film was only just finished before we left England. I have brought a copy out with me. It is typical of Des that he will make a detour of many hours over Namibia's far from perfect roads in order to show the film at park headquarters at Okaukuejo. It is his way of thanking the wardens and rangers who helped him and gave him advice. It is, also, a way of cementing relations for the future.

The Ombika pride's territory is very close to park headquarters. There is a good deal of roaring on the sound track of the film, roars as challenges, as greetings, as mating advances. We showed the film under the stars in camp. Presumably, lions can recognise their own voices. As the story unfolds on the screen, a crescendo of roars builds up in the darkness beyond the camp. It is the Ombika pride talking to themselves and answering or perhaps challenging themselves on the sound track. You don't often get an audience reaction to match that.

The last call of the trip was, let's face it a joy-ride—weren't they all?— although it would be quite reasonable to put it down to reconnaissance. Des wanted me to see the Caprivi Strip. Come to think of it, he is a great one for strips. Several years previously, after weeks of filming in the Arizona and Nevada deserts, he dragged us all to Las Vegas to view the Vegas Strip, lit up at night. I recall rather priggishly arguing that nothing could match the sunsets we'd been enjoying in the desert. I was wrong. For colour and brightness, the lights of the Strip made desert sunsets look like guttering candles. There was a lot more going on there, too, including stripping.

But the Caprivi Strip was different. The Caprivi is a narrow finger of land, some two hundred miles long and maybe forty miles wide that runs along the top of Botswana and has borders with Angola, Zambia and Zimbabwe.

It isn't of much value to anything except wildlife. It is mainly swamp. But it is one of main homes of Lechwe, the marsh antelope, a beast I had never seen and about which I thought we ought sometime to make a film. The only practical way to get there is to fly, at least when the time available is limited.

No doubt Pat Evans came out of Des' little black note-book. She was an extremely good pilot, especially for aerial photography and she had her own Cessna. I think she could fairly be described as a tough little cookie and not too easy to get on with. Des, however, is extremely tolerant of human failings, including my own. If she could fly and fly well and, what was equally important to the budget of the film, fly cheaply, then Pat was the ideal pilot as far as Bartlett was concerned.

It's a long flight over featureless country but she was dead on course and inspired confidence when airborne. We had permission to land at a South African airfield and called them up when about forty minutes away. Hearing a female voice, the South Africa Air Force gallantly offered to send out a couple of choppers to escort her in. She shot that one down straight away. She was quite able to find their field unaided, she said. And so she was.

The South Africans choppered us with our camping gear to some tumble down huts far out on an island in the swamp. The flight was memorable for two things. There was still a war going on around the Angola border. The enemy at that time was likely to be SWAPO, the South-West Africa People's Organisation. Stuck on the nose of the chopper was the warlike slogan 'Swat a Swop'. At this moment in time it is perhaps ironic to note that the young airmen flying this chopper came from the same organisation that did such heroic work in saving their black brothers and sisters from the floods in Mozambique. Previously, they'd been deployed against the former regime in that country. It was the U-Boat/Submarine syndrome demonstrated once again.

Perhaps it was as well that we didn't have to swat a Swop or anything else on that flight into the swamps of the Caprivi. Shortly after take-off, the navigator warned my wife that he was going to have to fire our heavy machine-gun. It was a routine to ensure everything was in apple pie order. The gun fired one shot and then jammed. Oh, well, that sort of thing can happen in the best regulated air forces.

The expedition? A success, I suppose. We met a three-legged lioness who didn't seem at all pleased to see us and could move surprisingly fast on three legs. We saw lots of lechwe, too, and magnificent they looked, leaping and crashing through the swamps in clouds of spray. Undoubtedly, Des would have to make a film about them. Perhaps when he'd finished his ten year stint on the Skeleton Coast. With Des, I had learned, it was no good trying to rush things.

I said earlier that Des nearly, if prematurely, got his wish and ended his days in Namibia. About the second year of the filming featuring the desert elephants of the northern Namib, Des and Jen took a vacation in Florida to buy and learn to fly two Drifters, flying machines about midway between a genuine light aircraft and a microlight.

In the wastes of the northern Namib these became invaluable tools. One fine afternoon, without a cloud in the sky, Des was flying one Drifter and Jen the other. They carried a passenger apiece. Jen had the girl vet from Etosha National Park aboard and Des flew with Mary Plage, Dieter Plage's wife. They were flying in ideal conditions about half a mile from each other. Suddenly and literally out of a clear blue sky, Jen realised Des was missing. She flew round and was horrified to see his Drifter upside down in one of the few swamps in the area. Jen landed beside the crash. Mary hung in her straps with what was plainly a badly injured back. Des was unconscious and trapped in his seat with his legs buried in the swamp.

Jen and her passenger got Mary out and laid her down in the shade of one of the few trees. There was no moving Des. The Bartlett's truck was two hours away at Mowe Bay. There was no one there to answer a radio call. So Jen left the lady vet with the casualties, flew back to Mowe Bay, put out a radio call for aerial assistance and returned with the truck two hours later, not knowing whether she would find her husband alive. No one kills a Bartlett as easily as that. When they finally extricated him, one foot was practically turned back to front.

Two operations and three years later, Des is off crutches and back filming in Namibia. Mary Plage has fortunately recovered. Jen was in Florida again learning to fly a twin-engined Drifter which will play a vital part in the next ten years filming.

A one thousand foot Namib dune close to the sea at sandwich harbour. The cold Benguela current washes the sand northward and the wind piles it up inland.

Relic on the Skeleton Coast. A carved wooden head found on a lonely beach. Perhaps a figurehead from an East Indiaman or a Portugese galleon.

Beauty in the Namib Desert. Sossus Vlei, one of the desert's few flat areas or pans. At some time, a flash flood had killed these trees.

Pelican Island
Leslie would have charged at Culloden

If it hadn't been for Leslie Brown, the world, or anyway some of it, would still have been wondering where the three million flamingoes of the Great Rift Valley nested. If it hadn't been for Leslie Brown, the same could be said about the thousands of great white pelicans that migrate up and down Africa from Ethiopia to Namibia. Leslie cracked both ornithological mysteries and in the process nearly cracked himself, or at the very least lost his legs.

Why do I equate Leslie with the forlorn Battle of Culloden? Because whenever I think of him I see him beard aflame, sporan askew, kilt aflying and claymore awhirling, hurtling down on the Duke of Cumberland's forces at the battle that finally put paid to Bonnie Prince Charlie's hopes. I have absolutely no doubt whose side Leslie would have been on: Charlie's.

If it hadn't been for Leslie Brown. I would never have experienced Pelican Island and a great deal more besides. He's gone now, no doubt to a Scottish Valhalla where the clans still gather. This book is to some extent about eccentrics. Leslie must come somewhere near the top of the list, at least in Africa. Many eccentrics are famous for being, well, just eccentric. Leslie, it must be said, was a great deal more than that. He was probably the world's leading expert on birds of prey, and, as will shortly emerge, knew more about flamingoes and great white pelicans than most ornithologists have forgotten. I have several especially cherished memories of Leslie Brown.

On Lake Naivasha, where he was advising us on the habits of fish eagles, he encountered a 50 hp outboard motor that refused to start. Leslie was not one to take recalcitrant outboards lightly. Whirling it round his head, and muttering strange Celtic oaths, he taught it a final lesson by hurling it, as if putting the shot or tossing the caber, far out into the waters of the lake. In a forest reserve in Ethiopia he encountered a hunting party of Galla, the local tribe, who wantonly speared a black and white colobus monkey. Leslie, at some personal risk, took the spears from the offenders and smashed them over his knee. No one argued.

Only Leslie could have had a brother called Marmalade. On a foot safari on the Omo River at the north end of Lake Rudolf, Marmalade suffered from chronic constipation. Leslie and John Blower solved his problem by giving him an enema with a stirrup pump.

Like many irascible people, Leslie Brown had a warm and kindly attitude to his brothers, black and white, unless he considered that he had been unnecessarily provoked. As an ornithologist, his greatest feat was the unravelling of the great flamingo mystery.

Three million greater and lesser flamginoes and no one knew where they nested! There was a clue, though. The Masai tribesmen believed that the birds were actually hatched out of the sodary waters of Lake Natron in Kenya and walked ashore when they were ready to fly. They based this magical theory on the fact that they sometimes saw fully-fledged young birds standing in the shallows.

Leslie Brown, then Chief Agricultural Officer for Kenya, decided that he must learn to fly in order to search the horrible pink soda wastes of Natron. If the Masai had seen young birds on the shore, then maybe Natron held the answer. From the air he saw what appeared to be two large colonies several miles offshore. The only way to find out for certain was to reach the colonies on foot.

Leslie set out on his own, equipped with only a canvas water bottle. At first the going on a hard crust of soda was good. But soon he began to break through into stinking black ooze. Next he encountered a half mile of shallow water covering even softer, sulphurous-smelling mud. At one point he was on all fours to save himself sinking. When he drank from his water bottle he found that the soda had penetrated it, fouling the contents and making them nearly undrinkable. By the time he decided that he must turn back if he hoped to survive, he was totally exhausted, dehydrated, and had drunk most of his remaining water lest it become more polluted. He was still far short of the colony he had hoped to reach. Halfway back to shore he was almost certain that he would collapse, become anchored to the mud and simply die of exhaustion and heatstroke. By good fortune he hit a ridge of harder soda crust that enabled him to make ten or more paces between halts. He reached the shore, took off his boots and found that they were filled with crystalline soda. His legs were red-raw with blisters and turned black as he watched them. He still had a seven mile hike back to his camp and a 45 mile drive to the nearest help, the Magadi Soda Company at Lake Magadi. There he lay in the company's hospital semi-conscious for three days. The legs took six weeks to recover and had to be repaired by skin grafts.

In 1957, he tried again, this time reaching a flamingo colony by walking over comparatively firm brown mud at the southern end of the lake. The mystery of the flamingoes had been solved.

Solving the mystery of the Great White Pelicans in the Ethiopian Rift was not quite as hazardous, though hazardous enough. In some ways it was a repeat performance, though one in which Dieter Plage and I could become involved before the curtain came down on the final act.

There are many thousands of great white pelicans in the northern half of the Great Rift Valley. Once again, the nesting grounds were unknown except for one far to the south in Tanzania. Once again, there was a clue in local folk-lore. In the Galla language, the word *Shala* means pelican.

Lake Shala is by no means as hostile to man as Lake Natron but it has its own hazards. It lies about one hundred and twenty miles south of Addis Ababa in the Ethiopian Rift. The lake itself is about thirty miles long. The mountains on the southern shore rise almost vertically from the water's edge and continue dropping at the same steep angle to the lake bed eight hundred feet below the surface. They act as a funnel to sudden and vicious winds. There are several small islands at the western end of the lake but none of the locals ever goes there. Shala holds no fish worth catching and the native population does not go boating just for the fun of it. The reason there are no large fish in Shala is that the lake is sodary, though in a fairly low concentration. On the north shore of this long narrow lake the scrub-covered hills are not nearly so steep though they rise to three thousand feet. A lake that holds no big fish does not suggest itself as a natural home for a nesting colony of several thousand large fish-eating birds and their young. Pelicans need about four pounds of fish a day. But then Leslie Brown got to hear through Dr Emil Urban, head of the Zoology Department at Addis Ababa University, that a local Ethiopian ornithologist had seen large numbers of pelicans in the vicinity of Lake Shala.

Following up this lead Brown and Urban determined to reach the small islands at the western end of the lake. The nearest of these is twelve miles down the lake from the most accessible end. So they borrowed a metal cockleshell of a boat from the Game Department, a craft that was certainly no match for the sudden winds that whip down the length of Shala, and set out to see for themselves.

Several times during that first voyage, sudden squalls nearly capsized the boat and half filled it with water. But the risk, they reckoned, had been worth it. On a flat, volcanic island about two and a half acres in extent nearly 5,000 pairs of great white pelicans were nesting. If they disturbed the colony the whole lot might easily desert. So they made the return trip, fortunately in calm conditions, and prepared to wait until the end of the breeding season before making their next move. Once the breeding pelicans had left the island, they set out again in a more seaworthy craft to build a hide from which to study the pelicans unseen when they returned to nest next year. And this is where Dieter Plage and myself got in on the act. And what an act it turned out to be.

In 1970, Emperor Haile Selassie and his court were still in power. Addis Ababa didn't seem to have changed much since Evelyn Waugh wrote *Black Mischief*. Begging appeared to be the chief home industry. My wife made the mistake of giving a small coin to a small boy. Next day and every day we were in town he was waiting for her outside the slightly dilapidated Ghion Palace Hotel with a large well-nourished grin and his begging bowl. Dieter warned against leaving a vehicle in the main street while you went shopping for supplies. You could easily find that you had no tyres and probably no wheels by the time you came back. I was constantly reminded of Prince Philip's story of his luxury marquee that had no modern or even ancient convenience beyond a simple hole in the ground. Hygiene was not of a high order. Squatting took on a different meaning in Addis. Citizens who felt the urgent need to relieve themselves thought nothing of doing so in the nearest gutter.

The story was going the rounds that the USA had offered aid to instal a modern sewerage system for the city. The government thanked them but said they would rather have an imposing new post office. As a status symbol of modernity, a post office is a far more visible asset. As a result you were well advised, even in the most modern hotels, to put the seat down on the loo if you wished to maintain a breathable atmosphere.

On the subject of drains: my wife once took me on a tour of the ruins of ancient Greece. I am not a great enthusiast for beautifully arranged classical rubble. So I spent the time eaves-dropping on two retired American civil engineers making the tour of a lifetime. Looie and Maureece were interested in ruins up to a point, the point being how the Ancients constructed their sewage systems. When we got to King Minos' palace in Crete, they were considerably impressed. Looie said to Maureece, or maybe the other way round: "You show me a great main drainage system and I'll show you a great civilisation." There's really a lot in that. I kept wondering how they would have placed Addis in the civilisation ratings. On the other hand you could have eaten off the floor in any of the royal stables opposite our hotel.

Dieter, Joan and I intended to stay in the city only as long as it took to organise the supplies needed for a stay on Pelican Island in Lake Shala. In those three days quite a lot happened. To begin with, and nearly to finish with, our hotel went on fire. We were eating in a restaurant about one hundred yards from the Ghion Palace when there was a sudden rush of two or three hundred people in the direction of the hotel. Dieter's opinion was that it was only a street riot and was best and, more important, safely ignored. But then the restaurant began to light up with a lurid red glow. Bells were ringing. "Christ." said Dieter, "it looks as though the Ghion Palace is on fire." And so it was, or anyway one wing of it. We battered our way through the crowd and with less difficulty through a half-hearted cordon of police.

"My cameras!" If the whole of our families had been in the burning building, his cry would have been the same. First things, first. I am not suggesting that Dieter wouldn't have rescued his loved ones had it been necessary. But to cameramen, cameras come very high on the list of loved ones, especially if there are about £50,000 of them threatened by the flames. We reached our rooms to find that the fire was in the next wing some twenty yards away and that a strong wind was keeping it there.

A fire engine arrived and connected up its hoses. A fireman manned a large brass water cannon on top of the engine but no water emerged from the spout. At this point, a policeman climbed on the roof with a revolver and shot out the upper storey windows, a far from ideal move as it allowed in gusts of air to feed the flames. The fireman in charge now climbed heroically onto the roof covered by the man with the water cannon who, perhaps for dramatic reasons—who knows?—kept him covered with muzzle of his brass gun. At which moment, Addis Ababa's hydrant system came unexpectedly to life. A powerful jet caught the fireman on the roof in the small of the back and knocked him off the tiles into the arms of the crowd down below. After that the fire burned itself out, completely destroying one wing of the hotel.

Having made sure the cameras were safe, we decided to try to get some food in the hotel dining room, much of whose floor, possibly as a result of the fire, but more likely due to a freak rainstorm earlier that evening, was under several inches of water. It had been a lively night and wasn't quite over yet. Three joyfully singing and obviously inebriated figures came splashing between the tables. Prince Bernhard of the Netherlands has always shown a keen interest in wildlife. It doesn't get much wilder than a foot safari in the Simien Mountains looking for the rare Simien fox and the even rarer Simien Ibex, especially if your guides and companions have been Leslie Brown and the great John Blower, first met in Uganda and now planning officer for UNO's Food and Agriculture Organisation. The trio disappeared still singing into the smoke-filled night. Pelican Island might seem quite tame after Addis.

Dieter was between marriages. He hadn't yet met his second wife, Mary. His former assistant Rod Borland was operating on his own in Namibia shooting his prize-winning 'Empty Desert'. Perhaps only Dieter would have taken on the pelican island assignment single-handed. His single-handedness was only exceeded by his single-mindedness. Both qualities were accurately portrayed by the life-style he described to us before setting out with him to the island. He had been living and sleeping under a tarpaulin. A tin trunk in the shade of the island's only tree contained all his provisions. The coolest position under the tarpaulin— and cool is only a relative term in this situation—was naturally reserved for film, tape recorders and off-duty cameras. My wife took all this in her stride but visibly brightened when he told her that he had erected a two-man tent as a guest room. Mrs Baker-Willock's reaction to this was feminine in the extreme. When we scoured the shops and stalls of Addis for provisions she somehow managed to find a large packet of paper napkins. By now I had travelled to enough wild places with her to know that it would be unwise to question the purpose of this purchase or, for that matter, any other purchase. It was the handbag and beauty box syndrome once again. As it turned out, the paper napkins were an extremely good buy. Dieter had forgotten to stock up with any toilet paper in his tin trunk.

We made the voyage out to the island in a large rubber boat. These rubber zodiaks will go almost anywhere, and at any speed when pushed by a powerful outboard motor. The zodiak might have coped perfectly well despite the fact that we had nearly one thousand pounds weight of stores and humans aboard, had not the 50 h.p. Mercury engine chosen that moment to develop magneto trouble. Had Leslie Brown been a passenger on that trip that outboard would, without doubt, after a quick whirl round the head as in throwing the hammer, Highland Games fashion, have ended up 800 feet down on the lake bed.

An eleven mile journey that should have taken fifty minutes took well over two hours. This would have been enjoyable enough in normal circumstances. The lake was in one of its benign moods, green slopes reflected in blue water so that you couldn't see the joins. We were accompanied most of the way by large rafts of panicky little grebes that dived en masse as we puttered and stuttered towards them. White-winged black terns fluttered and stooped for insects and took the occasional small fish off the surface. Meantime, the sun beat down. Lake Shala lies at an altitude of over 6,000 feet. Because the atmosphere is appreciably thinner, the ultra-violet light cuts through it and is multiplied by reflection from the lake's glassy surface. The effect on my wife's trim ankles was to make them swell to double their normal size. Dieter's, lips already blistered from the ultra-violet effects of previous stays on the island, began to break out in cold sores. The Beauty Box to the rescue once again. Out and on with the sunblock cream never to be neglected for a second thereafter.

Small wonder that Pelican Island is invisible from the shore. The heat haze was so intense that we were within half a mile before we could make out a faint white blur. We smelt Pelican Island long before we could spot any pelicans on it. The guano produced by fish-eating birds is notoriously high in nitrates, phosphates and stench.

The island resembled an aircraft carrier. The 'flight deck' which accommodated a nesting colony of some 10,000 birds was at the bow. At the stern, the aft section of the island dropped in one step of around twenty feet to a lower deck level. Close to the step was a single stunted acacia tree. Under it was Dieter's tarpaulin shelter and tin trunk. Twenty yards away, we spotted a small orange blob, the guest room Dieter had rigged for his visitors.

The first thing Dieter did after we had pulled the zodiak ashore and unloaded our meagre supplies was to get the cameras into action. What else would a wildlife cameraman do? To reach the hide that Leslie and Emil Urban had built, the three of us had to creep along, bent double, below the ridge of a small, crumbling lava cliff. Dieter mounted two Arrififlex movie cameras in the hide, side by side. Why two? Both commanded exactly the same view.

"The second one is for Leslie."

"But he isn't here and anyway I didn't know he shot film."

"He doesn't. The second Arrie hasn't got any film in it. I've just got into the habit of setting it up. Anyway, you never know I may need a spare. But it's really self-defence. When Leslie's sharing the hide he keeps on telling me to shoot things I've already shot. So I press the button on the empty camera and he hears it whirring away. It keeps the old bastard happy and saves me thousands of feet of film."

Dieter looked out over the shimmering water apprehensively, as if he expected to see Leslie walking towards us on the lake's surface. I understood his nervousness. Leslie was violent in his enthusiasms and tended to irritability when his recommendations were ignored.

I spent many hours with Dieter in that stifling, stink-ridden hide. The heat was about that you would expect in the stoke-hold of a coal-burning freighter in the Red Sea in August. Joan and I were mere visitors. But to spend hour after hour, day after day in that situation! For that you have to be a monomaniac or wildlife cameraman which is another way of saying the same thing. When Dieter carefully lifted the canvas covers over the camera slits, a wonderful sight was revealed. Three feet away, the nearest of the great birds conducted their family life. With the drama unfolding almost in your lap you forgot, at least momentarily, the stink and the heat.

The terminology with which Dieter described that action had been coined by Leslie himself. Four or five days before they are ready to mate, great white pelicans develop a fatty knob above their bills. Leslie had christened these birds the knobbers. Pink-faced knobbers were female: yellow-faced knobbers, the males. Courtship routines included a ridiculously dignified gait described in Leslie's lexicon of ornithology as 'the strutting walk'.

Pods of grey-plumaged young birds huddled together waiting for their parents to return with food. Egyptian vultures attempted to steal eggs from unguarded nests. In Kenya these birds have learned to pick up large stones in their hooked beaks They then drop these on such targets as ostrich and flamingo eggs to smash them. The Pelican Island 'gyppies' obviously hadn't learned the trick: either that, or there were not any suitable heavy stones on the island to drop. Occasionally fish eagles and tawny eagles swooped in looking for titbits. Perhaps the strangest predators of all were the sacred ibises who had their own nesting colony nearby on a small island consisting of columns of basalt. The ibises were on the look-out for any titbit they could find even if it was no more than a fragment of smashed eggshell with some yolk still stuck to it.

After the scorching, shadeless heat of the day, evenings and nights on the island, despite the laval lumpiness under the sleeping bag and the tendency for pelican ticks to get in bed with you, were superb. Sitting there in the moonlight, dining off Dieter's potato salad which he swore would last a week if made in a plastic bucket and kept in a cool-box but never made it beyond forty eight hours, it was easy to sense what the astronauts felt like on the moon when looking back at earth. As a main course Joan cooked Ethiopian mutton chops on a primus stove. From their muscular elasticity we guessed that they must have spent most of their lives attached to sheep galloping around on the precipitous pastures of the Simien Mountains. The first night we talked about lighting a fire. But the lava rock held all the heat we needed. Dieter feared a fire might attract the swarms of lake fly that hovered in clouds over the water. I think, however, that all three of us felt that a fire would somehow break the spell. It would reveal our isolation to the rest of the world— not that anyone was likely to be looking. Far away 'on earth' a fire winked in the darkness, perhaps a Galla village or more likely a bush fire.

The 'after deck' didn't afford much privacy but privacy is a fad of civilisation with which you soon learn to dispense in such circumstances. As to creature comforts: there was no shortage of luke-warm bath water in which the soap lathered wonderfully. The only problem was that the water was so sodary that when you emerged from the lake you had to rub yourself down with a towel very quickly or you instantly turned white with drying sodium carbonate. Perhaps that was the real story of Lot's wife! Dieter, however, had suffered far worse problems with the waters of Shala. In order to get close-ups of pelicans swimming he had persuaded Emil Urban to lend him a stuffed pelican from the university museum. Dieter had mounted this on an inflated inner tube, taken the stuffing out of the pelican's belly and placed a movie camera inside. Swimming in a wet suit and pushing the decoy pelican ahead of him, he got so close to swimming birds that young pelicans even pecked at the camera lens in the hope of persuading the decoy to push predigested fish down their throats. Great footage! The price paid in getting it was that after spending over forty hours in the water filming, the soda had removed most of his skin, not all at once fortunately, but it peeled off bit by bit.

Ten thousand pelicans and their young need an awful lot of fish each day and there are no fish big enough in Shala to satisfy their needs. So having found the nesting colony, the next problem facing Leslie Brown and Emil Urban was to discover where the pelicans went fishing.

Ten miles away, beyond the three thousand foot ridge of wooded hills on the north bank, lies Lake Abiata. Like Lake Naivasha in Kenya, Abiata is fresh probably because a small river flows into it. It is full of fish, mainly tilapia, weighing a pound or more. A pelican needs between three and four pounds each day to feed itself and its young. The pelicans' problem was to get there and back every twenty four hours without burning too much energy. As Leslie and Emil watched during their first trips to the island they saw how it was done.

The pelican airlift to Abiata starts around nine in the morning. Each day we would watch parties of adults fly out and assemble like convoys far out on Shala. Around mid-morning some parties took off and start circling, at first using wing power and then setting their wings and soaring. What they had been waiting for was a thermal of warm air rising on the far shore. Sometimes they spotted a spiralling dust cloud, but mostly they seemed to know by instinct when a thermal was building up.

On the ground, a pelican is a large ungainly bird weighing twenty five pounds. Wings-set, on a rising column of hot air, it becomes a gracefully efficient sailplane. Up and up and over the crest of the distant range of hills the first squadrons soared, to be followed by party after party as the day wore on.

In mid -afternoon, the birds who had been away at Abiata fishing for the past twenty four hours made the return journey, using the same soaring technique to cross the mountains but this time with a crop packed with fish. The great birds would approach the island several hundred feet up, then, partly closing their wings, descend like falling bombs and with much the same whistling sound, levelling out to touch down in the colony. The young and parents knew each other instantly, whether by sound or sight, I could never tell. The parent bird would make the grey youngster chase it before allowing it to feed, a principle of having to 'sing for your supper' repeated in many bird species as part of the learning process. A delightful aftermath of each spectacular landing was a gentle snowfall of breast feathers wrenched from the descending birds by the slipstream.

For the Abiata end of the story we needed Leslie Brown. to help us find where the Shala birds went fishing. So, at the end of a week, we made the eleven mile voyage back to the mainland with the motor still misfiring and my wife's ankles still swelling to make a rendezvous with the great man. This time it took two and a half hours and the water was decidedly choppy. We deflated the zodiak and stowed it on the roof-rack of Dieter's Land Rover. This still had not only all four wheels and tyres but some petrol in the tank due to Dieter's foresight in paying quite a large sum to the villainous-looking head man of a Galla village backed up with the threat that, he, Dieter, personally knew the Emperor. Next morning Leslie drove into camp nursing a considerable hang-over acquired at a farewell party for John Blower who was moving on to set up an outpost for UNO's FAO in Indonesia. In passing I should add that John Blower was always moving on to another country on behalf of the Food and Agriculture Organisation. Being a most efficient man in the most laid-back fashion, John always managed to come up with a conservation strategy for the country concerned which the FAO financed and the government of the country concerned sometimes tried to implement. As a parting gift he had left Leslie this king hang-over.

The morning did not start well. To begin with we had to re-inflate the zodiak using a foot pump like a large black beach ball. The theory was that if you stamped heavily and repeatedly on this, air was driven up a black rubber hose into our rubber boat. A gang of young Galla, lead by a gangly youth who was plainly too big for his sandals which were cut from an old motor tyre, gathered to watch us perform this feat. The youth would obviously have been trouble in any society. He found Leslie's attempts to pump air into the boat amusing. Even without speaking a word of Galla it was fairly obvious that his comments were disparaging. Leslie tolerated this longer than I had expected. Then, seizing the pump by the rubber hose, and whirling the black beach ball round his head, he charged the gang of Galla delinquents shouting: 'Sons of bitches and jackals' and caught the offender in the stomach with the beach ball. Shades of Culloden! The Galla fled.

We tied the now inflated zodiak to the roof rack and prepared to drive the twenty miles to Abiata. Leslie was purring sweetly after his victory over the Galla. All might have gone well had not a really stunning, bare-breasted Galla maiden passed along the track just above us.

"Ach," exulted Dieter, "a dolly-knobber." It was after all a fairly harmless adaptation of Leslie's own pelican-speak. Leslie, I am fairly certain, would have approved of this usage had not Dieter in his excited state put the Land Rover into reverse instead of first and backed the rear wheels over the edge of a small precipice. One hour later, after a good deal of jacking up and winching out, and some fairly vivid gaelic, we were on our way to Abiata.

This trip became a voyage of discovery. It had been established that the pelicans caught their fish in Abiata but it is a large lake so where exactly did they go fishing? It quickly became clear that, having crossed the mountain range, the skeins landed far out in open water. If this was where they were fishing, Dieter's task of filming them was not going to be easy. But great whites, unlike the African pink-backed pelicans, fish as a fleet, dipping their beaks in unison and driving the fish ahead of them, often cornering a shoal among reedy inlets. To succeed they must obviously do this in shallowish water.

For once we had got lucky. Close to shore was an area of former woodland. The numerous trees had been killed when the lake level rose as the African lakes tend to do from time to time. The trees were full of cormorants and nesting darters, kingfishers, ducks, including shoveler and mallard, and herons of several species. A bird city with plenty of trees in which camera hides could be safely built. And to top it all, the great white pelicans of Shala were fishing among the bird city's busy streets. A cameraman can hardly ask for more. Even Leslie was mollified and was already demanding that Dieter get some hand-held shots of the knobbers fishing.

So Dieter immediately got the camera whirring to keep Leslie happy, knowing perfectly well that the real stuff would have to be shot from the steady platform of a tree hide and not from a rubber boat rocked by the hero of Culloden's vigour and enthusiasm.

Lest I give the impression that Leslie was all fire and brimstone, let me quickly say that he was a delightful companion from whom I personally learned something new at almost every sentence, if only a new gaelic oath.

There is a postcript to the Shala-Abiata story. Two mornings later, when Dieter, Joan and myself were Land Rovering along the rough track to the Abiata fishing ground, there was suddenly a hoarse chortling in the sky. A flight of something, or rather somethings, that gave you an idea of what the flight of our long bowmen's arrows must have looked like at Agincourt, passed in front of the windscreen and descended, like a flight of arrows, on a small sandy beach by a stream to our left.

"Stop," Dieter. "Sand grouse!"

We stopped. In the next six and a half minutes—no more and no less—clouds of these beautiful dove-like birds appeared as dots far out on the savanna, poured onto the beach, marched down in packs to the waterside, took five or six sips and flew out again. They came with a noise of wings like the roar of a jet engine. They came in one side of an acacia tree and flew out on the other. The traffic pattern never altered. They came and came. Each party did the same thing. Each party flew out the same way to be replaced by another one. And then suddenly, the beach was empty, the sky silent. For once, even Dieter was caught flat-footed. He hadn't even got his camera out of the case.

"Tomorrow morning. At the same time," I said.

"Will they come again?" Joan asked.

"There's a good chance."

"Why this tiny little beach? Aren't there other places to get a drink. All those birds. Thousands of them."

"Did you see what they were doing apart from drinking? The males spread their breast feathers to trap water there. The feathers are specially adapted. They'll carry the water in those feathers twenty miles back to their young."

"Only the males?" my wife asked.

"You females can't have it all your way when it comes to rearing young."

"Amazing. How do you know all this about sand grouse?"

"Didn't you know? I'm a wood pigeon fanatic. Sand grouse are a distant relation."

So we came back next morning, a little earlier to set up the cameras. And at a quarter to nine on the dot the chortling started and the arrows flew and the film whirred through the camera.

Leslie had just returned from a trip to Addis. I told him about the sand grouse.

"Chestnut-bellied sand grouse, I expect". I told him we already knew that. Dieter and I reckon there are ten thousand of them.

So Leslie came next day. Another repeat performance. After it was over he said: "You boys can't count. More like 50,000 of them."

I wasn't going to argue with the great man. Besides I suspect he was right. The chestnut -bellied sand grouse kept it up for five days. On the sixth day not a single bird showed up. But then that's sand grouse for you. And that's wildlife filming for you. Sometimes, as I said earlier, you get lucky when you least expect it. But never tell anyone that it's luck.

Great white pelicans migrate along much of the Rift Valley. The site of their main breeding colony was a mystery until Leslie Brown and Emil Urban discovered it on an island in Lake Shala in the Ethiopian Rift.

Lake Shala pelicans coming into breeding plumage. The bird preening on the left is a 'knobber'. The knob on its bill developes when the bird is ready to mate.

A movie camera inside a stuffed pelican enabled Dieter Plage to film close-ups of swimming pelicans. Young birds even pecked at the camera hoping to be fed.

Thesiger's Walk on the Wild Side.

I had much more to lose than my wife. Wilfred Thesiger had had a great deal more to lose than either of us. In our case my wife couldn't possibly lose what I was putting at slight risk. To begin with, she didn't have any.

In 1934, Wilfred, now *Sir* Wilfred, a young man, fresh from university, collected a small caravan around him and, against the best advice then available in Addis Ababa, set out to solve the mystery of the Awash river.

Has it ever struck you that an intrepid someone, starting with Bruce, Burton, Baker and Speke was always setting out into the interior of darkest Africa to solve a mystery? The mystery of the Nile sources, both Blue and White; the mysterious whereabouts of Dr Livingstone; the mystery of the Mountains of the Moon and the course of the Congo river; the mysteriously late appearances of Lakes Baringo and Rudolf upon the map; and, as lately recounted, the mysteries of where three million flamingoes and 10,000 great white pelicans nested. Now here, in 1934, was another mystery. Where did the Awash River go? It poured down from the Ethiopian highlands, disappeared into the desert, headed in the approximate direction of Djibouti but never reached that port on the Gulf of Aden.

Wilfred Thesiger was determined to find out where the river emerged. The main hazard of his exploration, apart from the usual ones of hunger, thirst and disease, was that the Awash flowed through Danakil country or, to give the people and their desert their more accurate name, the Kingdom of the Afars.

Now the Afars have never taken kindly to strangers in fact they have always made a habit of killing and castrating them and wearing the dried testicles round their necks as trophies. This, for a young man in his twenties, was daunting to say the least. But Thesiger does not and did not daunt easily. A boxing Blue at Oxford, World War Two service in the Long Range Desert Group and SAS, a DSO and two post-war crossings of the Empty Quarter of Arabia testify to that.

He recruited a young Danakil guide, who probably saved Thesiger several times when an attack threatened. The young explorer reached the Sultan of the Afars in his capital Asaita and obtained permission to continue his exploration. The Sultan's word in Danakil country is the absolute and only law. Eventually, he reached the end of the Awash river. He found that it simply disappeared into a huge soda lake below sea level, its waters evaporating as fast, and sometimes faster, than they flowed in. The lake should perhaps be called Lake Thesiger. It is, however, known as Lake Abbaye.

Now the proposal was that we, that is myself, Dieter Plage, and inevitably my wife, should follow in Thesiger's heroic footsteps and record the story of the Danakil and their country before it was too late.

The mind behind this proposal and the instinct that guided it was that of *Survival's* chairman Aubrey Buxton. He felt that as a leading, perhaps at that time the leading wildlife and wild places film unit, we had a duty to record this wilderness and its magnificent if terrifying occupants before civilisation disposed of it, destroyed it or corrupted it. In this instinct he was perfectly correct.

I will freely confess that at the outset that I was not entirely relaxed about the project. Losing one's testicles, even in mid-life, is not a prospect any red-blooded man relishes. We had, however, several things going for us. An intrepid amateur explorer friend of Aubrey's, a stockbroker called Brian MacDermot, had several times ventured into the land of the Afars and had emerged intact. Brian (pronounced Bree-an) took the view that if we could reach the Sultan and win his support, then, like Thesiger, we had a fair chance of surviving to make our film. When we parted, Brian made his most encouraging remark to date. "Remember," he said, "that the locals are far keener on black balls than on white ones."

At this point, I must say that I had only to survive the reconnaissance. Dieter Plage faced a much more daunting prospect. It might take him as long as six months to get his footage, at any moment of which some Danakil warrior might be tempted to take a pot shot before drawing his castration knife. Would the Sultan's protection—if we could get it—last that long? At that point, no one could possibly say.

Our other trump card was that we had friendly relations with an international trading company called Mitchell Cotts. The company had large cotton plantations at Tendaho in an enclave on the edge of Danakil country. The Sultan, a highly commercial ruler, had cotton plantations of his own and stood to benefit greatly from the success of the Mitchell Cotts operation. Another way to put it was that, rather like Al Capone, the Sultan was selling Mitchell Cotts protection. He would keep his wild tribesmen under control in return for technical advice and financial support, a perfectly proper procedure in most African countries and a matter of routine politics where the ruler of the Afars was concerned.

While staying with the Mitchell Cotts plantation manager awaiting the long-drawn out negotiations necessary to get an interview with the Sultan, we had a vivid demonstration of the protection system at work. Word came that Danakil tribesmen had been invading the Mitchell Cotts plantations at night and grazing their camels on the cotton. The evening was interrupted by the arrival of the Sultan's chief of police, the *Feterari,* a civilised-looking, hawklike man in a white robe with a long-barrelled revolver stuck in his belt. Incongruously he wore glasses with brilliants in frames reminiscent of Dame Edna Everage. The resemblance ended there. The *Feterari* demanded that the plantation manager accompany him in his Land Rover. When they came across a party of Danakil illegally grazing their stock, the *Feterari* ordered his police to seize one of the men, bind his legs between two short poles. A third pole was then inserted and levered about until the sinews twisted and the bones grated. Lesser miscreants, I learned, were sometimes hung head-down over a pit of burning pepper or had their legs flayed by being rubbed with roughened, wetted planks.

The other great advantage we had over Wilfred Thesiger was that we didn't have to walk to Asaita. Mitchell Cotts owned a twin-engined Aztec flown by a pilot called Tuckwell to whom John Blower had said on being introduced: And what else do you do well? Funny how one remembers these social pleasantries long after much more absorbing things have been forgotten.

So we flew down to Asaita accompanied by Mitchell Cotts' Danakil interpreter who might have been, and probably had been, educated at Oxford or Cairo. He spoke excellent English. More important, his Afar was fluent.

We landed in a dust cloud about a mile from the Sultan's capital. The desert looked like one big airstrip, yellow, level and lacking in trees though I suspect the Sultan had had a few of his lads flattening the odd termite mound and rolling rocks out of the way. Captain Tuckwell put us down with scarcely a bump and we walked into town,

I had a distinct feeling that I now knew what Omdurman had looked, smelt and felt like in the Mad Mahdi's heyday. The streets were naked lava floes. One of the first things we passed was the graveyard, an area of level ground covered with cairns made of laval rock. This was how the Danakil buried their dead, presumably because they couldn't dig them in. Ahead lay a group of squat rectangular yellow buildings and the mosque. Surprisingly, a battered pick-up truck came to meet us and take us to the Sultan's palace, or rather the ante-chamber that turned out to be the waiting room of Asaita's leading and possibly only brothel. In our forty minutes wait, several customers passed through. Not one of them was Danakil. They were all *ferengi*-foreigners-men from the high plateau imported to work on the Sultan's cotton plantations. That these despised outsiders were able to survive at all was a tribute to the Sultan's absolute power. Any Danakil who had laid a knife on them would undoubtedly have been strung up above a pit of burning pepper, or worse.

In fact, the prime targets of Danakil trophy hunters were the neighbouring tribe, the Issas. If you look on a good map you will see this barren area in the Horn of Africa described as the territory of the Issas and Afars. To my eyes, the two tribes looked identical. Danakil men were tall, lithe and athletic with their fuzzy hair piled high on their heads. Issas likewise. The young women, bare-breasted and slim with fine ancient Egyptian features, could have held their own on any *haute couture* catwalk in London, Paris or New York. Among their own kind the Danakil we watched through the brothel window appeared gentle and courteous, both men and women kissing hands on meeting and greeting. And these were the people who considered it the height of fair play to shoot the identical looking Issa men in the back and chop the testicles off the corpse! There has to be, or so scientists will tell you, an anthropological explanation of such apparent behavioural contradictions. In this case I am inclined to believe that the anthropologists had got it right. The savagery, and particularly the castration ritual, was at base inspired by the shortage of water and waterholes in the Danakil desert. The obvious way to limit the number of rival users of this limited resource was to kill them and give a potent signal that further increase in the Issa population would be unwelcome and ill-advised.

Despite MacDermot's encouraging words about the relative attractiveness of black and white testicular trophies, both Dieter and I began to feel, as the minutes ticked by, that passing Danakil warriors were regarding us from the waist downwards with increasing interest. As small boys and bullies will, we laid off our anxieties by taking it out on the softest target, in this case my poor wife. We constantly reminded her that, since this was a Muslim community, she was less than the dust and might give grave offence if she forgot to walk well and humbly to our rear when we were finally admitted to the Presence.

The Sultan's palace was not, well, what you might call palatial, perhaps more like a territorial army drill hall set down in the middle of a desert. Our entry into the precincts was, however, impressive. The Sultan's bodyguard swarmed around us. It seemed to be composed of dark-skinned buccaneers whom Henry Morgan might have rejected as being too rough for the work he had in mind. The bodyguard was armed with rifles from every army that had ever fought in the deserts of Africa—the stalwart of the British Army in two world wars, the Short-magazine Lee Enfield (SMLE); the earlier Lee-Metford; Italian carbines; German Mausers; American carbines. The members of this villainous looking gang were, I discovered later, mostly related to the Sultan, about as good a life insurance policy as you are likely to get in Danakil country.

The plans we had outlined for my wife held up extremely well in our advance through the courtyard. As instructed, she did walk well in our rear. However, the moment we entered the palace, things began to go wrong. The Sultan, an enormous man in a flowing white robe, a walking marquee rather than a mere human tent, singled the lady out for greeting and indicated that he sit beside her at the plain wooden council table. This was not at all what we had expected. The Sultan overflowed his chair and the table on which was set an alarm clock. We had been warned that this clock was pre-set and that, when the alarm went off, that was the end of the interview. We began our dialogue, our interpreter adding to it a good ration of flowery flattery. I'd seen this sort of thing in the movies. I just couldn't believe that it was me taking part in this stilted and long-winded exchange. I seem to be playing a part in one of those made-for-television series about big business negotiating with an unnamed Arab potentate for the oil concession. In fact what this was really about was to get permission to film in the Sultan's highly lethal country without getting chopped up, or, worse still, off.

I heard myself saying: "Please tell His Excellency that he has a truly exciting country." (Understatement of the millennium).

Long pause while this was encoded into Afar.

A lot more deceptively cherubic smiling from the Sultan followed by a cascade of words about half the length of the Koran.

Shorter pause while this was decoded into English which came across as simply. "His Excellency wishes you to feel welcome."

We kept this verbal knock-up going for more than ten minutes. I began to fear that the alarm was about to go off at any second, leaving a great deal of business unfinished.

We weren't through the preliminaries yet. We exchanged lengthy insincerities such as: "Please tell the Sultan we would be delighted to welcome him in London if he would honour us with a visit."

Christ!I thought. What am I saying?

Later I discovered that this visit might, indeed, have come about. Mitchell Cotts had already flown him to Nairobi in Captain Tuckwell's Aztec and were seriously considering the advantages of a diplomatic pilgrimage to Claridges. M. Cotts had far bigger bucks at stake than we did!

The Sultan next paid extravagant compliments to my wife. Serve her right, I thought, if he's considering her as an addition to his harem. This took another five minutes at the end of which the Sultan turned off the alarm (good sign) and clapped his hand for refreshment to be brought.. Would we care for coffee? The coffee arrived in half gourds. It smelt strongly of ginger and maybe pepper. Beyond this was a distinctive but elusive flavour. It was only later that I discovered that the Sultan's kitchen staff, possibly to conserve water, frequently scoured out the pots with camel urine.

The alarm clock never did go off. In ten minutes, over the coffee, the Sultan wound up our business as efficiently as any chairman of a nationalised industry. It seemed that he actually wanted the outside world to know about his country. Not only did he approve of our plans but he guaranteed Dieter a safe-conduct in the form of his nephew who would accompany him wherever he wished to go. The assumption was that since no one would dare to lay a finger on the Sultan's nephew, no one would dare to attack the *ferengi*, Dieter Plage.

There was one big surprise in store. When the audience was over, the Sultan led my wife out into the courtyard whereupon the piratical bodyguard instantly prostrated themselves in the dust. Previously, no one had ever dared to ask the Sultan if he minded having his picture taken. It was just assumed by all concerned that he *would* mind. This turned out not to be the case which is how the only still picture of the Sultan of the Afars came to be taken—by Mrs Baker-Willock. It hangs on the wall of our downstairs loo to this day.

What made the Sultan so willing to give us permission to film his forbidden kingdom? My belief is that he was an extremely sharp operator who saw that the feudal Kingdom of the Afars hung by a slender threat of history. Sooner or later the old regime in Ethiopia would disappear. In fact, it disappeared far sooner than any of us expected to be replaced by a communist regime with little sympathy for independent and possibly rebelliously savage states within it boundaries. The Sultan no doubt saw that the more closely he could integrate with the outside world and with the West in particular, the better his and the Danakil's chances of survival. When, a year or two before, the Queen of England visited Emperor Haile Selasse in Addis, the Emperor had sent a message to the Sultan requesting that he attend the court in her honour. To which the Sultan replied that he wasn't going all that way just to meet some foreign woman. Such glorious days of feudal independence were numbered. I believe that the Sultan of the Afars was astute enough to realise this.

The Sultan was as good as his word. But his nephew was not always able to accompany Dieter. This was this marvellous cameraman's most hazardous assignment and I believe 'The Forbidden Desert of the Danakil', although not a wildlife film, was his greatest achievement. Dieter faced ambush and death several times. His closest call was when a party of Afar threatened to, and came very close to, throwing him and his camera into a boiling volcanic spring.

My plan for the film was that it should follow as closely as possible Wilfred Thesiger's exploration of the Awash river. At the time we made the film, Thesiger, who lived in a remote part of the Northern Frontier District of Kenya, came to London once or twice a year. Each day, in bowler hat, wearing a pin-striped suit, and carrying a rolled umbrella, Wilfred Thesiger, the archetype London clubman of an earlier age, would walk to the Traveller's Club. He allowed us to film him doing so, a remarkable contrast to the nomadic peoples among whom he spent much of his life.

I persuaded him to tell the story on film of the exploration of the Danakil country he made, as a twenty three-year-old, nearly fifty years previously.

He recalled the Danakil as a happy people... "though they might be jumped or ambushed at any time, they avoided the stresses and strains of so-called civilised man." He went on:

"You had no status as a man unless you had killed several men from the rival tribe. I arrived in a village where the head man had just died and his son had taken over. But the son had no standing. He had only killed one rival. So the next morning he went across the river into Issa territory and shot three men. He probably shot them in the back, in Danakil country there's nothing wrong in that.

After all, if you're hunting lion you don't warn the lion that you're there. Of course, there was a great celebration in the village when the boy returned. The day after we left, the other lot came across the river and wiped out the boy's village."

Thesiger added in a phrase that has never left me: "I took a rather good photograph of the boy when he returned from his raid" (pause)... "*Nice* lad!" I've somehow always treasured those two words. Even more have I treasured the phrase with which Wilfred Thesiger ended that interview.

"These ancient cultures and civilisations," he said "are *vanishing like snow on the lawn in a hot sun.*"

The sun melted the snow very soon afterwards. The Ethiopian revolution deposed the Sultan who fled to Muslim friends across the Red Sea. Four hundred Afar were slaughtered by government forces from Addis. The Sultan's palace was bombarded by tank shells and machine-gun fire. It all vanished like snow on the lawn in a hot sun.

Sir Wilfred Thesiger outside the Travellers' Club. In 1934 he took his life in his hands to follow the Awash river through hostile Danakil country.

Danakil tribesmen perform a war dance to get themselves worked into a fighting mood before a raid. The knives at their belts are for castrating enemies.

A Danakil warrior guards a precious waterhole. Castration and the wearing of 'trophies' symbolises the need to limit their rivals' population.

Gorillas in the Mountain Mist

The moment you got into Zaire you started to think about how you were going to get out. The welcome had not been warm. Joan and I arrived at the Customs Post at the Rwanda-Zaire border. It was the sort of set-up you see in very 'B' movies. The guard, you could hardly call him a customs official, sat with his feet up on a rickety table and showed no inclination to look at our passports. Dieter who had come to meet us on the Zaire side in a clapped-out Toyota called across to be patient. Dieter was a master of dealing with reluctant, hostile or bent customs officials. Usually all these qualities are combined in one person. But then our ace wildlife cameraman had had plenty of practice and knew exactly how much cash to slip into his passport in Sumatra, India or for that matter Zaire. This he intimated across the national boundary, symbolished by a pole and a couple of petrol drums, was not the time to try bribery.A lady from the American consulate in Bukavu who had come to collect the diplomatic mail confirmed this.

"Try to bribe them and they can stick you in gaol and it will cost you twice as much to get out." She told my wife: "You're lucky the woman isn't on. If she's in the mood she can body-search you and confiscate your cosmetics as an encore." I had half hoped that the consulate lady packed some clout that could ease our passage into the Republic of Zaire. No such luck. At the Rwanda-Zaire border there was no such thing as diplomatic privilege let alone immunity.

After half an hour, the duty customs officer took his feet off the table. He examined our passports and pointed out that the immigration officer in Kigali where we had landed had stamped Joan's passport but not mine. No doubt this had been deliberate. Technically, I was an illegal immigrant. In the circumstances, the fine of 40 US dollars seemed a far better alternative to a visit to the local gaol. We paid the fine and the customs man waved us through. We were in Zaire.

Dieter waved cheerily to the customs man. "He's okay. He knows I'll bribe him when the time comes to get out."

On the way into Bukavu, Dieter, who viewed the ways of unstable African states with a mixture of intolerance and amusement, filled us in on the local situation.

"We should be okay with the police today. It's near the beginning of the month. They've just been paid. In two or three weeks time they're liable to stop you and tell you your headlights aren't working which is not surprising since it's broad daylight. They'll fine you on the spot. For God's sake don't argue. Just pay the fine. It's their only way to make up their pay."

In their white steel helmets and 'shades', the Bukavu police reminded me forcibly of Papa Doc's Haitian *tons-tons macoute* as described by Graham Greene in *The Comedians.*

The Toyota lurched from rut to rut. "Mobutu", Dieter explained, "visited here about three weeks ago. So the locals filled in all the pot-holes with mud and painted white lines over them. After he'd gone, it rained like hell and all the mud and white lines washed away. Typical! Oh, and by the way, about President Mobutu. They run up the flag every morning and everybody stands to attention and sings the Mobutu anthem which starts *Mobutu Sesso Seko...* I think the words go on to describe their beloved President as the cock who fertilises all the hens in the district... So stand up and,whatever you do, for God's sake don't laugh."

I was already feeling that Zaire had a very black atmosphere about it.

Adrien Deschryver restored one's sanity. Adrien was the man we had come to work with and the man with whom Dieter and Lee Lyon had been working for the past few months. Adrien owned what was now the Kahuzi-Biega National Park for Gorillas. A good many people had heard of Diane Fossey's work with the mountain gorillas in neighbouring Rwanda. Until that moment no one had heard of Adrien and, to tell the truth, I believe he would have preferred things to remain that way.

It all came together like this. Professor Bernhard Grzimek, Director of Frankfurt Zoo, had been a good friend of *Survival* since its start. Bernhard Grzimek (pronounced *Jimmek*) was really a one-man World Wildlife Fund. He appeared on his own, to us, crashingly boring TV wildlife show in Germany and he ran a magazine called *Das Tier* through both of which he raised enormous sums for conservation worldwide. Soon after World War Two, he and his son Michael learned to fly and bought a Fieseler Storch, the light communications and spotter monoplane used by the Luftwaffe. They painted it in zebra stripes and flew it out to East Africa. There, on the Serengeti, they made a famous film called *Serengeti Shall Not Die.* Film and book had a great impact on a world increasingly aware of the need to conserve African wildlife.While making the film and flying out of the Ngorongoro Crater in Tanzania, Michael hit a vulture, crashed and was killed. Bernhard adopted Alan Root almost as a surrogate son and certainly as a filming partner. From that moment on, Bernhard became an invaluable ally of *Survival*, introducing us to Alan and later to Dieter Plage. He poured money into worthwhile conservation projects through the Frankfurt Zoological Society. One of the latest of these projects was that of the Belgian Adrien Deschryver in Zaire.

Adrien remains one of the most impressive people I have ever met. A quiet, soft-spoken, extremely reserved man, he and his family had in Colonial days owned extensive tea and coffee plantations on the twin mountains Kahuzi and Biega in what was then known as the Belgian Congo. When you met him, you knew that you were being summed up and somehow would have to pass a test, the best way of doing so was not to try but just to be yourself and hope that that was good enough. In return you felt that if you were ever in a bad spot this was the first man you would pick to be on your side. In another setting, you might have taken him for a bank manager, or maybe an officer in the Foreign Legion. He was utterly self-contained and yet radiated authority, the sort you don't have to use except in extreme emergency.

During the Simba uprisings of the civil war in the Congo, Adrien had turned his house into a fortress, clearing all the bush around for fifty yards to give him a clear field of fire should be find himself under siege. Instead at a time when the main street of Bukavu was piled high with dead Adrien had gone over to the offensive and rounded up 500 Simba rebels with a Jeep and a heavy machine-gun. At the moment he judged most dangerous to his African wife and three small children he had evacuated them at night across Lake Kivu. A man who preferred a peaceful life but definitely a good man to have on your side if the going got otherwise.

Dieter and his now fully fledged assistant Lee Lyon had had to pass such a test, though in a much more rigorous way than either Joan or I. At least we started with Dieter's and Lee's recommendation. When Grzimek suggested to Adrien that Dieter and Lee were the right people to film his beloved gorillas, Adrien was cautious. He had already had one bad experience with a TV documentary crew. He was not anxious to expose himself or his gorillas to another mob that just wanted dramatic shots of the great animals. Grzimek explained that this pair were specialists, dedicated to filming the whole story of the gorillas and Adrien's work with them.

So Adrien met Dieter and Lee in Bukavu, took them into the forest and introduced them to Kasimir. It was the Boadicea story all over again. Kasimir was the six-foot male silverback who dominated the gorilla family that Adrien had been studying. If Boadicea's charge was impressive, Kasimir's was shattering. After this huge animal had rushed at them screaming, mouth open, great arms flailing, Adrien looked round for Dieter and Lee, expecting to find them prudently retreating. Instead, they were both calmly filming. Adrien realised that he was dealing with something different.

I assume we passed the test or maybe it was Dieter's good word that persuaded Adrien to take us each day walking in his forest looking for Kasimir and his family. Once again, my wife came up trumps. It wasn't exactly easy going for a housewife from Surrey, even one with a good deal of safari time on her clock. In fact conditions of undergrowth and tree cover were so tough that Dieter himself had not been optimistic about the filming possibilities. He had promised himself that if he had ten minutes of useable film in the can after six weeks he would persevere and try to bring home at least a gorilla half hour. However, a powerful chemistry was at work in the forests of Kahuzi-Biega, though in one respect none of us realised just how powerful that chemistry would prove to be.

By the time we joined them it was obvious that Adrien, Dieter and Lee had formed a strong bond of friendship. Adrien's original reticence had turned first into guarded co-operation and then into complete determination to see that his gorillas were fully documented on film. But Dieter still had to overcome Adrien's reluctance to have his own work with the gorillas recorded. Gradually this obstacle fell away, too, and we were on course for making a splendid one-hour record of both the gorillas and the man who studied them..

Like many of the best practical conservationists, Adrien was no scientist. Once the civil war was over, he decided that he had seen enough violence and killing. Now all he wished to do was to study and save the magnificent animals who lived on his mountains. So he spent four years in company with one or two pygmy companions, notably the little shrivelled man known as Patrice, just getting to know one family of gorillas. Patrice's knowledge was invaluable. He and his companions had spent their lives hunting gorillas for food. Though they undoubtedly thought

Adrien was crazy, they were happy to help him. Apart from the fact the pygmies were being fed and paid, they undoubtedly admired what he was doing—another tribute to the magnetism of the man. I often heard Patrice tease his boss. Once after a close encounter with Kasimir, he told Adrien; "He doesn't like me. He knows my family ate his father." It was probably true.

Even with the help of Patrice, the study wasn't easy, but gradually, Kasimir and his family of some twenty odd animals came to accept Adrien. By the end of four years, he probably knew more about the mountain gorilla than anyone with the possible exception of Diane Fossey in the Virunga Volcanoes in the adjacent country of Rwanda. Unlike Fossey , who was eventually mysteriously murdered, possibly because she took too possessive an attitude to both gorilla habitat and the gorillas who lived on what she sometimes regarded as *her* mountain, Adrien had no such sense of possession. In fact, he gave his family estates as a gorilla reserve and Mobutu recognised his work by gazetting Kahuzi-Biega as a National Park.

Each day started by finding the whereabouts of Kasimir's family. Sometimes during the filming, Dieter and Lee walked—hardly the word for progress through the mountain forests—for twenty four hours before they caught up with them. To a certain extent, their whereabouts was governed by what they were eating at the time. There were other signs: the nests of branches which the family had built in which to spend the night; droppings; wild banana trees that had been ripped apart as a desert course; and at a certain season, the *bwamba* trees, a large oak-like tree that bore a fruit that was apparently the gorilla equivalent of caviare.

Realising our inadequacies when it came to rain forest travel, Adrien posted one of the pygmies to go ahead and slash the worst of the undergrowth with a panga. It helped but it still wasn't exactly a rural ramble. Joan did gallantly. Again, I think she was running on pure adrenaline—I know I was. The thought that somewhere just ahead or—so one hoped—were up to twenty four of some of the most powerful animals on earth lent extra power to tired leg muscles.

Often, though you couldn't see them because the gorillas didn't want you to see them—you knew that the family was all around you. Grunts and calls and, most exciting of all, the beating of gorilla breasts told you that they were only thirty or forty yards away in the dense undergrowth.

Early travellers in the Congo— and a good many feature films—reported and portrayed this beating of the chest with cupped hands as aggression. Adrien and

Diane Fossey, however, believed it to be a means of communication between individuals in a gorilla group and I'm pretty sure that this is the truth. Whenever a male gorilla made a threat charge there was certainly no breast beating, though a great deal of vocalisation and slashing of branches with the arms. I recalled Douglas-Hamilton's words about elephants: Never forget that elephants have been perfecting their threat charges for millions of years. My impression was that gorillas had been at it just as long.

So you followed Adrien's lead and kept slogging away through the forest. Almost invariably Kasimir would 'agree' to meet Adrien at some point in the day. It was almost as if the great silverback was granting an audience. Usually Kasimir would chose a comparatively open space and recline in the undergrowth rather like an emperor holding court. Behind him, females, young and lesser males would hang about, appearing from time to time, seemingly assured that if the head of the family thought it was all right to confer with this strange troupe of near gorillas—us—then they could relax, also.

Adrien believed that Kasimir took him as the leader, albeit a fairly junior one, of another gorilla group. I think it was a fair bet that this was true. The drill that we all had to follow when these meetings took place was well-known and rigorously obeyed. I had the very distinct feeling that if we ignored the rules, then we could be in bad trouble. The pygmy trackers had their own rules.

With the exception of Patrice, they withdrew well to the rear. The pygmies did not like gorillas and I think it is pretty fair to say that the gorillas didn't like them. Dieter said it was because they bore too close a resemblance to each other. In fact he knew, as we all did, that the dislike was based on old enmities. The pygmies had hunted the great apes and the great apes recalled that it wasn't so long ago since these little forest men had been their sworn enemies.

Though Kasimir as a fully mature silverback was the undoubted boss of the clan, there were two subordinate adult males. One, Hannibal, was easily recognisable because his mouth was permanently twisted in what looked like a rather superior grin. The second male, Musharamena (he who eats with his mouth open) took a special delight in discomforting the pygmies. Knowing that most of them served as bearers and walked at the rear of our small column, Musharamena would delight in spending hours outflanking us so that he could charge the pygmies from the rear. It was hard not to imagine that this was a gorilla game. If so, the pygmies did not regard it as fun. When Musharamena put in his charge there was a sudden explosion of little black men in the forest to the rear scattering in all directions. No one ever got hurt. Adrien regarded the whole thing with amused tolerance and a Gallic, or rather Belgique, shrug.

Even Adrien would approach Kasimir with great respect, usually talking to him softly in French. *Du calme, Kasimir. Du Calme*...and, if Kasimir showed signs of restiveness, *Assez, Kasimir. Assez*...It invariably was enough. Adrien would then sit down close to the great clan leader, and likewise sometimes with Hannibal, who was definitely number two in the family, pretending to be eating whatever it was that the gorillas had been eating. Often the mock meal was a handful of *galium*, the weed that grows in British hedgerows and gardens and which we call 'bedstraw'. But there was a ritual to be observed with this. If you have handled bedstraw you will know that it feels sticky to the touch. Examine the weed and you will find that its leaves are covered with little hooks. The gorillas quite understandably do not relish 'sticky' plants and so they roll the *galium* up into a ball before swallowing it. Thus Adrien, when mock eating this weed, would first roll it into a ball before putting it to his mouth. Kasimir and Hannibal both seemed to appreciate the reality of his mime.

Meantime the rest of us followed the drill as laid down by Adrien. We formed single file behind him so that at his first approach we did not appear to the gorillas as a menacing mob. Later, when the 'audience' was established we were allowed very slowly to move a pace or so to one side in order to get a better view. Kasimir appeared to notice this but accepted it as non-menacing. Cameras were allowed at the second or third meeting and then only if you moved them to your eye very, very slowly. The worst thing you could do was to point. Gorillas, rightly, hated being pointed at. Almost certainly they regarded this as a potentially menacing movement.

And then, after perhaps ten minutes, sometimes more, Kasimir would intimate that the audience was over, simply by rolling over and gradually moving off into the undergrowth almost in slow motion. I never saw him stand up when concluding a meeting with Adrien. If he had done so,then we might all have had something to be concerned about.

In his increasingly rare unsociable moods, Kasimir would sometimes charge. I suppose gorillas have moods just like their distant human relatives. Kasimir's charge which happily stopped short of an actual assault took a great deal of getting used to. Once again Douglas-Hamilton's reassuring words came back to me. "Always remember," he had said. "that these big animals don't really want trouble. They're big enough to know that they are not really threatened but that doesn't stop them threatening you." He'd said this about elephants but it applied, I always told myself, equally to mountain gorillas. When Kasimir did come barrelling out of the undergrowth you could see that he was quite an old gentleman. His open mouth showed his teeth were badly worn. Some teeth were even missing. With a vegetarian this can only mean that old age is taking over. When you watched him demolishing a large wild banana tree single-handed , you wouldn't have suspected that he was probably in his declining years.

Towards the end of a six month, day-in, day-out filming in the forest mists of Kahuzi-Biega an extraordinary event took place that shook Dieter, Lee and even Adrien.

As curator of the Kahuzi-Biega National Park, Adrien was given charge of a baby gorilla whose mother had been killed by poachers. Together with his African wife and children, Adrien reared the baby with one object, eventual release in the forest. Adrien taught it what foods to look for and how to gather and eat them. At last the day came when he judged the baby was ready to be returned to the wild. The obvious home for her was among the family with whom Adrien identified most closely—Kasimir's.

On the chosen day, Adrien made a gradual approach to Kasimir's group cradling the baby in his arms. From the outset it was clear that all was not normal. The whole family was wildly excited. Hannibal, with whom Adrien normally had exceptionally friendly relations, was unusually noisy and put on a potentially dangerous demonstration. There could be no question of a strategic withdrawal for Dieter, Lee or Adrien. They were surrounded by the family on all sides. The baby in Adrien's arms cried loudly. Suddenly Kasimir came straight for Adrien in full charge. "At that moment," Adrien told me later, "I thought I was dead." He did the only thing possible and dropped the baby on the ground. Kasimir snatched her up, barking and screaming with his mouth wide open, all the while keeping his eyes on Adrien as if expecting a counter-attack. Kasimir retreated into a small clear space in the undergrowth while the family gathered round to inspect the infant gorilla.

True to form, Dieter had kept the camera running all this time. It was still running when Lee, white-faced and crying, stepped into the shot. She couldn't explain the tears but said afterwards to me that if was sheer relief to find Adrien unscathed; "I honestly didn't think any of us would escape alive." In view of what was to happen later ,Lee's concern for Adrien's safety stuck in my mind.

I believe the baby would have survived but for two things. There was no lactating female in the group to feed her. A period of exceptionally wet, cold weather followed her release. Alas, she didn't have the stamina to survive the hailstorms and drenching rain.

The Dieter Plage-Lee Lyon partnership had worked wonderfully well. Both were, tough, determined perfectionists. The gorilla film they jointly shot was a masterpiece of wildlife camerawork under the most difficult conditions. But on the personal level at which it had started out, the relationship had long ago come apart. Dieter had plainly hoped for a partnership that would flourish both personally and professionally. Beneath the surface there was a constant if fairly well suppressed spirit of competition. One illustration of this was that when the couple were in Nairobi preparing for the gorilla expedition, both decided to learn to fly light aircraft. Lee got her license in almost record time. Dieter took nearly twice as long though he turned out to be the safest bush pilot with whom I have ever flown. Flying with Dieter was like buying a ticket with Luft Hansa. Flying came almost as naturally to Lee as it does to a bird. Dieter never resented this but he would obviously have liked to have sprouted wings as quickly, or preferably more quickly, than his protogée. Never mind: he was more than to make up for it later.

Once 'Gorilla' was in the can, a project had to be found for Lee Lyon on which she could work on her own. It was plain that she wouldn't have it any other way and we judged that she was ready to go solo. We picked her subjects in the Virunga National Park (formerly Le Parc Albert) at the northern end of Lake Khivu. One concerned a fishing village in the Park called Vitshumbi—the place of the salt—where the fishermen shared the village with hundreds of pelicans, storks and egrets. So-called tame elephants walked the streets between the huts. The extraordinary thing about these elephants was they behaved in a totally docile fashion in the village but once outside on the lake shore they became *kali* - wild again. In fact, Dieter very nearly got demolished by a bull on the lake shore because he overlooked for some strange reason this change in elephant personality. He escaped the charge at the last moment by unhooking himself from the battery belt of his camera and running. The elephant stopped just short of him and showed its displeasure by stamping on his camera. Though none of us realised it, the incident was an omen and sad warning for the future.

What none of us realised also, except no doubt Dieter who was still in Zaire filming at the summit of the active volcano Nyiragongo ,was that a passionate though slow-burning love affair was building up between Lee and Adrien Deschryver.

Kahuzi-Biega National Park for gorillas now had an African warden and staff.Adrien had been displaced by Africanisation, a common enough occurrence. Adrien found plenty to fill his life. One of his activities was flying supplies down to a breakaway faction in the south of Zaire. In passing I should perhaps add how Adrien learned to fly, since it is fairly typical of the man. He told me that when most of the Belgian colonials were fleeing the country they sold many of their bulkier possessions to anyone who would pay a fair price. One such possession was a twin-engined aircraft. Adrien bought it for a knock-down price and then decided to take to the air. I asked him how he had learned to fly it.

"Pleese." he said, giving me that slight, gentle smile. "I practice landings and take-offs up here." We were flying up to the Virunga Park in his old single-engined Bonanza at the time. "Christ," I said, "look out Adrien, there's a bateleur eagle just ahead." "*Pas de probleme*," he said and banked steeply to port.

Lee often flew with him on his freight runs to the south. Always *gallant*,Adrien gave Lee his hut by the make-shift airstrip where they landed and since it was a fairly dangerous area sat outside all night with a loaded Colt. 45 automatic. On this particular night it was pelting with rain and freezing cold. After half an hour or so, Lee took pity on him, opened the door and said: "you'd better come inside." Adrien accepted, no doubt with a Charles Boyerish charm. After that he, so to speak, never came out again.

The story, however, has a tragic ending. After she had nearly completed two half hour films in the Virunga National Park, Lee heard, as indeed we did at base in London, that an unusual and exciting operation was about to take place in Rwanda. Rwanda has more people per square yard than any other country in the world. It certainly has no room for elephants. Nevertheless, one 'pocketed herd' existed in a swamp in the middle of this throng of people. With good reason, the villagers feared and indeed hated the elephants. So most of the adults had been wounded with inadequate guns or bore the burn marks caused by broken wire snares. Twenty or thirty very savage and mainly wounded and therefore dangerous adults remained. But among this much harried and persecuted herd were a number of calves.

The plan was was to shoot the adults, capture as many calves as possible, sling them beneath choppers and airlift them to an acclimatisation camp. After they had settled down in the bomas there they would be taken by road to Rwanda's one national park,Kagera. There they would be released on a headland jutting out into a lake.This had been sealed off against lions by electric fences in the hope that the young elephants would have a good chance of establishing themselves.

In London we got to hear of the story through, once again, Bernhard Grzimek. Some, including Alan Root who was on a rare visit to HQ, felt that the shooting of the adults, however necessary, was too grim a story to show on television. I argued fiercely that it was too good a story to miss. Aubrey Buxton came down on my side, with the provision that we presented the story fairly and without sensationalism.

By the time we had argued it out, Lee had flown to Rwanda in her own aircraft backed up by Adrien Deschryver driving her transport. The airlift of the first babies went splendidly and Lee shot marvellous footage. The luck held with the first releases in Kagera Park. On being released from their crates one or two of the babies made token demonstrations and then escaped into the bush as released animals, even adult ones, usually do.

It was on one of the last releases that things went tragically wrong. A calf weighing about three quarters of a ton came down the ramp from the crate and kept going—straight at Lee Lyon. She had taken every sensible precaution. She had drawn up her Volkswagen Kombi so that it was directly behind her camera position with the door open. The one safety precaution she had ignored was to be free of her camera battery belt. This seems extraordinary in retrospect because she had been there when Dieter, because he had been attached to his camera by his battery belt, had nearly been flattened by that bull elephant at Vitshumbi. But to say this is to overlook the nature of cameramen and women. It is the shot that counts. Maybe, the scene seems less real and immediate when the eye is glued to a view-finder.

The elephant kept coming. There would still have been time for Lee to unhitch herself and escape into the open door of the Kombi. By the time the elephant was only yards away, it was too late. It wiped her down the side of the truck and knelt on her. Adrien and others rushed to drive the elephant off. Lee just had time to look up and say "Adrien" and died.

She is buried in Kagera National Park.

I got the news that she had been killed from a young man in the American Embassy in Grosvenor Square. My first thought was that she had flown her Cessna into the side of a mountain. The young man handed me a cable from the US consul in Kigali stating that she had been crushed by an elephant. The young embassy official gave me a little homily about girls doing unsuitable jobs. I couldn't answer or argue or even tell him that Lee wouldn't have considered any other job suitable. The impact had just hit me and I was choked.

There was a lot of talk of witchcraft. Even Peter Scott asked me what I thought of this theory. I replied that I fancied witch doctors could put spells on people but hardly on young elephants.

Adrien Deschryver died a few years later. His heart gave out.

Adrien Deschryver, the Belgian settler who made his family estates in Zaire into Kahuzi-Biega National Park for lowland gorillas.

Kasimir, the senior male silverback, whose family Adrien studied. It took four years of cautious work to get the gorilla family to accept him.

Lee Lyon in African dress.

A gorilla's charge is formidable with much shrieking and beating of vegetation. Despite this, gorillas are basically peaceful animals. Here, Kasimir demonstrates.

Permission to Leave

The thunder rolled: at least I thought it was thunder. The lightning danced and flickered: at least I hoped it was lightning. The *Tumpang Jalang* did a little rolling and dancing on her own. In the Indonesian tongue, *Tumpang Jalang* means 'permission to leave'. No harbour master in his right mind, at least no western harbour master, would have given the *Tumpang Jalang* leave to do anything under his jurisdiction, let alone leave harbour. We were on our way, Dieter Plage and his newly married wife, Mary, my wife and myself, to look at Anak Krakatoa, 'the son of Krakatoa'. It was no thunderstorm that we had seen and heard below the far horizon but the young Krakatoa, still fifty miles away, flexing its muscles to receive us. We were setting out on another recce with the aim of making a wildlife programme no one had yet attempted. The story would tell how the great eruption of 1883 had created Ujun Kulon, the isolated national park which was the home, perhaps the *last* home of the one-horned Javan rhino.

There is no easy way to reach the place in the Sunda Straits where the young Krakatoa rises 2,000 feet from the seabed close to the spot where the old volcano destroyed itself in 1883.

Two friends had tried to reach Anak Krakatoa a few weeks before in a hired motor boat. The engine had packed up when well out of sight of land. Their special skill was studying tigers in the jungles of Nepal, not navigating in small boats. Now they were adrift with very little nautical knowledge and no sail even if they had known how to use one. With the currents setting southward, their next stop would have been Australia or Antarctica had not a Japanese tanker, on a thousands to one chance, sighted them.

Heavens knows whence Dieter had dredged up the *Tumpang Jalang*. It seems likely that he had consulted John Blower, (still moving round the world and now UNO's Food and Agriculture Organisation conservation planner for Indonesia) who probably drawled: "try a local fishing boat, old boy."

Somehow Dieter had come up with the *Tumpang Jalang*. She was about seventy five feet long and narrow with it. The deck was raked fore to aft, rising quite steeply at the bows, a design I hoped that had evolved to cope with the sudden nasty blows that can arise in the Indian Ocean. The only shelter was a wheel-house aft, from which, on the port side, rose an eight foot metal pipe about two foot of which was loosely wrapped with asbestos string, presumably as insulation. This was the exhaust from the diesel engine. When the captain called for full speed ahead the unguarded parts of this pipe glowed a nasty red. The boat had no guard rails. Safety was plainly not a main consideration aboard her. She carried not so much as a life-belt let alone a dinghy, rubber or otherwise. I doubt if any of her crew could swim. In fact when the enormous man whom Dieter called the bo'sun went ashore in deep water he relied for flotation on an empty plastic barrel clasped to his chest. The other duties of the bo'sun consisted of cooking, swearing at the four man crew and sleeping flat on his back on deck. At all times and in all weathers he wore a woollen scarf tightly wound round his head as a turban. Dieter swore that this was to keep his brains in. It did not seem unlikely.

The cooking element of ship's life worried me a bit. What if we had a fire on board miles from anywhere? Beside the wheel-house on the starboard side was a blazing brazier. The only insulation between this and the wooden deck was a steel plate that glowed with the heat. On top of the brazier, stroked by naked flames, stood a huge black cook pot, into which anyone passing tossed anything from a shark's fin to a fish head. As ship's cook, the bo'sun confined his contributions to generous handfuls of curry powder and exotic herbs. These gave the resulting bouillabaisse the rich green colour of a pond covered with duck weed. Anyone could help themselves, at any time, with a large ladle hanging on the wheel-house door. Alain Compost, the charming young Frenchman Dieter had enlisted as temporary assistant, declared the fish stew to be delicious.

Once well out of sight of land I couldn't help wondering how the ancient brown mariner who was our skipper knew where we were. The tiller had long since broken or rotted away. In its place a long iron bar had been welded to the head of the rudder post. Our captain, reclining in the port side scuppers, kept one large spatulate big toe glued to the end of the iron bar. It seemed possible that the toe had become flattened as the result of years of contact with the *Tumpang Jalang's* rudder bar. As land was left further and further astern, I asked Alain Compost if he would enquire of the captain how he knew our exact position on the ocean. The captain listened courteously to Alain's question and then replied: "My toe knows where we are." After that I stopped worrying. When you've got the right sort of big toe aboard who needs radar and satellites to fix your position?

Anak Krakatoa had quietened down a little as we got nearer to Ujun Kulon but the mountain was still grumbling away and we could see the column of black smoke rising high above the young volcano still hidden from view. No one could tell whether the son of Krakatoa would match the performance of its terrible father. The eruption of 1883 has been calculated to have generated the power of 3,000 of the atomic bombs that destroyed Hiroshima. The violence had largely been caused by the ocean pouring into the magma chamber beneath the mountain. The hundred foot tidal waves—*tsunamis*—produced by super-heated steam had swept miles inland through the Sunda Straits that separate Java and Sumatra, drowning 36,000 people and leaving a Dutch gunboat marooned a mile inland. The big bang was heard 2,000 miles away. Apart from that, all the rest of the world knew about Krakatoa's eruption was that the dust hurled into the upper atmosphere caused the most wonderful sunsets for several years to come.

The big wind came from nowhere. Five miles out of Ujun Kulon we were hit by something approaching a Force Six. The *Tumpang Jalang* stuck her bows into a nasty short sea of six foot waves, cut through the first, threw up her head and crashed down into the next trough. She was obviously pretty good at handling seas like this, not that this helped her passengers. The four of us were sitting on deck in the bows when the squall hit. It was no place to be. The wheel-house seemed a long way away. Dieter told Joan to slide aft on her backside and not to try to get up. She was doing fine when the bo'sun, no doubt with the best intentions, dashed out of the wheel-house, seized her by the arm and bundled her upright. Unfortunately, as they drew level with the diesel exhaust, the boat rolled instead of pitched. Joan hit the red hot exhaust only for a split second but it was enough to sear the skin from elbow to shoulder. Alain got her in the wheel-house and took out a bottle of mercurichrome antiseptic from his kitbag. A burn like that is the last thing you need in the hot and humid climate of the Java seas where wounds easily turn septic. Alain saved the day and may even have saved her arm

Next day we circled Anak Krakatoa who was obviously in a foul mood. Several weeks before Dieter and Mary had landed on the volcano to get some establishing shots. Dieter had climbed to the lip of the crater which that day was producing only a curl of smoke and steam. In the middle of the night, Anak Krakatoa woke up and hurled lava and rocks high into the air. One of the latter about the size of a small cottage came rumbling down the mountainside, passing within fifty yards of their tent.

To a biologist—and for that matter to a wildlife film-maker—-Anak Krakatoa posed some fascinating questions and provided a few answers. Among the questions was how long would a newly created volcanic island take to acquire a population of flora and fauna? How quickly would the coral reefs destroyed by the great eruption take to re-establish themselves? In both cases there was a definite date as a starting point. In the case of the reefs, 1883. The new volcanic island had poked its head above the surface in 1928. Already the island had acquired nearly thirty species of plants, insects, birds and reptiles. So where had they come from?

Seabirds, of course, are ocean travellers. Seeds are borne on the wind. Larger fruits and seeds are carried by the ocean currents. Some immigrants might raft to the new island on fallen tree trunks. Many reptiles like snakes and lizards are excellent swimmers.

This is the point where the stories of Ujun Kulon and Krakatoa inter-mix. Barely twenty five miles of sea separates them. The great eruption had flattened and reshaped Ujun Kulon. But the most important result, at least for the Javan rhino and other wildlife, was that Krakatoa had denuded the area of people. They had never returned to resettle it, perhaps because of the fear of a repeat performance.

The *Tumpang Jalang* took us past sharp needles of rock jutting like fangs above the surface. It was an eerie feeling. We were sailing over the exact spot where the loudest bang the world has ever heard took place.

To one side of Anak Krakatoa stands the only part of the original volcano that did not disappear in dust. This island is now heavily wooded. A white-tailed sea eagle was soaring along the slopes of what remained of the original crater. This shattered relic gave you a good idea of what the slopes of Anak Krakatoa will look like in a hundred years provided it doesn't blow its top in the meantime.

The national parks of Indonesia are vastly underfunded like almost everything else in that nation of islands. Nevertheless there was a willing and helpful warden at Ujun Kulon and a hut which was infinitely preferable to sleeping on the deck of the *Tumpang*. Anyway she was off for the night about her real business—catching sharks.

Before we sailed for a recce next morning, the warden told Alain Compost there was something he would like to show us if we would take a short walk in the jungle. After leading us for about a mile through dense undergrowth, the warden stopped and pointed to a the base of a large tree. The snake might have been hard to spot but for one thing. Python colouration matches their background splendidly. Even quite a large python can made itself practically invisible if it cares to. This was a very large python indeed. The warden said that it was at least twenty feet long. One feature made it easy to spot. Sticking out of its distended jaws was the head of a stag, antlers and all. A rusa deer is a close relation of our own red deer and nearly as big. The python had caught the stag about a fortnight previously. Its digestive juices had done a good job of breaking down the carcass but when it came to head and antlers it realised that it had a problem. But pythons are in no hurry about such matters. A big meal like a deer will last them a long time. In the meanwhile it was relaxing, waiting for the head to decompose sufficiently for the antlers to drop off.

The *Tumpang*, her holds full of the night's catch, was waiting to take us to the location Dieter hoped would give him the best chance of seeing and filming a Javan rhino. On a previous trip to Ujun, Dieter had found a small river, the Cigenter, on the opposite shore of the park. The jungle was so dense—which suited the rhinos fine—that there was little chance of filming them except at points where they crossed the Cigenter. Tracks made it plain that they occasionally did so.

We lowered a dug-out canoe from the deck of the *Tumpang Jalang* and precariously lowered ourselves into the hollowed out tree trunk that was to take us ashore. The bo'sun meantime assaulted the beach clasping a plastic tub and thrashing frantically with his feet. The sands at the mouth of the Cigenter bore Krakatoa's trade-mark. It looked just like the coal dust you sometimes see on otherwise unblemished Welsh beaches such as Porthcawl. In Wales, the black tide mark is coal dust. Here, one hundred years after the big bang, Krakatoa had scattered the black ashes of its spectacular suicide.

Hollywood could not have created anything like the Cigenter even for a Tarzan movie. Trees with grotesque twisted roots like cathedral buttresses clawed their hold on the banks. Creepers and ferns roofed the narrow waterway. Leaf monkeys, whooping with fright or joy, leapt these walkways like trapeze artistes. At least three species of kingfishers dived for small fish and, most, remarkable of all, one species of fish shot back, though not at the kingfishers. Archer fish lay in wait below over-hanging leaves for insects tight-rope walking the slender leaf stems in search of food. If you sat still and watched you might be lucky enough to see a beetle knocked off its leaf by a bullet of river water. The archer fish specialises in shooting down its prey with a high-velocity jet which it propels with the power of its gills through a mouth like a pistol barrel. Indeed, it is more like a gunman than an archer. Either way it is no mean feat to hit its small target and knock it down into the water. It must instinctively allow for the bending of light—the angle of refraction—between water and air. Occasionally, an archer would put his weapon aside and simply leap out of the water to snatch its prey off the leaf above.

The Cigenter was worth a film on its own. But how much more so with the addition of a Javan rhino! If they could be got they would be the first scenes of one of the world's rarest creatures shot in the wild on colour film. TV audiences, I had long ago learned, are not impressed by such filmic 'firsts'. They want excitement, adventure, sometimes beauty and what the Americans call jeopardy, in other words risk, or anyway threat of risk, to life or limb. But wildlife cameraman are impressed by such 'firsts'. And so, long after fly-by-night people like myself had left the scene, Dieter Plage was there on the Cigenter, day in, night out, until he got his rhino. In fact, a pair of rhinos, male and female. But that is the nature of the beast, God bless them, the wildlife cameraman, and sometimes the wildlife camerawoman. They are truly a breed apart.

There's always a footnote to every walk on the wild side. My wife had been lucky to get away with a badly burned arm. I was not so lucky but then it was all my stupid fault. I should have known better.

One day when Dieter was deep in the jungle of Ujun Kulon filming flying-foxes, I decided to take a swim. Flying foxes were Cigenter habitués. They came to rob the wild fig trees of their small hard green fruits. Of course, they are not foxes at all. But they have red foxy faces. They also have a three foot wingspan. Flying foxes are the world's biggest bat and you find them in many tropical places from Africa to the Far East.

Dieter had sequences of them taking figs, now he wanted film of their roost. Since they roost in hundreds, hanging like huge string bags from the topmost branches of trees, they make excellent footage. And being at least partly diurnal, the camera is bound to catch some of them flying and landing in the tree tops, the mothers with young clinging to their breasts.

It was a sweltering day. The women had found some jungle shade. The *Tumpang* wasn't due to pick us up for an hour. The water looked wonderful. So I stripped off. Unfortunately I failed to observe one basic rule; always keep something on your feet. On the edge of the coral, I kicked off and felt an excruciating pain. I'd plunged both feet into a nest of long-spined sea urchins. These creatures have a very effective defence mechanism. The tips of their barbed spines break off and inject venom into their attacker. At first I thought that, like Moira Borland, I'd tangled with a Portuguese man-o'-war. Or maybe a lethal box jellyfish loaded with neurotoxins. A sea snake? Or even a scorpion fish. There are so many nasties in tropical waters that the unwary bather has a considerable choice when it comes to doing himself an injury.

I somehow got ashore without repeating the injury, crawled up the sands and lay there feeling very sorry for myself. The soles of my feet looked as though they had been peppered with dust shot.

It was no good shouting and I certainly couldn't walk. After a time, I thought, someone will come looking for me. I hope I'm still alive. After half an hour the pain was still just as bad though I was obviously going to survive. Whatever had happened wasn't fatal. Just bloody foolish.

And then two fishermen in a dug-out canoe fishing with a cast net appeared. They might have been poachers. They could have been park staff. Who cared? I waved my shirt and shouted. The dug-out passed by and then the netsman turned to make another cast and, as the circular net flew out with that deceptive ease that captivates the eye, he saw my waving shirt. At first I thought they weren't going to stop. If they were poachers they almost certainly would not stop. But then the man at the paddles swung the nose of the dug-out round and beached his canoe with careless skill. I did notice that both wore ancient flip-flops, tied to their feet with cord. In passing I should add that the entire year-before- last's output of the Bata flip-flop factory seems to wash up on Indonesia beaches at least once a day.

I held up my feet and pointed to their black and blue punctured soles. The paddler shook his head sadly as if to say: tough! Then he picked up a stout stick and made beating motions with it. Oh God, I thought, they're going to mug me. You feel worse about that sort of thing when you are stark naked.

The netsman pointed to his own feet and, standing on one leg, tapped the other foot quite hard. He smiled and pointed to my feet. Plainly they were experts in bastinado. Next he stroked my injured feet very gently. He had one word of English. "Okay?" I nodded. What had I to lose?

It was extremely painful, but not nearly as painful as the original stings. For about ten minutes they beat the soles of my feet with varying degrees of never unbearable force. The pain began to ease. Plainly this was an ailment they were familiar with and a treatment they recognised as effective. I imagine the beating broke up the spines, restored the circulation and dispersed the poison.

They stopped at last and gestured to me to stand. To my surprise, I found that I could. I could also limp a few steps. Both fishermen smiled happily and shook my hand. "Okay?" ... "Okay" I said and shook their hands warmly in return. I had some money in the pocket of my shorts but felt it would have been an insult to offer it. I am sure that I was right about that, if nothing else.

Half an hour later I reached the wives at the mouth of the Cigenter.

"Where on earth have you been?"

"Swimming"

"Wasn't that a bit unwise?"

"Very," I said.

Twenty five miles away Anak Krakatoa roared as if to say: "are you really up to this sort of thing?" At that moment I was sure that I was not.

A shark fishing boat *Tumpang Jalang* in which we sailed to Krakatoa. She had no life rafts and the Indonesian captain steered her with the aid of his big toe.

Deck space and accommodation was limited aboard the *Tumpang Jalang*. The open deck was fine until we hit a storm in the Sunda Straits.

In 1928, a new volcano erupted from the sea bed on the site of the old Krakatoa. The mountain of rock and ash it threw up is already over 2,000 feet high.

Anak Krakatoa, son of Krakatoa. Its parent exploded in 1883 drowning 36,000 people. Dieter Plage filmed from the crater lip just before a recent eruption.

The Men of the Forest

It was as if God in a errant moment of creation had locked away paradise inside a sauna. The trees stood one hundred and forty feet high. Creepers coiled their trunks like fluffy scarves carelessly but artfully thrown round the throat of a coquettish woman. Siamangs, or to give them their more accustomed name, Gibbons, *who-whooed* with their unearthly cry as they looped and swung invisibly through the forest canopy. If you took a swig from your water-bottle, the liquid left your body within seconds in sweat through the skin of your bare arms and legs. Try to recycle it with a quick lick and, if you were lucky, you got a brief energising shot of salt. So to keep up the saline level you swallowed a salt tablet. You saw all this, did all this, experienced the discomfort of all this and wondered at the marvel of it all because you were in the Sumatran rain forest. At Bohorok to be precise. We had come to film orang-utans.

The approach walk to Bohorok might have tested the less fit entrants in the London marathon. It wasn't more than a mile or two and the track was not particularly difficult. It was the humidity that got to you. Even Dieter Plage, who had made the trek before, sweated a few pints. My wife and I simply felt wrung out. Though neither of us would have admitted it, I think we both wondered whether we would make the finishing line. But, of course, you can get used to anything provided you want to do it enough.

The Bohorok river restored everyone's sanity. Clear and sparkling as a Highland trout burn, it divided the majesty of the buttressed trees on either bank as a nave divides the columns of a cathedral. You don't find many Jack Russell terriers in cathedrals. Come to that, you seldom find the little brutes in the dark green denseness of a Sumatran rain forest. There, on the far bank pricking her ears and yapping as only a terrier can yap, was an undeniable Jack Russell. Suni belonged to Regina Frey, one of the two Swiss girl orang-utan experts we had come to see and, as we hoped and prayed, whose work with orang-utans we planned to film. We crossed the white water of the Bohorok in a dug-out canoe. A helper from the Indonesian wildlife service was waiting to take us to Regina Frey's and Monica Borner's camp.

In one sense this wasn't a wildlife story. Perhaps it would be more accurate to call it a wildlife story in reverse. Orangs exist in diminishing numbers only in

Sumatra and Borneo. Undeniably, they are the most attractive of the great apes, Gorillas have it for majesty. Chimps for their mischievous and apparent sense of humour or at least what we imagine to be a sense of humour. Gibbons and Siamangs, the fourth of the ape group (the family *Pongidae*), delight visitors to zoos with their seeming ability to swing through the trees without touching the branches. But orangs, and especially young orangs, have an appeal, even to hardened cynics like myself, about which it is almost impossible to avoid the sin of anthropomorphism. They are so darn cuddly. And that is where the trouble starts.

Rich Indonesians are as susceptible to the charm of young orangs as all of us at Bohorok were. The difference is that they wish to own one and keep it captive. No doubt when the animal is small their children find the orang a perfect pet, just as western children keep guinea pigs and rabbits. The difference is that guinea pigs and rabbits do not, as they grow up, take the place apart. Orangs are sometimes called 'the mechanical ape' because of their intelligent use of planks, poles and bars as levers to wreck their cages. The Indonesian owner's answer is to confine the unfortunate creature in more secure which usually means smaller cages and enclosures. Result: one very depressed and possibly dangerous orang-utan. There is another element to all this. To Indonesian owners an orang-utan is as much a status symbol as owning a Porsche sometimes is in the West.

Monica and Regina, two attractive young Swiss scientists, had been picked by Professor Bernhard Grzimek to win back as many orangs as possible from their Indonesian 'owners' and retrain them so that they could be returned as soon as possible to the wild. That was the purpose of Bohorok orang-utan station.

There was one thing going for the two girls in this situation. Many 'owners' had become tired of their 'pets' and were happy to be rid of the responsibility and trouble of keeping a full-grown orang. Monica and Regina had the necessary powers from the authorities to take orang captives by force if necessary. But rightly they used argument and persuasion. In such a country it can be a poor look-out to make enemies in high places. Cunning old Grzimek had known this and picked the girls for their tact and powers of persuasion as much as for their scientific knowledge.

There were at that moment about twenty five orangs at the station. Except for the fact that none of the new arrivals was on drink or hash, the treatment was very like a course at a human rehab clinic. Often the new patients were psychologically damaged through close confinement. You might compare their condition to that of a pilot shot down in Vietnam and kept in squalid and cramped conditions and subjected to mental and possibly physical torture. Some of the new arrivals were in a very similar state. So the first step was to build up their confidence in their human guardians. This, in itself had its problems since the ultimate object was, once their pysche had been restored, and once they had learned to live wild again, to make them independent and release them in another part of the forest. So new patients were at first kept in large quarantine cages, fed by hand, shown kindness and taught to trust their guardians until the point at which they could be let loose during the day to wander off into the forest on their own. But they had to be in for evening roll call. This was the highlight of everyone's day, including Dieter, his camera assistant, Mike Price, and ourselves.

It took place at the feeding station about four hundred and fifty feet above the level of the river, late in the afternoon. Monica or Regina with a couple of Indonesian wildlife helpers would climb the hill laden with canisters of milk and bunches of small green bananas. The orangs who were, so to speak on parole, knew the hour of tea time to a minute. Promptly at five o'clock they would come swinging and chattering through the tree tops to the feeding station.

Dieter had a special affinity with the orangs and it was if they recognised it. Unlike most wildlife cameramen on our team he had a tendency to see human qualities in attractive animals. This never overflowed into his work. He never committed the unforgivable sin of pretending that his animal subjects were people. But his sense of humour prompted him to see human likenesses and qualities in some creatures. Don't we all, or anyway most of us? Once in Sri-Lanka, where we were making a one-hour Special about leopards, we were watching a troop of langur monkeys feeding in the grass. Something scared them, possibly the distant cough of their arch enemy, the leopard. Twenty monkeys rushed for the trees on the edge of the clearing. One turned and ran back, apparently searching frantically for something in the long grass, "He's lost his Swiss Army knife," said Dieter. It was a neat, almost cartoon-like instant observation. We had all, at one time or another, mislaid that invaluable tool. An anthropomorphic comment, maybe, but both funny, observant and endearing at the same time..

So, when Dieter arrived with his movie camera to film the orangs' tea party, the apes were waiting for him and leapt from the trees to cling to him. Often he arrived with four orangs draped round his neck. "Okay, you guys," he would say good-humouredly, shifting his hold on his precious Arriflex to accommodate a fifth ape.

Dieter had his own names for most of them. Presek, a lowering ape with a tough manner and an extremely small brow was known as the oil man. Why the oil man? Because he looked like a driller on an oil rig, Dieter said. He had a vast and complete memory of feature films that had impressed him so I assumed he had seen some oil-prospecting epic in which a look-alike for Presek had appeared. Then there was 'the thinker', who continually struck a pose like Rodin's famous statue and Suka, an especially attractive and mischievous baby from Borneo (the orangs from Borneo are slightly redder than the Sumatran race). Suka was named after the character in a TV advert for Swiss cheese. The most courteous of all was Oyong, the Indonesian name with which he arrived at the station. Oyong was continually kissing my wife's hand, or so she liked to think. In fact, I think he was sexually sampling her. She probably exuded some subtle female pheromone (I know she does this for wasps). True to her sex, she took this as a compliment, which, however you looked at it, it undoubtedly was. She had Oyong almost literally eating out of her hand.

The tea party began when the last orang had returned from his or her paroled day of freedom in the rain forest. In my experience, no one was ever missing from the daily hand-out. Their table manners left a lot to be desired. There was a good deal of childish squabbling and tantrums. Oyong, especially, could put it on when he felt cheated, passed over, or deprived. Like a naughty child he would pound himself or the boards of the roofed cages on which the tea party took place. There was never any aggression or serious bad-temper, simply temperamental outbursts apparently aimed at the real or imagined unfairness of life. Just like us? Impossible not to make the comparison.

The tea party had its subtleties, however. Orang-utans are not especially hooked on bananas, not in the wild state at least. Bananas seldom grow in their forests. They would far rather feed on wild vines, leaves and creepers. So Regina and Monica purposely feed them on a boring diet of bananas, knowing that when they were ready for release into the rain forest they would instinctively look for and feed on the foods that were more natural to their tastes. Occasionally, a young wild male would join the party, scooping up five bananas in each hand and swing off back into the treetops.

Gradually, one became accustomed to life beneath the hundred foot trees and the suffocating humidity. There was always the Bohorok river rushing and gurgling seductively past our tent. At least once a day we would strip off and body- surf down the rapids into the pool below. It did a lot for the sanity. Dieter and his new assistant Mike Price, had built a lean-to shelter of bamboo and agricultural polythene. This was where at dusk we enjoyed the happy hour. As far as Dieter and I were concerned, the nightly tot or two of Scotch was not nearly so important as the brine in which the pickled cucumbers were immersed. Dieter and I had never really fallen out about anything on any wildlife location that we had shared around the world. But who got the first or maybe the largest slug of brine from the pickled cucumber jar was something quite different. Dieter and I were both natural sweaters. We needed the salt replacement and the cucumber brine had it. In those circumstances, it was the most addictive and alluring drink either of us had experienced. No one else seemed to feel the same terrible urges. So we agreed to one equally measured slug per night taken from plastic cups of precisely the same size and volume to be poured and drunk simultaneously. You could feel your burners light up before the liquid had hit the pit of your stomach. Even ten-year-old single malt has never matched Del Monte cucumber brine for effect. Later, in more civilised parts of the world, Dieter and I searched for a pickled cucumber liquid that would give us the same lift. We went through the whole range on offer in the world's grocery stores and supermarkets but nothing ever hit the spot like Del Monte juice in a high humidity Sumatran rain forest.

We ate each night in Regina and Monica's camp, a sort of log cabin whose walls were decorated with some of the largest cockroaches in the world. Then Joan and I somehow found our way to our tent and slept on an over buoyant blow-up mattress. One morning, when we went down to the river for a pre-breakfast wash and brush-up, we found tiger pug marks within six feet of our two man tent. Not a lot of people ever meet a Sumatran tiger. In fact, Monica Borner's husband, Marcus, had just obtained his PhD for his study of the Sumatran tiger *rarely having actually seen one.* His study was based on pug marks, kills, droppings and other signs that a Sumatran tiger had passed that way. The race is far more rare than all other tigers and appreciably smaller than, say the Bengal or Siberian. However, these are small consolations when you discover that one has been sniffing your tent in the night. Dieter's opinion was that it had gone down to the nearest Indonesian village in search of a dog, to which tigers are particularly partial.

When a batch of orangs was judged ready to return to the rain forest we crated them and took them at least ten kilometres up the Bohorok river so that there would as little incentive as possible to return to the station for a free meal. I've spent quite a large part of my leisure life from Kashmir to Exmoor wading in rough and rocky rivers when trout fishing. But I'd never experienced anything like the Bohorok. Every stone seemed to have been greased for maximum slippability. I had enough trouble and I'm supposed to be used to these conditions. One of the Indonesian bearers held my wife's hand and I freely admit that I needed a helping hand almost as much. The reason? Possibly the rain forest and the blinding sunlight that reached the river produced a different sort of super-slippery algae. At one point, the bearers carrying one of the crated orangs lost their footing and disappeared into a deep pool. The orang sailed down until the crate grounded in some shallows and appeared not a bit put out by the mishap.

At last, the moment came to release our friends. Oyong and Presek were among them. For several minutes they seemed unsure, like apprehensive children looking for help to mum. Regina herself looked as tearful as any mother seeing her children off to boarding school for the first time. And then somewhere in the forest a wild orang called. Oyong and Presek seized a creeper and disappeared like ascending firemen into the tree canopy above. In two years, Monica and Regina had returned 30 orangs to the forest, perhaps not many but every ape counts when the world population of orang-utans is down to 10,000 and shrinking fast largely due to deforestation.

They had regained their true title. Orang-utan means 'Man of the Forest'.

The next stop was to be Nepal. When you've come this far you might as well look for and recce future projects in the same general part of the globe. For some time, we'd planned to move on from Indonesia to Nepal. Dieter had in fact already flown his Cessna 206 from East Africa to Kathmandu in anticipation of filming in the Himalayas. This was no mean feat for a pilot with less than a year's flying experience. In fact, during the long crossing of the Indian Ocean and the intricacies of landing among the Jumbos and DC 10's at Delhi he had occupied the co-pilot's seat. Very wisely he had persuaded a commercial pilot friend to take the left hand seat. Just the same, his friend had let him solve the problems such as: what do you do when your wings are icing up one thousand miles out over the ocean. Dieter had come through the trip with, well, flying colours. Once in Nepal he had hit a problem. Apart from three or four registered mountain pilots, no private pilots were licensed to fly in Nepal. With his considerable powers of tact and persuasion, Dieter had got round the authorities, provided he was checked out for Himalayan flying by one of the four authorised mountain pilots.

Dieter's instructor, an American mountain pilot called, of all things, Jay Klinkenbeer, gave Dieter several pieces of homely Himalayan flying advice. One piece was: "Dieter, there are a lot of clouds up there and some of them clouds have got rocks in them." Another item of essential wisdom concerned landing at a particularly hairy mountain strip. "Dieter," said Jay Klinkenbeer, "Landing there like parking your car in the garage at eighty miles per hour." Dieter obviously took these words to heart. He not only flew in and out of all these appaling places but stayed alive up there.

So now with the orang film in the can, Nepal, Everest, the tigers of the Royal Chitawan National Park and a short take-off and landing Cessna 206 were waiting for us. And I, for one, couldn't wait to get a piece of the action. As it turned out, I got more than I had bargained for.

A week or so before we arrived at Bohorok, the wardens of PPA, Indonesia's struggling conservation organisation, had brought in an obviously sick adult female. She'd been kept in the worst possible conditions. The PPA men had taken her from her 'owners' more or less by force. For the regulation time, she occupied, as did all new arrivals, the big quarantine cage. She sat huddled in the corner, like a sad mental patient. Apart from her obvious state of depression, she had what appeared to be the orang equivalent of 'flu. She sneezed and coughed continuously, while mucus dribbled from her nose and mouth. The kindest and most obvious thing would have been to have given her a lethal injection and put her down. But this, the girls argued, was not in their brief. Their remit was to return every orang possible to the forest, even if it took two years to do. So, of course, there was never any question of a lethal injection for the sufferer. Instead, at the end of her quarantine period, she was allowed to roam free with the other inmates in the fairly reasonable belief that this would cheer her up. Whether it did or not I cannot recall. What I do know is that when Dieter, Joan and I left Bohorok she was still dribbling and coughing as badly as ever.

Our route to Nepal called for a brief stop-over in Singapore to pick up some new camera equipment. What else? Dieter collected cameras and lenses like other people collect stamps. Then a flight to Delhi, arriving in the early hours to catch the Royal Nepal plane for Kathmandu in the morning.

At the end of the first day in Singapore I was feeling pretty sick. We called the hotel doctor who understandably diagnosed Asian 'flu, advised a day in bed and doses of Paracetamol.

We hit Delhi airport at one in the morning. In my experience Delhi is not the liveliest airport to get things done at all, let alone in a hurry. I once waited an hour in the immigration queue while the passport officer had forty minutes shut-eye. This, the Indian businessman in front of me told me, was quite normal. The best thing to do was to relax and read a book.

On this occasion I wasn't expecting quick results. Dieter had over a ton of camera equipment, some of it newly acquired. The registration numbers of the numerous lenses, cameras and recorders should have been checked. But at one a.m., in Delhi International Airport! I sat huddled and shivering on a bench with my dear wife who was beginning to fear for my life while Dieter blitzed the freight department. The spirit of General Guderian still lived. The freight department might have been hit by a panzer division, but a panzer division firing rupees instead of 88mm shells and persuasive words in place of machine-gun fire. *Schwerpunkt,* the panzers' word for a breakthrough, had been achieved in forty minutes flat. We were through with over a ton of unchecked freight. We took a taxi to a very strange Indian motel called 'The Golden Cockerel' where I sweated a great deal and wished to die or go home or both. Instead we caught the Royal Nepal 727 to Kathmandu in the morning. Climbers could have heard my teeth chattering on the summit of Mount Everest.

All I remember about arriving at the shed-like airport building in Kathmandu was that Dieter forecast that by the time our luggage arrived from the plane the porters would have pinched the piece of rope that was holding my suitcase shut. He was right. Rope must have been in short supply in the Nepalese capital. Some friends of Dieter's who had written an illustrated book on the birds of Nepal came to meet us. I remember trying to shake hands and finding that I was in a state of semi rigor. Now even I was beginning to believe that I might never see Surrey again.

Old friends to the rescue once more. John Blower (who else?) had completed his wildlife conservation plan for Nepal on behalf of UNO and had, as already reported, moved on to Jakarta to do the same for Indonesia. His faithful sweep-up man, none other than Frank Poppleton, last met as head warden of the Uganda National Parks, always moved in behind Blower to tidy up and put the conservation plan into action. It was an excellent, if fast-moving, combination. Now I am coming to it: Frank was operating out of Kathmandu and had a house there. At the moment of our arrival, he was away on a field trip, his charming Danish wife Inge with him. They had left word that we were welcome to use their house while they were away. We moved in direct from the airport. I just about made the first bed I saw and carried on dying. If Joan and Dieter hadn't been there I might just have done exactly that. Both hit the ground running. Kathmandu may be one of the most romantic places in the world in which to peg out. It is also one of the cities best equipped to speed your exit. In those days there was not a lot to be bought in the shops or bazaars except any kind of dope which you could get over or under the counter. Hygiene everywhere was of a decidedly low standard. There was a hospital but the local word was not to get admitted. It was said that they only changed hyperdermic needles when they had injected enough patients to get the one currently in use blunt. Nor was the town over-supplied with doctors.

When Dieter had flown in in his Cessna before tackling the orang project he had made a number of friends and contacts. That was invariably the Plage style. One of these was a very able young scientist Andrew Lawrie, studying the one-horned Indian Rhino in Royal Chitawan National Park. Dieter planned to make, and eventually did make, an excellent rhino film with Andrew. Another was Lisa Van Gruisen, immensely capable Girl Friday to the travel entrepreneur Jim Edwards. Jim ran the highly successful wildlife lodge, Tiger Tops, in Chitawan National Park. Both now came galloping to the rescue. Lisa took my wife shopping though there was not much to sustain an invalid other than Oxo cubes and scrawny chickens whose neck was wrung while you waited. The unappetising nature of the fare didn't matter a lot to me as I couldn't keep anything in my stomach except the Oxo. I suppose you could keep alive on Oxo. Anyway I did. Andrew Lawrie advised that if I had to go to hospital, for God's sake forget the local abbatoir. Dieter should fly me to the Gurkha hospital at Pokhara. Meantime, Andrew organised the King of Nepal's physician, Dr Mala, who mercifully had been trained in Edinburgh.

Mala was an excellent doctor but confessed that he was baffled. There were, he said, so many unknown viruses that could attack Europeans in the Far East. Had I been in contact with any sick persons recently? I said not that I knew of, but, almost jokingly—not that I felt like joking—that I had been in close contact with a sick orang-utan who seemed to have severe ape flu.

"Did you know," Dr Mala said, "that apes and humans can sometimes transmit illnesses to each other? Polio, for example." A bell was ringing but I didn't care to ask for whom it tolled. That sick female orang. I had handled her often. I even remembered wiping her snot off my sleeve. We couldn't be certain, of course, but it seemed the most likely explanation. Treatment? Dr Mala knew better than I did that antibiotics don't do much when faced with viruses. Nevertheless, antibiotics had to be tried. So he prescribed and kept prescribing different antibiotics. It was comforting, especially to Joan, to have this wise and kindly man on our side, but not even Dr Mala claimed that we were making much progress. After about the third course of anti-biotics the inside of my mouth started to break out in ulcers.

Then came a heavy culture shock. Frank and Inge Poppleton had returned from their mountain trek and understandably wanted to use their own house. Jim Edwards kindly suggested that Joan and I moved our sickbay to his residence which was a sort of caravanserai for anyone, particular Everest climbers and their sherpas, passing through Kathmandu on their way to the high Himalayas. The jollity was tremendous and the noise colossal. I felt that my last grip on sanity was slipping away fast. In this extremity, my old Uganda friends Frank and Inge suggested that I might have a better chance of recovery if we moved back in with them. They were right. I lay for a fortnight watching a Nepali family opposite my window harvest their rice. I could write a book of instruction on rice harvesting but somehow have not got round to it. Meantime my fever refused to go away. Oxo cubes became less and less attractive. Mrs Baker-Willock once again showed her true metal. She must have been scared witless. I know I was. Everyone was most kind. Lisa took her to Tibetan villages. Dieter flew her down to Chitawan and up the Everest valley. He even flew me to Chitawan in the hope that my passion for light aircraft might raise my morale. It did, but only briefly. My stomach objected strongly especially when we had a dog fight with a black vulture that didn't seem to understand the rules of air combat.

Eventually, Joan and I decided to run for it. Flights were booked to England. I was shovelled onto an Air India flight in Delhi in the middle of the night. I arrived home in good old Surrey, opened the door to our garden and threw up in a rose-bed.

I went to see the experts at the Tropical Diseases Hospital as everyone in our trade sooner or later does. They were delighted with my theory about the sick orang-utan. They'd never had a patient before who'd caught anything from an ape.

"Can you," a grave young doctor in a white coat in all seriousness asked, "get a swab from the orang-utan in question?"

When I'd stopped laughing I said that she was either dead or one hundred and forty feet up in a tree in the Sumatran rain forest.

"In that case," he said, "you probably can't."

Only much later did I discover that she had died, taking with her the baby Suka and three or four other orangs to whom she had transferred the virus.

For the next two months, I got through the day but developed a temperature and was sick promptly at five thirty every evening. Then as mysteriously as it had caught fire, the virus burned out.

But I had very nearly taken my last walk on the wild side.

Dieter Plage gives three young orang-utans a lift to the feeding station at Bohorok. Each afternoon at feeding time the orangs would leap on him from the trees.

Orang-utans are called 'the mechanical apes'. They are adept at using tools such as branches as levers. This one, Oyong, merely wanted to be a camera assistant.

When ready for release into the wild, the orangs were carried ten kilometres up the Bohorok river. This orang escaped this mishap with a ducking.

Regina Frey organising the orangs tea party. Manners often left a lot to be desired.

The orangs who lived wild all day in the forest received a free hand-out of milk and bananas. The orang with back to camera gave the author a nearly fatal virus disease.

Envoi

I know that I have written more about Dieter Plage in this book than about my other good friends and companions in the field. I make no apologies for that. The fact is that Dieter and I were not only a team, we shared many of the same interests and certainly the same sense of fun. We made more films together, went to more exotic locations together, although my other old friend Des Bartlett, the daddy of all wildlife cameraman, runs Dieter pretty close. I don't know anyone who failed to find this larger -than-life highly anglicised German the best possible company.

When we were working together on the orang-utan rehabilitation story in Sumatra, Dieter repeatedly said to me that one day he wanted to return and make a film about the Indonesian rain forest before some smart politician sold it all for a knock-down price to his brother-in-law so that they could share the profits when the trees were cut up and flogged in Japan. Or words to that effect. He wasn't far wrong. Soon after we filmed the Bohorok story,they cut and sold all the trees on the opposite, non wildlife reserve bank of the Bohorok river. Would the reserve be next?

Now, if Dieter had a professional weakness, it was for gadgets. He played with model aircraft that were supposed to carry cameras aloft with fish eagles. He put a camera inside a remote-controlled tortoise to film elephants. An elephant trod on it! In the Galapagos he proposed to place a small camera inside a bomb that could be dropped from a microlight aircraft to imitate a blue-footed booby diving and hitting the water. I told him that (a) we had had quite enough of German bombs and (b) he'd be lucky if the camera filmed the splash as the bomb hit the water. As related, the one gadget that did work was the camera inside the stuffed pelican mounted on a blown-up motor tyre. But then anyone who has decoyed ducks could have told him that it *would* work. So I always successfully opposed and, as his boss, sometimes downright banned his more outrageous ideas for gadgetry. Dieter, being Dieter, laughed good-naturedly and began a long explanation to my deaf ears which invariably began with the words: "*Ach!* Colin..."

After I retired as head of the *Survival* unit, Dieter got his wish to return to the Sumatran rain forest. The difficulty with filming rain forests is that ninety per cent of the life in them exists in the canopy at the top of the huge trees. The cameraman therefore has to solve the problem of first getting there, second staying there, third moving about there, fourth achieving a steady camera platform and lastly actually finding and filming the birds and insects that make the story.

Various methods have been tried, some with varying degrees of success—towers, platforms, rope walkways, series of hides and combinations of all these.

Dieter's solution was a helium-filled, bicycle-pedal operated dirigible. It had been developed and tested quite successfully by the science department of Southampton University. Apart from getting stuck under a bridge, it had passed all its acceptance trials but in the comparatively calm and normal conditions of southern England. It was in fact the ultimate in gadgetry and as such appealed to Dieter as the perfect solution to filming above the rain forest canopy.

Had I still been in charge at *Survival* I would have fought its use with all the powers at my disposal. I might have been over-ruled but I know that Dieter would have listened to my protest. I could probably even have persuaded the directors of the company to have put a veto on it. I know I would have tried. Had I succeeded Dieter would be alive today.

The filming started well. The mini airship behaved well despite all the difficulties of transporting and maintaining the thing in a rain forest environment. The ground crew consisted of one of the designers, Dieter's wife, Mary, and Friedemann Koester, a fellow German who had been Director of the Darwin Research Station in the Galapagos and who had worked and filmed with us on the five one-hours we made about those islands.

One morning, when everything seemed to be going as normal, Friedemann on the ground noticed the fuselage of the little airship was starting to bend. At that critical moment, the ground-to-air radio failed. By the time Friedemann managed to attract Dieter's attention, the framework had buckled further. Dieter was provided with a life-line fixed to a tree trunk down which he might have *abseiled*. But his first and only thought was to attach his Arriflex camera to the safety rope.

He fell over one hundred feet. He was alive after he hit the ground. Friedemann and his wife Mary carried him over a mile, across several streams until they reached a track. Before a vehicle could be brought he was dead. Both Joan and I who had shared so many adventures with him feel we can never miss a great friend more.

Dieter Plage was killed while filming more than one hundred and forty feet above the Sumatran rain forest while using a pedal-driven drigible. While he was trying to secure his camera, the frame of the little airship buckled. This picture typifies the man, deadly serious about his work but always ready to make the most of the lighter side of wildlife film-making.

Notes

The reader may find it useful if certain points in the text are amplified or brought up to date.

1. The Uganda National Parks suffered severely during the terrible years of Idi Amin's bloody rule. The northern parks were probably worst hit. An elephant population of several thousands in Murchison Falls Park (now Kabarega National Park) was reduced to hundreds and all the big ivory was shot out. Rhinos, black and white, including those caught as described in Chapter Two, as well as a later capture of white rhinos, were shot for their horn. Paraa Lodge was looted and partly wrecked. Wildlife generally was decimated for food and trophies and not least by Amin's army. The northernmost park, the Kidepo, towards the Sudanese border, became a complete free-for-all for poachers. The Queen Elizabeth Park in the south of the country probably fared slightly better though the herds here suffered greatly also. At the moment of writing (September 2000) this park is recovering well with an elephant population of around 1,500. Both Murchison and the Q.E. have viable elephant populations, provided poaching can be controlled. Tourism is gradually being re-established, especially in the Q.E. though tourists in Murchison and the Kidepo are still regarded as at risk from the great number of automatic weapons in the hands of illegal factions.

2. Chiels Margach vanished without trace in the Idi Amin years, Bill Cowen died naturally during this period and Bombo Trimmer in 1976.

3. Frank Poppleton is currently living on Vancouver Island. After leaving the Uganda Parks he became an advisor to UNO's Food and Agriculture Organisation (FAO). In this role he served with John Blower who became Chief Technical Advisor to the FAO. I encountered them in various countries around the world, including Nepal and Indonesia, Blower usually carrying out the original survey of conservation problems and Frank Poppleton moving in behind him,as Project Manager, to carry out and implement the basic plan. After Amin was deposed,

Frank, with his wife Inge, went back to Uganda on behalf of FAO as Chief Technical Advisor to sort out some of the conservation problems of the largely derelict parks.

Roger Wheater, now Professor Wheater, moved to Scotland, first as Director of Edinburgh Zoo and later as Deputy Director of SNH and more recently Director of Council for the National Trust for Scotland. John Blower retired to Herefordshire.

4. Sadly, the great wildlife wardens, Ted Eales, Billy Bishop and Josh Scott described in Chapter Four are now dead. Kenzie Thorpe died in the early 1970s. The first three had special responsibilities as wardens of nature reserves. I have always felt that such great characters would have felt less inhibited living wild and free as their ancestors had done before them on the north Norfolk coast.

5. The list of superb wildlife cameramen and women who filmed for 'Survival' is too long to give in this book. Naturally I have written about those with whom I worked most closely. But there were many others, men like Richard Kemp who began life in 'Survival' as an assistant film editor; Chris Knights one of East Anglia's biggest carrot growers who showed himself as highly skilful with a camera as he was at combining intensive farming with wildlife conservation on his farms. Nor must one forget the female partners and camerapersons, including Cindy Buxton, Aubrey Buxton's daughter, who, with her partner Annie Price, defiantly sat out the Argentine invasion on South Georgia and carried on filming throughout. Liz and Tony Bomford did some fine work together. All these people were genuinely a breed apart, utterly dedicated to the job and prepared to sit out the most trying and sometimes dangerous conditions to get their film. They, truly, lived a life on the wilder side.

6. Manyara National Park is still one of the jewels in Tanzania's wildlife crown. The elephant population remains stable as in Iain Douglas-Hamilton's days of research, although the herds that he studied, including Boadicea, were mainly shot by poachers several years after he completed his work there.

7. To reach Luderitz you must take the one road through the Sperrgebeit, the forbidden diamond area. A special permit is required before you may even dismount there. Just before you reach Luderitz, you come to the ghost mining town of Kolmanskop. In the 1930s this settlement produced more diamonds than any other town in Namibia. In the 1950s the diamonds ran out and the miners moved on. Some of their sand-filled, German-style houses are now being restored.
The Caprivi Strip runs for 280 miles from the north east corner of Namibia eastward towards the Zambezi River. It varies from 20 to 65 miles wide. Most of it is an extremely flat plain lying on the swampy northern border of the Kalahari. The strip, named after Leo, Graf Von Caprivi, the German Chancellor of the period, was ceded by Britain in 1884 to give the then German colony of South-West Africa riparian access to the Zambezi.

8. As Wilfred Thesiger said of primitive tribal civilisations such as the Afar tribesmen of the Danakil Desert: "They will vanish like snow on the lawn in a hot sun." Shortly after we completed our film 'The Forbidden Desert of the Danakil', Emperor Haile Selassie was deposed by a revolutionary government. The Sultan of the Afar was not long in following, taking refuge in exile in Riyadh. The last pictures I saw of his palace in Asaita, its walls were pock-marked with machine gun fire and holes made by cannon shells.

9. Sadly, there can be little doubt that the mountain gorilla is a species bound for extinction. Since we made our film in Kahuzi-Biega National Park, Zaire, the park has been closed to visitors because of civil war. Only two of the families formerly habituated to meet tourists now exist. Gorilla watching, unknown at the time of our filming, is now a fairly well organised specialist tourist attraction in Volcanoes National Park, Rwanda, as well as in the small Ugandan section of the Virunga Volcanoes. Gorillas can also be seen by hardy tourists conducted by skilled guides in Gabon and Congo-Brazzaville. Poaching pressure everywhere is such that the ultimate extinction of both mountain and lowland gorillas seems certain.

10. Since we filmed at Bohorok, the trees on the bank opposite the rehabilitation station have mostly been felled for sale as timber to Japan. Though conservation work continues both in Sumatra and Borneo, the future of the orang-utan in the wild, largely because of deforestation, would seem to be extremely short-term.

WPA PUBLICATIONS

The World Pheasant Association is committed to the conservation of all the world's gamebirds. The sale of its publications not only helps the educational side of its work but also the raising of funds for its international conservation projects.

PEAFOWL
their conservation, breeding and management
T P Gardiner

At last a book which does justice to this fascinating group of pheasant related birds. Tim Gardiner has ten years' experience in answering queries on peafowl to draw on and has added to that by meticulous research into all aspects of their behaviour, reproduction and distribution.

Hardback 103 pages 62 photographs (6 colour)
1 colour plate 6 maps
ISBN 0 906864 30 5.......... **£29.95**

PARTRIDGES & FRANCOLINS
their conservation, breeding and management
G E S Robbins

Over 90 paintings and photographs have been used to illustrate this book which provides practical advice and guidance on the captive breeding of these species. Emphasis is placed on the importance of properly co-ordinated captive breeding projects in ensuring the long term conservation of these game-birds

Hardback 114 pages 101 photographs (96 colour) 6 figures
ISBN 0 906864 45 3.......... **£24.95**

INTRODUCTION TO ORNAMENTAL PHEASANTS
K C R Howman

This book will prove invaluable reference work for those planning to keep their first pheasants, while being of more than a passing interest to those who are already advanced in keeping these birds.

Hardback 128 pages 56 photos (32 colour)
11 figures
ISBN 0 88839 381 4.......... **£14.95**

QUAIL – their breeding and management
G E S Robbins

Now in its third re-print, this book is the bible for all who wish to keep quail and learn more about them.

Hardback 108 pages 25 photos (22 colour)
4 illustrations 1 map
ISBN 0 906864 02 X.......... **£14.95**

THE NEW INCUBATION BOOK
Dr A F Anderson Brown
and
G E S Robbins

This book is essential reading for anyone wanting to incubate eggs of any type, whether they be pheasants, waterfowl, ratites or even crocodiles.

Hardback 276 pages 60 photos
51 figures 10 tables
ISBN 0 86230 061 4.......... **£14.95**

PHEASANTS OF THE WORLD – their breeding and management
K C R Howman

Keith Howman's thirty years of pheasant breeding is combined with the most specular collection of colour photographs ever assembled.

Hardback 184 pages 341 colour photos
8 figures 1 table
ISBN 0 88839 280 X.......... **£45.00**

CHENG AND THE GOLDEN PHEASANT
Yang Qun-rong
Edited by Derek Bingham

A fascinating biography of the life of the late Professor Cheng who for nearly 70 years was China's leading ornithologist. His life spanned war, civil war, the emergence of the Peoples' Republic of China and also what he called the 'Cowshed Years'.

Hardback 286 pages 28 photos 3 maps
ISBN 0 906864 20 8.......... **£19.95**

PHEASANT JUNGLES
William Beebe

Pheasant Jungles captures the excitement of the solitary pursuit of these scarce and secretive birds. A birding classic reprinted. Anyone who has visited Sri Lanka, the Himalayas, China, Malaysia or Indonesia or plans to do so, will find this book a fascinating read.

Hardback 268 pages 8 colour illustrations
68 photos
ISBN 0 906864 20 8.......... **£19.95**

Available from: Game Conservancy Limited, The Sales Centre, Fordingbridge, Hampshire, SP6 1EF.
Tel: 01425 651003 Fax: 01425 651026-7 email: sales@gct.org.uk

For further information on the World Pheasant Association, Tel: 0118 984 5140 Email: office@pheasant.org.uk